OFF THE RAILS

One Family's Journey Through Teen Addiction

SUSAN BURROWES

SHE WRITES PRESS

Published August 21, 2018
Printed in the United States of America
Print ISBN: 978-1-63152-467-7
E-ISBN: 978-1-63152-468-4
Library of Congress Control Number: 2018930867

For information, address:
She Writes Press
1563 Solano Ave #546
Berkeley, CA 94707

Interior design by Tabitha Lahr

She Writes Press is a division of SparkPoint Studio, LLC.

Names and identifying characteristics have been changed to protect the privacy of certain individuals.

We must be willing to let go of the life we've planned,
so as to have the life that is waiting for us.

—Joseph Campbell

Preface

When our daughter Hannah was in ninth grade, my husband Paul and I felt like we owned the world. We had healthy children, good jobs, a vibrant social life, and a solid plan for retirement. Six months later our fourteen-year-old daughter shifted from moody to malicious. Another six months and we were out scouring the streets for her in the middle of the night. Six months after that, we were staring down at her in a hospital bed, near death from an overdose.

When Hannah's behavior turned destructive towards herself and others, we found ourselves in a vortex of shock, upheaval, dread, and shame. Shock because things like this just didn't happen to nice families like ours. Upheaval because we were completely unprepared to address the terror that our daughter introduced into our home. Dread because we had no idea whether we were taking the right steps to help our daughter. Would our attempts to help Hannah scar her, drive her deeper into addiction, or push her further away? Finally, shame, always shame, at our inability to "handle" our own child, and shame for the things that she did that fell so far from the values with which she was raised.

Over the next two years, we exhausted our financial and emotional resources, grappling with what had gone wrong with our family, and struggling to make it right. Life as we knew it fell apart. We found ourselves lost in the frightening world of therapy, educational consultants, and troubled teen programs, uncertain of how to find the right support and professional services for Hannah. We didn't know how to save our daughter.

But ultimately we learned, and that is our story.

As we came to the end of our harrowing journey, I found myself spending hours on the phone speaking with other families who had gotten our number from programs, professionals, or friends. Dozens of families contacted us—wounded, looking for a balm, praying for a cure. I never met Melissa, who called, worried about her daughter, but I knew her, and I knew her familiar story.

"My daughter is getting in some trouble at school," she began tentatively, as they all did. Eventually her story spilled out, all in a rush like she couldn't stand to linger in the words. "I think she's using, sometimes she's completely spaced out, and there's blood in the bathroom. I think she's cutting but she won't show me . . . I don't know what to do."

More than anything, I wanted to assure her that everything would be okay, but we both knew that it was too soon to tell and too hard to know. Instead, I did the only thing I could do. I answered Melissa's questions as honestly as I could. She asked me, "What happened to your family? How do you know when it's more than just regular teen behaviors? What programs did you consider? How did you choose? What was it like? What did people think of you? Are you sorry you did it?" Big, important questions that made me feel small and ill-equipped. I gave Melissa the only thing I had. I gave her our story.

I am not a therapist, and do not claim any special expertise in parenting. Quite the contrary. I made many mistakes and took many wrong turns before finding my way back to my daughter. During our two years of treatment, I learned that there can be more than one truth, more than one way of thinking, and more than one path back to love.

While this book reflects our family's journey, I hope that it helps as you make your own difficult decisions about your at-risk teen. *Off the Rails* will show you what life "looks like" on the inside of several teen treatment programs, giving you a glimpse of this alternative universe—a glimpse we wish we'd had before committing our daughter into their care.

This book is about teen addiction, but it is first and foremost about my relationship with my daughter, and how we saved each other, with help from our family, and lots of people who supported us along the way. My hope is that our story will bring clarity, community, and courage to those who may be going through similar challenges, or those who know someone who is.

I began writing together with my daughter, but she decided that she wanted to look to the future, not the past. In the end, this book is my perspective of the events that took place over the course of nearly two years, based on both my daughter and my journals, notes, boxes of letters, and hours of conversation. I have worked to acknowledge my daughter's shifting feelings about her experiences, and her request for balance. I also tried to stay true to her wild spirit, humor, creativity, and her wise and soulful view of the world.

Some names in *Off the Rails* have been changed to protect the young people who played such an important role in our journey.

Chapter 1

Mom

I watch the ugly bruise form on my upper arm, while I struggle to keep driving on the narrow rural road. Hannah remains poised for battle in the passenger seat, her pale porcelain skin flushed with anger, her lovely, long-fingered hands still clenched into fists. Her pretty cherub's lips, in a permanent pout these days, part to scream at me, "Fuck you, you fat cunt, eat shit!" Spittle sprays from her mouth to water the bloom of black and blue on my arm. There's nowhere to pull over, nowhere to run, no way to escape this cage of a car. I'm trapped, just me and this wild creature, and though I look for my sixteen-year-old daughter, I can't see her at all. Who is this child-woman, and where did she come from? If she's willing to hit me, what else is she capable of? Will she steal? Will she kill? Am I the mother of a monster?

Hannah

She gets me in the car, and I'm her fucking prisoner, and she thinks she can torture me as much as she wants. She is driving and lecturing me the way she always does when she has me captive. It's as though all my pissed off feelings roll down from my head into my hand and form a fist, and I hit her. Stupid, right? I almost kill us when I hit her. She swerves into the other lane on our wanky little road out in the middle of bum-fuck nowhere, and I know the look on her face isn't fear of an accident, it's fear of me, and that makes me feel good. I watch the bruise form unevenly on her arm, like a map of the terrain we've just crossed, and I know that bruise will divide us forever.

Mom

The fact that Hannah was struggling was clear a long time before she ever hit me, before she turned angry, before she started tenth grade and decided that she didn't want to be anything like the person she was in ninth grade, and way before she became what she called a "therapy kid."

It seemed that every day of the summer between ninth and tenth grade Hannah was more distracted and less interested in her old activities. She asked me to drop out of our daughter-mother book group ("All bitches," she said), she tossed out her beautiful carved and gold-leafed gourd projects ("Crap," she said), and she gave most of her books to Goodwill ("They're just cluttering up my head," she said. "I need to think.")

I place the books in a box carefully, remembering how we read the alphabet book *Chicka-Chicka Boom Boom* over and over again, Hannah so serious as she traced the brightly colored illustrations with her pudgy fingers, later making awkward paper cutouts to express her own alphabet. I run my hand over the spines of the cheap set of classics we bought her— well-worn volumes of Mark Twain, Louisa May Alcott, and E.B. White. "I want her to be able to really read them," I told my husband Paul, and she did, the pages dog-eared and the margins full of doodles and notes. Hannah doesn't want her newest books either, and I tuck Sharon Creech, Barbara King-solver, and David Sedaris into the box, along with her book club books, the school books, the books that she bought with all of the gift cards, the books she found in used book bins, the books that made her laugh and think and, most importantly, connect with me and Paul over all these years. I pack away the laughter, the adventure, and the connection and seal the box.

Hannah

It's hard starting high school at fourteen. My birthday is in early October, right at the cutoff, so I'm always the youngest person in my class. I'm almost a full year younger than some of the other kids. I guess my parents talked to my kindergarten teacher about waiting, but they thought I was too smart. Then why do I feel so fucking dumb about how to act in high school? Ninth grade was a nightmare. It was a new school, and I didn't know anyone or anything about the "right" clothes or the "right" books or the "right" movies. I was just wrong. And there were plenty of mean and nasty people who were always looking for the chance to point that out. The only place I felt safe in ninth grade was the art studio, cuz I could hold my own there. Tenth grade is going to be different. I won't let those cows make me feel bad any more.

Mom

I don't know how to help Hannah. I don't want to be one of those helicopter parents. I can see she doesn't have a lot of friends at her new school, but she loves the art teachers and the beautiful, naturally lit studio space. I'm relieved when she finally makes some friends. She tells me that they are nice, and that she has been going out to lunch with them regularly. She tells me one of them is a writer, and that the other wants to be a doctor. I relax into the driver's seat as she talks. It had just taken her a little time, that's all. Everything will be fine now.

Hannah

Tenth grade starts off okay. I meet some cool kids that aren't part of the mean girl club. I like them, but by the time back-to-school night comes in October, they're all hooked up and coupled off. They're still pretty nice to me, inviting me along when they go downtown for lunch and asking me if I want to go to the park after school. I do go downtown with them once in a while, sitting in the backseat alone, or crammed in with another couple. I don't know where to look sometimes. I feel like some kind of perv, watching them squeeze and tease and do the kissy thing over lunch. It helps when I get a little high with them, cuz then I don't care as much that they're at each other, and I'm alone. I like being a little high at school too, because I've landed in some crap classes with a bunch of Mean Barbies. After school, my friends rush outside to get rides from their boyfriends. I'm left waiting on the steps, my little sister climbing and snaking through the railing waiting for Mom to come. I don't understand why she's late so often. She quit work to be a pudgy, frizzy housewife. How long does it take to clean toilets and cook dinner? It isn't all bad to wait though, cuz I really don't like to be seen in Mom's BMW—a relic from her old life, a pretty phony ride for the person she's let herself become. *Just kill me*, I think as I slide into the passenger seat, *if I ever let that happen to me.*

Mom

I am often late picking up the kids. The drive to school is pretty long, but that isn't it. I think I slow down, anticipating the bald hatred waiting for me in that parking lot. Hannah is always alone when I get there. I guess she didn't get into the same tenth grade English class as all her friends, so she doesn't see them after school. She gets a new teacher who specializes in Jane Austen, and I am filled with dread when I meet her at back-to-school night.

"This year my students will become familiar with the world of Jane Austen." My heart sinks as I watch the teacher wave her blunt hands over the imposing stack of novels that the teens will be expected to read. Especially when she starts reviewing the scholarly body of work that she herself has written about Ms. Austen. Hannah's favorite books that summer had been *Full Frontal Feminism* by Jessica Valenti and *Nudity* by our mutual favorite, David Sedaris. Given the fact that her friends are studying contemporary literature while she slogs through Austen with a self-proclaimed expert concerns me. Hannah asks me to go to the school office with her to help her transfer into the other English class. I am open to it, but the vice principal says no. "It will be a great lesson for Hannah," she says. "It will be an opportunity for her to expand her reading." Finally, she gets to the point, leaning back in her big blue chair and looking down at her desk. "We don't have seats available in the other class." I watch Hannah purse her lips and look to me for support, but I look away. Maybe it will lead to new interests. Maybe she'll meet new people.

Hannah

You'd think that when I finally meet Dylan, my friends would be happy for me. They aren't. Suddenly they're, like, relationship experts.

The minute I see Dylan, I decide that he will be my boyfriend. I'm still lost and self-conscious at my school after a whole year, but on his very first day, he strolls down the hall sneering at the Barbies and dropping into his desk like it's a Barcalounger. I make eye contact with him, and he smiles and moves his long blond bangs out of his eyes to get a better look at me. He is definitely less of a geek than most of the boys at school. He's a transfer from a military school, my little group of friends whisper, kicked out for having a knife. "I know that sounds bad," he tells me, leaning against my locker later that day, "but it was a fucking pen knife, and I borrowed it to open up a stuck trunk." He growls the words as he leans in towards me, and my heart races, and I think for a minute that he's going to kiss me—my first kiss—but he doesn't, and I am disappointed. I find out over the next few weeks that he's pretty pissed about the way he's been treated. He's pissed about his Mom's new husband, he's pissed about his bio-dad's indifference, and he's pissed about the attention his new little sister is receiving. Dylan's just pissed. All the time. Pretty soon he's pissed at me all the time too, always expecting me to prove to him that he comes first to me, and I guess he does.

Mom

I first find out about Dylan at 2:00 on a Tuesday morning in September. I wake up to a steady buzzing. Thinking that I'd left my cell phone on vibrate, I jump out of bed and fumble to answer a call that, in my mind, can only mean someone has died or disaster has befallen a family member. But my phone tumbles off my nightstand, silent until it cracks on the hardwood floor. By the time I follow the sound downstairs, the buzzing has been replaced by soft flirtatious murmurs coming from Hannah's room. "Hannah," I hiss in my best stage whisper, pushing her door open, "get off the phone."

"I have to go," she says into the phone, rolling her eyes towards the heavens. "My mom."

Hannah

I have no privacy. But I have a boyfriend. Now I just have to figure out how to get some fucking privacy.

Mom

I let myself think that Dylan is the problem. In a way, it's a relief to have something outside of the family to focus on, to lay blame for Hannah's increasing surliness. I ask Hannah to invite him over. "He's welcome here, Hannah." I smile, trying to salvage our relationship. "I'll make dinner."

As it turns out, Hannah doesn't want anyone to come over. "Please," she drawls, "middle class, middle politics, middle of the woods." She rolls her eyes to make sure I understand her deep shame at the bourgeois family we have become. Evidently our conventional lifestyle is hipster death. I bite back my retort as she pulls her $28 watercolor pad off her $175 easel. Is this what Paul and I have worked so hard to achieve? I turn away from Hannah's disdain, trying to remember her as a little girl, climbing on the tractor Paul rented to work on our big property every weekend, to make a home for us. In my mind's eye, she is wearing his sweat-darkened hat on her curly head and smiling at him with love. But on teenage Hannah, the fedora has turned into a grungy, gray knit cap, and the smile has turned into a sneer.

Hannah

They want me to "bring my boyfriend to dinner." Hah! I can hardly stand being with them and their middle-class morals, so why should I torture Dylan? Why should I let them judge him the way they judge me? Why should I let them into my life any more than I have to? Why doesn't she get it? I don't want to spend time with her. I try to imagine what we would talk about, sitting at the dining room table over steaming plates of the immigrant slop she cooks. "Dylan," she would no doubt say, "tell us about yourself."

Then Dylan, in my imaginary discourse, answers politely. "Oh yes, Mrs. Burrowes, I enjoy music and movies and blow jobs, especially when I'm high as a kite." No, I think I'll just keep Dylan to myself.

Mom

Finally, something Hannah and I can enjoy together. It's October, and that means Open Studio time in Santa Cruz, when many of the artists who live in town throw open their doors to visitors. As an "Arts Intensive" student at her high school, Hannah is required to visit studios, to sketch and interview artists. I am looking forward to the day. Art is the place where Hannah and I come together. I love art; it feeds and calms me. Hannah, well, she's special. Ever since she was a toddler, she has expressed herself through her art. I walked around for years with her sketchbook and pencils in my bag, and it seems as though every family picture includes our little Hannah stained with markers or spattered with paint. I first noticed her unique viewpoint in kindergarten, when the teacher tugged me over to the bulletin board. There, twenty-three children's drawings of an alligator adorned the wall. One child, our daughter, had rendered only the gaping mouth, teeth, and tongue at the forefront. "Cuz that's the part I'm scared of, Mommy," Hannah had explained. By third grade, the school asked us to find a private art teacher for her because she had "outgrown" their program, and so we did. I have loved watching her work through the years, her focus complete, her mouth moving as though chewing on all of the possibilities. Even now, I can get close to her without rebuff when she's working, as everything falls away for her except her art. Her long, pale fingers wrap around the brush as though it's an extension of her right hand, her left hand a troupe of brightly colored fingers that periodically have to dance on the canvas, making contact with the emerging image.

Hannah

Open studios are really interesting. As usual, there's a bunch of crap, but there are also some pretty cool pieces. I look at them and wonder if the artists were high when they made them. I know that my art is a lot better when I'm high. Dylan is helping me experiment with a bunch of different shit to see what kind of buzz works best.

Mom

The studio tours are great, and we end up going to more than the required three. Our last stop is Bruce Telopa, our favorite local artist. I wander around the garage studio, admiring his work while Hannah sketches for her homework assignment. It is lovely and peaceful, but only for a moment. On the way home, an angry fight flares. I am confused, not understanding how it snuck up on us—I didn't see it coming, not at all, and I don't know what we're fighting about. Suddenly at a stoplight, the car door opens, and Hannah jumps out, disappearing into the small but busy downtown area of Santa Cruz, a haven of oddness that masquerades as hip. Her homework assignment will remain unfinished, joining the heap of her paintings—half worked and abandoned in a graveyard of canvas in her room.

Hannah

Ha! Somehow I make it through the morning with Motherperson. I slip out of the car when we get close to downtown. I know Dylan is down here, and my girls too. I know where they hang. I should be able to find them with no trouble.

I almost don't answer the phone when it rings, but I know she will be a fucking robocaller until I answer, so I pick up. She's crying and can't push her words past the sobs. Is that supposed to make me feel bad? I tell her that I won't get in the car with her, but she can send Dad to get me later. Her hurt is a wave, and it feels good washing over me.

Mom

I find myself wondering if I could have helped my girls get along better. If I had, maybe they would still be living in the same room, upstairs, near Paul and me. But Hannah and her sister

Camilla didn't get along, and Hannah moved downstairs when she was thirteen, to a room that opens on to our deck, setting up a corner studio and pinning up her finished pieces in a private show by and for herself. It becomes her haven, until Dylan becomes her haven. Now she thinks of it as her jail, and Dylan as her destination.

Hannah

It's easy to get out at night. The "Brady Bunch" family I live with goes to bed before 11:00, and our dogs are totally useless. All I have to do is walk out of my room as soon as I hear the snores, across the property, and up the long drive where Dylan is waiting. He can't always borrow a car cuz his buddies freak out about him not having a license. On those nights, I just walk into our little mountain town and meet Dylan there. It's a dark five miles through a fucking forest, but sometimes I get lucky and someone stops and gives me a ride. One time a dude even gave me some Oxy, dropping the pills into my palm with his sweaty hand, smiling at me with his nasty meth teeth and stinky breath. Okay, I think, rolling the little pills between my palms. Why not?

Mom

People start telling me they "think" they might have seen Hannah out late. I have to know, so after Paul goes to bed, I wait on the deck outside her room, leaning against the wood railing, feeling silly and unsure of myself, like some terrible TV show detective. Before long, the door slowly cracks open, and Hannah's lovely, long, painter's fingers curl around the door's edge, followed by her slender body. Her other hand holds her little black ballet flats and, not seeing me lurking in the shadows, she walks off barefoot, a small smile playing about her mouth.

Hannah

Crap.

She is waiting for me on the deck, like some kind of fucking stalker, and she comes up behind me before I make the end of the driveway, scaring the shit out of me. Does she think she can stop me? I have plans, and I mean to keep them. What can she possibly do to me? Well, I'll tell you what she can do. She gets in her car and starts driving after me, lighting up the road ahead with her headlights, talking on the phone.

Mom

I call Paul first. He sounds confused and groggy, and I have a pulse of resentment that he is sleeping. "Where are you?" he asks.

I answer, pissed and panicked. "I'm just down the road. I'll be home soon." My next call is to the therapist I have started seeing, the one who is going to make me a more effective parent. She tells me I have a right and responsibility to put Hannah in the car and take her home. I drive past Hannah and stop the car, hazards blinking, in the middle of the abandoned road. I try to talk, to reason, to bargain with her, but soon I am gripping her arm, and she is pulling and screaming and collapsing on the ground, her voice reverberating in the quiet of the woods. Foul screams cut through the peace. "Cunt, let me go!"

Neighbors we have never met run down their long driveways, belting robes as they go. "She's my daughter," I blubber, as I manage to drag her back to the car.

Hannah

Yeah, I get in the car, but I don't waste time talking to her. I call the police and tell them I've been kidnapped. I tell them I am being abused. I figure that'll get them to come fast. Maybe I can still salvage my night.

Mom

The police pull into our driveway right behind me, and quickly figure out the situation, watching as Hannah gets out of the car, cursing me. "Fucking bitch, you can't keep me here."

The two officers don't mince words with her, stepping in close and speaking in clipped sentences. "Do you know that it's illegal to place false calls to the police? Do you know how many dead or raped girls we pick up on these roads?"

I don't know if they are exaggerating, but I hope Hannah is scared enough to back down. She is not. She tells the officers, "Fuck you!" then she throws a "Fuck you, too!" at me before spinning around and returning to her room. The police officers stand silent, witness to my impotence. I hang my head, not able to look them in the eye, and apologize.

Hannah

How dare she treat me like a fucking prisoner?

Mom

After that night, Paul and I decide to put a GPS finder on Hannah's phone. It's easy to do, and it will make my phone vibrate if she goes more than a mile from home. She notices, and resists, but we tell her that we've all added the feature, that it's to help her find her phone if it is lost, a partial truth. I tuck my phone into my pajama top every night, so the buzzing will wake me up if she slips out of the house. Later, to my horror, cancer will grow in that exact spot, as though the pain of being my daughter's jailer coalesced into a tight, toxic ball. I still feel the memory of those nights every time my hand brushes the scars on my breast.

Hannah

So, walking is out for the time being. Too easy for her to catch up to me, too much drama when she does. But if I can get into a car quick enough, she'll never know where I went.

Mom

In the end, it isn't the buzzing of the GPS tracker that alerts us to Hannah slipping out, it is the dogs. Generally useless, they are alert for once, barking their disapproval as Hannah makes her way up the driveway in the dark night. This time Paul is awake, and pulling on jeans, he slips into his car and follows her, making it to the top of the drive just as she pulls away in a car we don't recognize. He calls me, panicked. "I'm losing them, you'll have to track her with the GPS. Hurry."

The GPS is accessed through our phone carrier account, and I haven't used it before. By the time I get my computer on, manage to log into our account and then the GPS feature, forgetting our password, Paul screaming, me fumbling with the keyboard, they are out of sight. "Tell me where they went," he says brusquely, letting his anger at my ineptitude show. I try to give him directions, taking him on a wild ride along twisty mountain roads, dead ends, one-way streets, and unmarked driveways. Oh, he finds her. It is a high fence, but he can hear them, and smell them, the sweet drift of pot and the small fire pit guiding him in like runway lights calling an airplane down.

Hannah

OMG it's so creepy . . . my Dad's forehead and eyeballs looking over the fence like some weird pedophile. I could die when he calls my name, and it gets worse. Pushing out of the rickety lawn chair, I try to muster some dignity. Walking out of the gate in the dark, I fall right into a bramble-filled ditch. Sniggers follow me to the car. Dylan is getting so pissed at me. I'm worried that he'll find someone cooler, with more freedom. I can't let that happen. I won't let that happen.

Mom

"Sweet sixteen?" I snort. After arguing, Paul and I have decided to give Hannah a birthday party. Well, Paul has decided.

"We have to keep letting her know we love her," Paul insists. "We have to give her a way back to us when she's ready." He is adamant. "Sixteen is a landmark birthday, and I don't want her looking back and thinking she was short-changed."

I give in, reluctantly, thinking that we are the ones who are being short-changed. How do you give someone a birthday party when they don't want anything to do with you? We rent the party room at her favorite vegetarian restaurant and ask one of her new friends to invite people. The black lacquered table is low to the ground, Japanese style, with soft cushions in bright colors scattered around the floor like a field of flowers. White paper globes float above white place settings, the subdued illumination mingling with the glow of candles on the table, creating a pillow of light in the dark room. Camilla and I put a little cellophane goodie bag containing a movie ticket at each place setting, black bow holding a single red mum in place. Paul gives the restaurant his credit card to run. Then he takes my hand. Time to leave.

Hannah

Sixteen now, but they still treat me like six. I'm thinking I can at least get out for the night and celebrate my birthday. My girls tell me they have a surprise planned for me.

Mom

I let Paul pull me out of the restaurant by my hand, feeling like I'm being pulled out of Hannah's life. Camilla holds my other hand, and we pretend this is normal.

Hannah

Everyone is here! We have gobs of great veggie food, and tickets to a show downtown. The timing is great, we finish eating and walk right over to the theater. After the movie we head to the park and get lit, big time. Perfect evening until I find out that it's sponsored by the folks. Fuck them! Why can't they let me have anything to myself? Now that I'm sixteen, I'm going to have to lay down the law. They will not run my life this year.

Mom

We settle into a routine. Every morning I knock on her door. Every morning she responds, "Fuck you." Every evening is a battle over homework, over going out, over money, over everything, anything. Thanksgiving comes, and I sit at the dining room table grasping for gratefulness. We have a spattering of family there, and my two polite, ambitious, and accomplished nephews sit across from me, filling the silence with lively stories. They are so handsome, so well-meaning, so happy that I am envious. Why have they turned out so well? What didn't I do? Should I have been tougher? Easier? More distant? Less? I can't even look at my own daughter. I am distraught. I smile at the boys and offer more mashed potatoes.

Hannah

Un-fucking-believable. My Eagle Scout (no, really, they *are* Eagle Scouts) cousins grace our table and charm the shit out of my mother. I can see the wistfulness in the glances she tries hard not to send my way. Really? She would rather have them?

Mom

December comes, and it's tough. As advertising reaches its frenzied, seasonal peak, our situation at home becomes as grim as the Grinch's world. Hannah's grades hit an all-time low, but every day she begs to go downtown with her friends. We try to tie her outings to her grades, fishing around for some way to motivate her to work harder at school. The English class is the worst. Hannah hates Austen, and she hates her tyrannical English teacher. She does little or no work in the class in a misplaced attempt to gain power. In return, the teacher does everything in her power to make Hannah uncomfortable. She sits on the edge of Hannah's desk and tells Hannah gory, detailed stories about butchering (Hannah is a vegetarian), she confronts and embarrasses Hannah in class (did the teacher think this was motivational?), and she stands right at Hannah's shoulder during in-class essays (did she suspect cheating or was she trying to intimidate?).

I deeply regret not helping Hannah fight the school's decision when she tried to change classes earlier in the year. I watch, realizing too late that Hannah is not expanding her horizons or learning a valuable lesson about how to get along with people. What she's learning is that the school administration and her parents are unwilling to help, even when she does things properly. I learn a lesson that year too. Schools are not about children. They are about expediency, and lip service often stands in for sincerity. I learn that for every teacher who is a hero to a child, there is one who is cruel and uncaring and destructive. I berate myself for not choosing a public school, or maybe pledging more generously in the fundraising drive to curry favor with the administration. I sit at the parent association meeting, clenching and unclenching my jaw as they congratulate themselves for being so progressive and student-centered.

Hannah

I hate school, and the way they treat me there. Skipping school seems easier than going to school some days. I never plan ahead, not really. On school mornings I relax in the bathroom with the door locked. I pluck my eyebrows, work on my gauges, and consider my wardrobe choices until Mom and Camilla bang on the door. Then I scream, "I'll take more time if you don't leave me the fuck alone!" And I do. By the time I make it to the car, my mom and sister are sitting in stony silence. By the time we get to school, we are late, my sister furious, my mom shaken from her freeway fun. Camilla runs, but I saunter around the corner of the building towards the front door. The saunter is my tool. I know Camilla will be long gone before I ever turn the corner. And usually the front desk person is gone too, off eating her granola or some such shit. That's when I decide. Is my homework done? What is Dylan doing? Is it a good day to go and be free, be me?

Mom

It sounds pathetic, but I never knew that I shouldn't trust Hannah. I wonder how many parents have fallen into the same trap. She's a good kid, has always been a good kid, surly these days and a little mischievous, but she's just going through regular teen stuff, school stuff, boyfriend stuff, right? I read books about hormones, and about brain development—the loose dendrites in her frontal lobe. Not her fault. Just biology. A beehive head, I call it. Hannah is not amused. She calls me an idiot. She is right, of course. The warning flags are raised and waving. Her hair-trigger temper, bouts of deep depression see-sawing with manic energy, her open contempt for school, the growing clutter in her room, mysterious burn marks on her arms, and her constant need to be out. Red flags? Hell, her behaviors are more like klaxon horns and flashing lights. I am blind, deaf, and dumb.

Hannah

When I skip school, I usually head downtown. It's amazing there. The Santa Cruz scene is so cool. Everywhere you look, no matter what time, there is this wave of weirdness. Rich west-siders posing as hippies mix it up with street people wearing garbage bags. Protesters share their corners with drug dealers. Make hemp legal! Wanna buy some hemp? Street musicians dot the walk with musical droppings, hoping for what? A few bucks to pay for their rooms at the co-ops? Discovery and fame? And the kids! Bright hair in oranges, blues, and greens. Pierced parts with silver, bone, and gold. Tats on their arms, their necks, and peeking out of their waistbands. And always, the rich smoky scent of weed hanging in the air, swept away when the sea breeze comes through, then creeping back in like fresh-baked bliss.

Mom

I used to love to go downtown. It's great people watching, and there's a wonderful farmers' market there on Wednesdays. Sure, I run into aggressive panhandling from time to time, but as long as you're there during business hours, it's pretty safe. It was after Hannah started begging to go there every day, after she jumped out of the car to be there, that I started looking at the streets with new eyes. The weed, the begging, the lewdness on the streets. Hanging out downtown had crept up on us, just the way the rest of Hannah's behaviors had. "Mom, I'm going to a movie with the girls" turned into "Mom, drop me off at the cookie place, that's where we're meeting," and finally "Mom, I finished my homework at school so I'm just going to walk downtown with everyone; we're going to get a pizza before the movie."

Maybe I know something is wrong, and don't want to see it. When we go along with what Hannah wants, our home is pleasant. When we push for rules and restrictions, it is hell. Screaming, slamming, throwing, breaking, and finally that day in the car, the day when my daughter finally crosses the line and hits me.

Chapter 2

Hannah

We pull into the driveway and she just sits there, her eyes wide, holding her arm where I hit her, her mouth opening to dispense shame. I don't wait for her to guilt me. I get out of the car and go to my room, pulling the beer can out of my bag as soon as I close the door.

Mom

I follow her too-thin back (when did she get so thin?) through the kitchen door, meaning to talk to her, but there's a light blinking on the house phone. It's the dean of students at Hannah's school. Hannah has stepped over the line again. He would like me to call him. It's early, so I pick up the phone and call, the number long settled into memory from Hannah's many infractions. I expect the same old routine, him complaining, me complying, him assigning punishment, me supporting and augmenting his decisions. But this time is different. There will be a hearing with the Judicial Review Committee about an altercation involving another girl. I lean against the kitchen counter, the mottled granite seeming to mirror the pattern of the darkening bruise on my arm and ask, "Can you give me details?"

His response is a bit too quick, as though my question is anticipated. "No, we'll present all the facts at the meeting."

I hang up the phone and lean back against the cool metal of the refrigerator, then slide down the smooth front of it to the floor, wrapping my arms around my two big dogs. This can't be good.

I wait for Paul. He stops to pick Camilla up from Hebrew school, and they come in armed with the regular questions about dinner and my day. I chop onions furiously, tears forming while I tell him about Hannah hitting me, and about the call from the school. He stands silently in the kitchen, his mouth pressed into a grim line. Hannah's door is still closed, a thin wood wall against our siege. We wait, an army of two.

Hannah
They want to know what I did. What I did, not what that fucking bitch from school did. She's pissed that Dylan likes me, not her. First she tells Dylan I'm a lesbian. Then she tells him I'm a slut, fucking every guy at school. "Make up your mind, cunt," I tell her. She has all the Mean Barbies fucking with me too. They tell Dylan that they see me with other guys, they put up ugly pictures of me I didn't know they took on their Facebook pages, and they do little things to piss me off, like walk real slow in front of me down the stairs when they know I'm late for class.

Mom
We finally find out from Hannah that Dylan has been expelled for telling a girl to "drink cement and die." The school decided that was a direct threat and asked him to leave. I find myself in an uncomfortable position, siding with Dylan.

Hannah

What if he had asked her to board a fucking space ship or get in the ocean and start swimming? How is it a threat to tell someone to do something that they would never do? It's an excuse to get rid of him, he doesn't fit here.

Mom

Paul and I prepare for the meeting with the board the way we prepare for any big presentation, discussing how the committee will come at us and researching our rights. We hope to keep her in school. It doesn't occur to us that we might be hurting her by doing that.

Hannah

My parents, a.k.a. handlers, make me dress in soft colors and soft fabrics, buttoned almost to my neck. I wear my hair down over my gauges, and skip makeup for the day. I am a product that they are pushing. All that's missing is a jingle. I think about the art studio at school, and how important it is to me, and I decide to do what they want.

Mom

We think we're ready, but the school outflanks us. In the middle of a discussion about Hannah's grades, the dean of students pulls out a single piece of paper. "This," he announces triumphantly, "is from Hannah's Facebook page." I reach across the big maple table to take the page from his hands. It is an image of a bloody, mangled doll. Hannah has written a caption underneath the picture. It reads, "This is how you make me feel." Then she has posted another comment: "People who make others feel this way should get what they deserve." I cannot get words around the lump in my throat, and I let the paper drift softly onto the polished surface of the table. I look up to see the dean lean back in the fake leather chair, his job done, waiting to dole out punishment and close the meeting. From the look on his face, it has all gone according to his plan. But he hasn't planned for Paul.

"So?" Paul calmly asks, picking up the page, "What are you going to do about the person who is making my daughter feel this way?" It is the dean's turn to be stunned.

"This is a threat," he finally stutters, pushing his black-rimmed glasses into place.

"To whom?" Paul continues. "I don't see a name here. And I don't see any threatening action described either. What I do see is a single piece of paper, taken out of context, posted on a non-school site by a teenage girl who is so bullied in your school that she feels mangled."

We soon have a deal. Hannah will be permitted to continue in school after the winter break, but she is required to write a letter to the girl who felt threatened by the post, the daughter of a major donor. Hannah will be considered suspended until that time. We also agree to see a therapist to help Hannah deal with her negative feelings. This should have been the moment we took Hannah out of this school for good, but sadly, we missed it. Paul and I leave, satisfied with our negotiating skills.

Hannah

I really, really do not want to write a letter to that piece of crap cunt that got Dylan kicked out of school, but both of my kow-towing parents are on me. Finally, I come up with this:

"It was not my intention to make anyone feel threatened. It was a description of my feelings. I am sorry if anyone read more into it. The school year is half over and I hope we can ignore each other and mind our own business."

Can you believe they went for such a bullshit apology?

Mom

We submit Hannah's apology, and we wait. Everyone is gone for winter break, and we are left in limbo about Hannah's fate, which is resting in the hands of an adolescent girl who took offense at Hannah calling her out on her crap. I am angry, but still try to make some kind of holiday for the family.

Hannah

No holiday cheer around here. It is fucking agony to spend time with the family. Dylan is away at his bio-dad's house, everyone is busy, and I am stuck. Mom usually has people over, but this year she doesn't, and I know it's because she's ashamed of me. She pretends she's not, wrapping presents and asking Camilla and me to light the candles every night. She closes her eyes while we do, and I wonder what she's praying for.

Mom

Please God, help me. Help me know what to do. Help me be strong enough to do it.

Hannah

After the candles, Camilla and I get gifts. Mother-person puts the charity box out, and we are required to think about the poor kids who have nothing and throw some of our allowance in before opening our gifts. "It's me," I want to shout, "who has nothing." But I throw some coins in to ransom my gifts. Gift cards. How sentimental.

Mom

By the time the school and the girl's family finally accept her apology, Hannah has missed the beginning of the semester, and her last chance to pull it together academically. Our life turns into a horrible funhouse mirror of how family life is supposed to be. Hannah screams, inches away from my face, because I won't take her where she asks, spittle beading on my cheeks like tears as I try to stand strong. I run into our rabbi downtown while wandering the streets looking for Hannah, the rabbi's sweet face filled with concern while I, mortified, am unable to meet her gaze. A mass of unwashed street people and unwanted, drug-addled teens roam café to café amidst tourists and local shoppers, panhandling, shoplifting, and dealing drugs in the aisles of the farmers' market I had once enjoyed so much but now avoid. Santa Cruz, a town we love for its liberal ideals, embraces liberal parenting as well. So many teens without supervision, without curfew, without guidance that it begins to remind me of some kind of *Lord of the Flies* remake.

Hannah

They are mostly leaving me alone, and as long as I go to school and agree to see some bullshit therapist, I can see Dylan as much as I want. I win.

Mom

When she's home it's like a ghost is moving around the house. She is here but not here, her mind already downtown or at the park or wherever Dylan is. We try to have "family" in this spectral world. But our attempts lead to screaming fights, foul language, sarcasm, and tense silence. So we start avoiding each other. Camilla, always quiet, becomes silent, a spectator who somehow finds herself crouching in the corner of a lion's cage.

Hannah

I know what I want next, or at least I know what Dylan wants. It happens at his house. We drop some E, and sex seems like a pretty good idea. His mother is right there, in the other room, and he has a friend over too, lying on the floor, half passed out from hitting the flask. That's a little gross but exciting too. When it's over, I just can't figure out what all the fuss is about. All in all, a non-event. It's a big deal to Dylan, though; he starts acting like he owns me. He needs to know where I am all the time now, and who I'm with, and I have to be available when he wants me. It's a pain in the ass, but also flattering in a creepy way.

Mom

Hannah just doesn't have enough homework for prep school. I know with certainty that her grades will reflect the list of lies she is telling me about finishing her work. She keeps busy in her stink-hole of a room, sketching and painting and spending hours on digital art. The work is amazing, but it scares me. Gone are the soft colors of her childhood. Her canvasses are strewn around her room, a confetti of hatred. Faces scream in agony, limbs free-float, disassociated from bodies that are repugnant in unique ways—men with cages for heads peer out from between the bars, greedy babies wave their octopus arms, and women hang upside down, smirking men peering out from behind them. Dylan comes by the house sometimes, his head shaved, his thin face angry.

Hannah

Dylan is having a bad time at home. His bio-dad isn't much better than his step-fucker, so he really doesn't have anywhere to go. He leans against the stone wall at the coffee shop, drinking from his glass and then his flask, planning to move out on his own. Planning for us to be together.

Mom

Do you ever imagine that people who tell you bad news have a sort of secret glee about them? I think they're delighted that your problems make theirs seem smaller by comparison, and they can hardly hold their pleasure in. It reminds me of newscasters who speak about the day's tragedies with too much energy, bright eyes, and taut features barely holding back the smirk twitching under their studiously somber tones. I'm getting regular reports from people now, ranging from gossipy to concerned to casual. "I saw Hannah at the mall. At Victoria's Secret. Was that her boyfriend?" "I don't want to shock you, but I thought I smelled smoke on Hannah the other day." "Wow, Hannah sure is trying a new look." It's funny, I think, standing in my kitchen kneading my bread dough, pushing at it like it is the cause of my angst, how nobody ever warned us as newcomers to Santa Cruz, about downtown. Now everyone wants to tell us how much bad stuff happens there, and how our daughter is in the middle of it.

Hannah

Did you know that if you show the doorman at a rave your tits he'll let you in for free? Men are such goons. But raves are great. My recipe for a great night out is friends, a flask, some Ecstasy, and some bitchin' music.

Mom

Hannah wants to go out every night. If we won't drive her downtown, she punishes us. She screams in our faces, following us around the house, spitting on the floor or into my mother's precious heirloom vases or into my food. When she still doesn't get her way by punishing us, she punishes herself, with razors, knives, and scissors. If she can't find something sharp, she burns herself. She doesn't even try to hide it anymore. She screams, "I need control of my own life. I need to make my own decisions." She tells me that the cutting and burning are my fault. I start to see bandages, remnants from childhood boo-boos, Barbies and NASCAR and dinosaur bandages on the raw, self-inflicted wounds, cuts that lay open her tender flesh to reveal her agony. Is it my fault? I stand in the bathroom, my tears dripping on the empty bandage box, mingling with her bloody fingerprints.

Hannah

She knows I'm not really taking a shower, even though I lock the bathroom door and turn the hot water on. I have a piece of glass today, a bit of the last dish I broke in front of her, and I scrape it over my inner thighs, harder and harder until the welt starts weeping blood and my pain pours out. I am overwhelmed with the sweetness of it, the amazing release of it after waiting for it all day. I look into the mirror, but the steamy fog makes it hard to see myself.

Mom

After waiting nine weeks for an appointment time with a psychologist who specializes in adolescent issues, Hannah is finally starting therapy. She is silent after school, chewing at her lip the way she does when she's deep in thought. I am happy, trying not to hum, relieved that I will finally have professional support. It's difficult to get an appointment with this therapist. She is sought after, her practice is closed, but she is seeing us as a favor to our rabbi. We climb the concrete stairs of her office building and travel down a long, dimly lit hallway to an unassuming office door. We should come right in, the little brass plaque assures us. The waiting room has no receptionist, just a couple of beige couches and a bunch of magazines, including *Seventeen*, *Teen Vogue*, *Elle Girl*, and *Boy's Life*—no surprise, given the therapist's specialty. Hannah helps herself to a paper cone of water from a corner cooler, and then studies the table magazines, moving them around daintily with one finger, as though afraid of getting infected by normalcy.

An interior door opens and we are both ushered in and asked to sit by a stout, gray-haired woman wearing a loose black dress and sensible shoes. She would like me to sit in on the first part of the hour, she explains, and then leave her with Hannah.

A dog lies under her desk, maybe an Australian Cattle Dog, and I wonder if it is a therapy dog. I don't get a chance to ask because Hannah wastes no time, announcing "I'm here because I have to be." I feel a jolt, a warning that things are going to turn bad, but the therapist nods, unruffled. She proceeds to ask Hannah questions, met by silence.

"Why do you think you were asked to come here? Do you have any goals for our time together?"

I squirm on the nubby, uncomfortable side chair, but though I want to explain everything—why we're here, and how much hurt is in our lives—I manage to hold my tongue because she is asking Hannah, not me. Hannah snaps back a response.

"I don't think much of therapy, and I don't think much of you. I mean isn't obesity a sign of mental issues?"

The therapist smiles. "Well, Hannah, I have a busy practice and many young people who want to be here. If you don't want to be here, I suggest that you don't waste either of our time."

Is she serious? Is this a bluff? We have searched for and then waited more than two months to see this therapist. Now, twenty minutes after we arrive, Hannah fires her. I try to catch the therapist's eye, but she is looking down at her desk, making some notes, maybe happy that she won't have to squeeze our pain into her busy evenings anymore.

"That's it?" I ask, astonished and angry. "That's all you have for us after a nine-week wait?"

The therapist looks up and half smiles, smug. "I can't help her if she refuses to participate."

I want to scream at her, to ask her how she became known as an expert. How can she possibly help teens if she's not willing to work to earn their trust? I turn to leave instead, swallowing my anger and despair at the session, at the wasted weeks, at my inability to help my daughter. Hannah has already walked out, and waits calmly, even happily, in the waiting room, leafing through *ELLE Magazine.*

"Can I go downtown now?" she asks sweetly, as we make our way down the stairwell. I don't answer, afraid of the sudden impulse I have to push her down the concrete steps.

Hannah

What a bogus therapist. Writes a couple of articles about teens and thinks she's hot shit. I guess she's the chief brainwasher, but I'm not interested in being fixed. Mom stumbles down the stairs after me, frightened rabbit look on her face, her mind someplace else entirely.

Mom

The second therapist we try is the one I've been seeing. This time Hannah sees her alone. After fifty minutes, she returns to the waiting area, the expected question voiced before I even get up from my chair.

"Can I go downtown now?" I nod, defeated. That was our deal, my bribe to get her here and sit through an entire session, and she bounces out of the office happily. The therapist steps into the waiting room.

"Susan," she says softly, "there may be something else going on here." I suspect that in therapy-speak "something else" means "something serious" or maybe "something I can't figure out." I just nod again, numb and a little confused, and she puts a card into my hand. She is referring us to a psychiatrist.

A small part of me is happy that a trained psychologist can't figure out what's wrong with my daughter. How can I expect to, if she can't? I call the number, and I'm surprised that he will give us an appointment for the following day. Then I drive Hannah downtown, knowing that I'm doing the wrong thing for the wrong reason, knowing that I am enabling her, knowing that the deal I made with her is a bad one, an abdication of my responsibility, knowing that I have given up, that I am frightened of the screaming monster she becomes when I refuse her, the monster that is growing and becoming uglier and more dangerous by the day. She gets out of the car, and I can breathe again. There will be quiet for a few hours. I pretend that she's going shopping or having coffee with friends, but deep down I know better. I pray that the appointment tomorrow will help.

Hannah

I'm not fucking crazy, I'm just tired of being me. Tired of fighting, tired of being different, tired of other people controlling my life. I thought agreeing to therapy would get everyone off my ass, but they aren't finished looking into my head. They're sending me to another shrink. At least this dude is interesting. He lives out in bum fuck nowhere so he can keep horses, filthy beasts. He's a pilot, and flies out of the little airport in town. He tells me that stuff right away, like he's either trying to impress me or warm me up by revealing personal shit. But what really interests me is his painting. I can't stop looking at it, a big, dark painting of mice, their little skullcaps cut off, electrodes and wires bristling out of their heads. I think it's weird that he hangs such a wild ass painting in a place where he's trying to keep crazy people calm. But his questions are all the normal ones, and so I have my lies all prepared.

"Do you do drugs?" he asks.

"Not really," I tell him, looking him in the eye and shaking my head. "I mean I smoke every now and then, but nothing else."

He nods and makes a note. He doesn't press me, doesn't doubt me, and I smile at him. This will be easy.

Mom

I have been sitting in the psychiatrist's little blue anteroom for nearly two hours, not trusting my irascible daughter with a stranger. I have been playing a movie of the school year in my head, in case I'm asked about my daughter's transformation from a bookish artist to a ball of anger and spite. Now she steps out of his inner office and leans against the door, trying to look indifferent. The doctor appears behind her, a concerned look on his face. I set the glossy Arabian horse magazine on the little end table and stand up. I think I am ready for anything, but I am wrong.

Hannah

I want to be the one to tell her, and so I talk before he has a chance. "Evidently, I'm bipolar." The words make it real, and I feel numb and a little scared. I dig my nails into my palms and focus on the pain to stay level. The shrink waves his hands towards me, like he's a magician, and he's just pulled a crazy person out of his hat. Mom looks confused and worried. She takes a step forward, but doesn't hug me because I've made it clear that I don't like her hugging me. I get a small moment of satisfaction from that, and then sit down while she takes her turn in the doctor's office. His office doesn't smell bad, but the waiting room that he shares with other doctors in the building has an undertone of wet dog, or maybe manure. I breathe deeply and try to figure out what just happened.

I went to middle school with a bipolar girl. She wasn't really anything like me. She screamed and twirled when she was manic, and sat in the back of the class staring at the back of my head or sleeping when she was depressed. The only way we're alike is that she's an artist like me. A musician. The shrink told me that there seems to be a strong correlation between creativity and bipolar disorder. Maybe he's trying to make me feel better cuz I'm an artist. I mean, like, all artists are a little cracked, right?

Mom

I'm caught completely off guard. The doctor asks me for some background, but there's no history of bipolar disorder in our family that I know about. And though Hannah has been moody her whole life ("an artistic temperament," we used to call it), she tends towards depression—not the mania that marks half of this disorder. But the doctor is certain.

"Her mood swings like a pendulum," he observes.

"Like a wrecking ball," my inner voice silently responds. The news is serious, but I am uplifted. We know what's wrong. Selfishly I relish the idea that it isn't me or my parenting, it's a disorder. Maybe now we can fix things, we can find our daughter again. Is there a name for this emotion, the blending of despair and relief I am feeling?

Hannah

The ride home is silent. We stop at the drug store and Mom goes to the pharmacy counter while I amuse myself by looking at sharp objects in the cosmetics section. Manicure scissors, hairpins, maybe even a mirror. I run my fingers over them slowly, planning my evening. I wander into the housewares area and smile at all the things there are to huff. Glues, cleaning solvents, markers. I tuck the thought away for another day and join Mom in line. The pharmacist looks me over as he hands the little white bag to Mother-person and goes over all the shit that can go wrong with the meds. I try on looking crazy for fun, pushing my hair back so he can see my gauges, giving him some googly eyes and scratching at my armpit. He looks away.

Mom

Hannah is on lithium now. The psychiatrist suggests that we dole out the pills to her each morning, and that we check her mouth to make sure she swallows them. Have you ever tried to drag an oppositional teenager out of her filthy room and get her to say "Ahhh?" I wake up every morning filled with dread for the day ahead. There will be anger, pain, maybe worse. I will say the wrong thing. I will get a call from the school. I will be embarrassed at a public place. Something bad happens every single day, and every day I hope that the lithium will help. Why doesn't it help?

I keep trying, knocking on her door every morning, waiting for the inevitable "fuck off," then bravely opening the door, pushing aside the detritus of a damaged soul . . . first the bed itself, which she pushes in front of the door to keep me out, then the filthy, stinking clothes, balled up discarded sketches, books, and an odd assortment of art supplies, including used brushes, uncapped tubes of oil paint (the good kind), and half full cups of paint-stained water. It's an archeological dig of discarded undertakings: months of failed projects, abandoned homework, half-eaten and moldy food, and an odd assortment of unusual items . . . a mountain of bottle caps, wire, headless dolls, and other potential art that sadly never makes it past being junk. Today there is something else. It's a drinking glass, but the liquid in it is a muddled yellow color. Flat beer? I sniff. No. It's urine.

Hannah

I figure I must be pretty crazy for them to go straight for the big guns like lithium. It's a pain in the ass to be dragged out of bed every morning and given pills like a prisoner. Mom is supposed to check my mouth, but she doesn't. If I wanted to, I could be nice and open my mouth to show her, but why should I give her the satisfaction? It would just feed into her 1960s TV family fantasy. Both of my parents are like that. "Oh, we just want to be a happy family skipping through the fields of flowers holding hands and singing 'Kumbaya.'" But TV families don't take meds every morning just to stay even. And they don't tuck their meds into their cheeks in order to spit them out.

Mom

Summer comes, a hazy mix of medical bills and mayhem inflicted by our older daughter. I tell the psychiatrist that the lithium doesn't seem to be working, and he counsels patience. "I have to titrate her dose." I ask him why her moods change so quickly. "Ultradian," he explains confidently, "extreme rapid cycling. She's more bipolar than my most bipolar patient. Text-book case, really."

I work up the courage to stop taking Hannah downtown as often as she likes, and she starts calling cabs, using her savings to pay the fare. When her savings run out, she borrows money from her sister, promising to pay her back, but never doing so. Finally, Camilla refuses her, and Hannah seeks revenge by decapitating the animals in Camilla's beloved Beanie Baby collection, carefully balancing the detached heads onto their truncated bodies so that when Camilla lifts the little creatures, their heads fall off and roll away for maximum horror. The screams are terrible, and I rush into Camilla's room in time to see her picking up one animal after another, heads rolling around the floor in a macabre legless dance. Hannah stands by, smiling, clearly satisfied with the effect. Camilla flies at her laughing sister with her whole body, hands shaped into claws, but Hannah is quick. She pulls her arm back all the way and swings at Camilla with an open hand, the force of her blow meeting the force of Camilla's forward movement with a loud crack, leaving Camilla crumpled on the hardwood floor, sobbing. Sudden rage moves my arm in response, and I slap Hannah, slap the laugh right out of her before I collapse next to Camilla, holding her, ashamed that I am unable to protect her from the terrorist in our home, ashamed that I have been violent towards Hannah. I groan with the pain of it, and it sounds like someone else's voice, feels like someone else's actions. Who have I become? I turn Camilla's sweet face to me; her cheeks are wet from tears, and her freckles are concealed under the red of Hannah's handprint. Hannah, unremorseful, has stalked off to her room, and I hear her door slam, a final note to the cacophony that is our lives. When our house is finally calm, I dial the doctor.

"No," he tells me, "she's not a danger to her sister." *How does he know?* I wonder. I want to believe him, believe that Hannah wouldn't hurt us, not really, but what if he's wrong? She hit Camilla, she hit me. I am afraid that her violence is becoming a fact. I try not to leave the girls alone, and Paul tries not to leave me alone. Our home is a war zone; no place is safe.

Hannah

The shrink only sees me once a month to regulate my drugs. He keeps upping my dose cuz I'm still crazy. I still cheek 'em cuz I'm not that crazy. They are going to make me see another therapist weekly to make sure I don't kill my family in their sleep. Mom is calling around.

Mom

I am emotionally exhausted, defeated really, but Paul keeps trying to reach Hannah. He offers her a car if she does her summer school work, but she declines, yelling, "I reject your bribes." He tries other things. Behavior contracts, reward systems, varying consequences—none of them have the slightest effect on Hannah's conduct that summer. She rips up the behavior contract, telling us, "I reject your values." We offer her an allowance if she does some chores around the house, but she rejects our money too. Hannah is malice in a pretty package. We cancel our vacations, skip family reunions, turn off our phones, and hunker down. We talk about switching schools, thinking that moving away from the bullies and the boy might help, but Hannah tells us she needs the art program, that she'll make it work. We believe her. We sign the school's paperwork for another year, our misplaced trust in every pen stroke.

Hannah

Summer is amazing. I've been using Ecstasy since fall, but now it seems like it's everywhere, and so easy to score. E makes everything seem more open and fun. Dylan got me to take it for sex, but I really like it for painting. I feel like my art really happens when I take it. It's worth the low that comes after the high. Besides, the low only lasts until I use again. So I do. It's a crazy roller coaster, and I know it will help me roll right through the new school year. I'm happy that I'll be seeing my friends every day, and finally have some freedom from the parent people—they are such a pain in the ass.

"Blah blah blah tuition, blah blah blah education, blah blah blah behavior." Whatever.

Mom

Hannah has a great first week in school, and I feel the tickle of hope that at long last we have come through the other side. I think about other phases she went through, like her Goth years, when she wore heavy eyeliner and a long black trench coat from the Salvation Army. After she was done with the look, she didn't wear black again for years. Maybe this is another phase, maybe we are done with her idiocy, maybe she'll be serious about school this year. It's not too late, I think. She can still get into a good college if she buckles down. I mention it, lightly, but Hannah has other ideas.

Chapter 3

Hannah

The first week of school was mind-numbing, but this week is going to rock. It's going to be a kick-ass weekend, and I want to get started so I get my parents, a.k.a. keepers, to release me Thursday night. There's a rave downtown, my girlfriend has her house to herself for the whole weekend, and Dylan, who is living with his bio-dad now, is in town. All the moving parts are in place for some major merry-making. That's why I can't understand why I feel so fucking low. I mean low like, "Oh do I have to breathe? It's such an effort."

I think some E will help—it usually does—so when I get to the club Thursday night, I wash down a half with my flask. That's how I like to roll, a half every twenty minutes until I hit the sweet spot. I kill the time waiting by drinking and dancing. But this time I'm just not getting what I need. Nothing. So I decide to call it an early night and just go home.

It's pathetic how happy my fat cow mother is when I get there, thinking I must be wearing out on downtown. I slam into my room, just so she knows it's not time to make s'mores and braid each other's hair. I can't seem to stay up or down. I'm all wacky out of control. I haven't taken my meds in a couple of days, so I start taking the lithium I've been cheeking to see if it will help steady me. After some of those, I don't know how many really, I decide to take a walk. In the movies when people take a bunch of pills, their friends always tell them to keep moving. I keep moving, but the bad feeling just keeps moving with me. I'm scared.

Mom

Thursday is a school night, so I am happy to see Hannah come home early. But by the time I knock on her door to offer her some hot chocolate, she is gone. Hannah has discovered how to disable the GPS on her phone, and Paul has to hunt for her with no help from technology. We risk calling a few of her friends, but nobody knows anything. I sit with the phone, dialing her number over and over again, pleading into her voice mailbox, then screaming into it while Paul gets in his car and starts driving past her favorite haunts. Downtown, the park, the coffee shop. He searches for hours. I check her closet and her bathroom to see if she has left home as she often threatens, but as far as I can tell, her things are all in place.

Finally, about 4:00 on Friday morning, Paul finds her walking unsteadily down our street, alone. He calls to let me know, and I rush out on the deck, grateful to see his car roll down the driveway, my legs weak under me. My relief turns into anger as she spills out of his car and unsteadily scuffs past me into the house without speaking or looking at me. I lose control. I grab her shirt and pull her into the bathroom. "Take a shower," I tell her, "because you are going to school today." She sits on the toilet and puts her head between her knees.

"Mom, please, I don't feel too good."

"Of course you don't. You've been out partying all night, on a school night too."

Hannah

I don't know if she's ever been this mad at me, and I don't want to lose the rest of the weekend, so I do my best to get ready for school. *I can do this*, I think, *it's just one day and then the weekend.* But when we get to the school parking lot, I can't fight off the dizziness and curl up in the front seat while Camilla bounces off into the building. What is happening to me? I try to focus, try to move, but moving makes the dizzy worse, so I freeze in place. I move my mouth but nothing comes out.

Mom

"Get out." I hiss, turning to her, pale and unfocused in the passenger seat. She's done this to me before, refusing to get out of the car. She opens her door and leans out.

"Mom, I'm gonna be sick."

"Well, have the school call you an ambulance then." I feign disinterest, studying my nails. "You're making me late."

I knew the moment I said them that I would be sorry for those words.

Hannah

I can't move myself out of the seat, and we sit in the empty parking lot for a while, me trying not to hurl, she talking to me in that hissy, angry voice, her eyes narrow. I don't hear a lot of what she says. I'm feeling loopy and floaty and sick, but when I try to tell her what I did, she cuts me off and tells me she doesn't want to hear my bullshit, that I'm irresponsible and selfish and all kinds of crap like that, and I guess I am, but I need to tell her that I'm in trouble, something's wrong. "I'm sick, I'm sick," is all I can manage with my rubbery lips. Finally, she leans towards me.

"You will go into the school right now or I'm taking you to the emergency room."

I pick the emergency room.

Mom

I don't panic until I see the alarm in the admitting nurse's face. Hannah is sitting dizzily on the straight back chair next to the nurse's desk, slurring a laundry list of drugs, and the amounts she thought she might have taken during the night. The next thing I know, she is in a bed in one of the emergency room cubicles, with lines of fluids dripping into her intravenously.

"The saline will help to attract the lithium that is still being time-released into her bloodstream," explains a second nurse as she adjusts the tubes snaking down Hannah's arm, the needle a fang, piercing the delicate blue vein on the back of her hand. Blood tests show that Hannah has toxic levels of lithium in her system, twice as much as the highest therapeutic level.

The doctor is grim. "She's one or two tablets away from coma, or death." I know that there is some appropriate thing to say when you're told your daughter is near death, but I don't have it, I can't find it, I am stone, I am statue still, I am frozen in a moment of horror. The doctor turns away from my shock, marking something on his clipboard. "I'd like you to stay and speak to county social services," he orders, as though I would leave my daughter. "A social worker will be arriving shortly." I don't understand.

I ask the doctor why we are seeing a social worker. He is blunt, and his tone accusatory. "We have to consider that this may be a suicide attempt." He explains that Hannah will be interviewed to determine if she's a danger to herself, or if I'm a danger to her.

I try not to sound too defensive. "She's not suicidal, she just did something stupid." He doesn't react at all, and suddenly I feel like I'm the one who is stupid. I groan and sink into the chair that I had pulled up beside Hannah's bed. My daughter was overdosing, and I didn't even see it. I didn't see her. Did she try to kill herself? I sit in the chair, reliving the night before, looking for clues to a suicidal mindset, but all I find are the taunts of an oppositional teenager and my angry words. Did I miss something? What have I done?

Hannah

Oh fuck, I really don't know how many pills I took, I don't fucking know how drinking or taking E makes lithium stronger, but they keep telling me it does and that I'm screwed. The doctor's face looks like a fucking Halloween mask, his mouth turned down all wonky. Aren't they supposed to make me feel better? They're scaring me. I feel like shit. Mom sits next to me with her hand on my forehead, pushing back my hair, staring at nothing. I dig around for something snarky to say, but it's too hard, too hard, and her hand feels too good. I close my eyes and stay quiet.

They move us into the corridor when they need the room, and Mom drags her chair to the foot of my bed, resting her head on the gurney and trying to doze. That's what I see when I open my eyes, Mom's head and shoulders hunched, her arms crossed tight across her body like she's trying to hold herself together.

Dad and Camilla get here, and Dad pretends everything is going to be okay, joking a little too loudly for the hallway of a hospital, people glancing over like he escaped from some yuck-it-up lunch meeting and wandered into the wrong building. Camilla hangs back like she knows better, she knows things won't be okay, like she's the only one who knows me, knows everything about me, knows what's going to happen. It occurs to me then that things might not be okay, and that makes me feel even sicker.

Pretty soon, a lady from the county gets there. She sends everyone away and talks to me for a long time, pulling up the chair Mom was trying to sleep in.

"Do you think of hurting yourself often?" she wants to know, balancing a beat up carry-on bag full of papers in her lap, and fumbling around the bottom of it for a pen. "What is

it like at your house? Does anyone hurt you there?" I consider
fucking with her, but I'm too tired.

Mom

I stand in the bustling hallway with Paul and tell the lady from
the county that Hannah is under the care of a psychiatrist.

"Good," she replies. "We may be able to release Hannah
in the care of a psychiatrist. I'll need to check in with him, and
he'll need to monitor her drug levels closely."

She calls him. Then we call him. The hospital calls him
too. He doesn't return our calls, then or ever. I dial him over
and over, leaving urgent messages, wishing I could slam a
receiver down for emphasis, the end button on my cell phone
inadequate to the task. Suddenly I realize what she said. That
she *may* be able to release Hannah. What is that supposed to
mean? What else would she do? Worry and exhaustion push me
against the wall, and I let it hold me up.

Hannah

That lady, the county hag? She seems pretty sure I tried to kill
myself. I try to tell her I didn't, that I just wanted to party with
my friends and that I felt really flat, really down and that they
have me on fucking lithium and that's what it's supposed to be
for, right, to help my moods, so I took it, but by the time she
finishes asking me questions I'm not really sure any more, and
that freaks me out. I work at the edge of the bandage holding
my IV in place and try to figure out what happened, and she
stands up and looks at my hands but not my face and tells me
to get some rest.

Mom

"No psychiatrist, no release." The social worker breaks the
news to Paul and me in a borrowed office—a tiny closet
really—already cramped with a desk, three chairs, and lots of

medical equipment covered in opaque plastic that is the same grey as her hair.

"What exactly are you saying?" I try to interpret her words, but they seem to be another language, one I don't understand. "You mean you won't release her from the hospital? You won't release her to us, her parents? How can you do that? What are you saying?" I struggle to remain calm, trying to hear what she's saying, what she's meaning.

"Hannah is clearly in trouble and needs support," she states. "Your psychiatrist seems . . . um . . . unavailable, and we shouldn't take any chances. Since the ER has some questions about Hannah's motives and has put forth the possibility of suicide, we can keep her safe at the behavioral hospital while she detoxes and we assess the situation."

I push down the panic and anger. "Assess the situation?" I search through my anger and disbelief for my next words, grateful for Paul and his unerring way of asking the right questions.

"Where will you take her?" (Fremont Behavioral Hospital.) "How can we be sure that's the best place for her?" (We can only put her where we have an opening.) "How will she be transported?" (An ambulance.) "Can we take her ourselves?" (No.) "Can we see her there?" (Yes, after twenty-four hours.)

I am hearing the conversation from the bottom of a deep shaft; it echoes and swirls around me like noxious gas. I cannot count the humiliations to which we have been subjected over the past year, there are too many, but this is worse, much worse. I have been holding my breath for such a long time, waiting for the conversation to change, waiting for the air to clear, to feel safe. These implications, though, they are too poisonous. I take a deep breath and bleed out the words I have been stanching.

"Do you think we've been hurting our daughter?" The shame of slapping Hannah rears up, and I push it away, clutching at myself. Paul puts his hand on my arm, so gently, trying not to wound me further.

The social worker looks sad as she replies, "I was really torn, but I think this might be best for your family."

What does she think is happening here, this gaunt woman in clothing too heavy for the weather? Am I supposed to trust her judgment? She doesn't know anything about our family. I am in the Parent Association. I bake for all the bake sales. I make posters for the mentor program. I make sure my children eat well and have decent clothes, send them to a private school, take them to museums and movies and travel. *I am not one of those bad parents.*

"How can you take my child away?" The year of frustration and fear pushes my question out. I am too loud, and the county lady stands too quickly, bumping into one of the plastic-covered machines, sending it skittering into the wall. I need her to answer me. "How can you just take her?" I demand. She silently hands Paul yet another business card for another therapist, extending her arm as far as she can to keep her distance from me, from my reaction, then turns and leaves us alone with our new reality.

Hannah

Honest, the loony bin is more like a jail than a hospital. They take my belt and my shoes, and even take the string that holds up the pajama bottoms my mom brings for me. I am put into a small windowless room, and at night the heavy wood door is locked behind me. They check on me through a little mesh opening every two hours. So creepy. During the day I go to sessions where everyone explains how they ended up here and how they feel, sitting on brown pleather couches and orange plastic chairs that look like they have been stolen from a cafeteria. Lucky for me we aren't required to speak. So I don't. And I don't speak when the parents visit either, except to tell them to go away and not come back. But they do come back. They bug me every single fucking day that I am there. One or both of them, even though I refuse to see them. Pathetic.

Mom

The doctor clears his throat and opens the hospital file. He stares at it so long that I wonder if it's the first time he has seen it. Paul and I sit on orange plastic chairs in a tiny conference room, holding hands and waiting. Finally, he speaks, the lovely singsong of his Indian accent in stark contrast to his words.

"Your daughter had a close call."

Is that supposed to be news to us? I shift in the uncomfortable chair, waiting. He looks up from the file and continues. "It will take us approximately a week to reduce the toxic levels of lithium in Hannah's bloodstream. After we lower her blood levels we can transition her to an alternative drug, Depakote. She may have to take more than one medication, but it will be safer."

"I thought she was here for three days." I say, pushing at the edge of the table, which is bolted securely to the floor. I am distracted. Why would they bolt the table down, but leave the chairs loose? What is the point?

"Well," answers the doctor, an assortment of pens threatening to fall out of his pocket as he leans forward over the table, "it will be much safer for her here. We can monitor her blood levels during her transition."

I bristle. How can I know what to believe, who to trust, how to move forward? The doctor gets up and leaves, and I turn to Paul. "What should we do?" He doesn't answer right away, tapping at the table as though he is expecting a message to come through in reply.

Maybe it does, because he looks up at me and says, "It's time to try something new."

Hannah

Fuck. They're keeping me in lockdown. I sit on my narrow bed in the little cell they keep me in and listen to the doctor explain something about detoxing me. He leaves, and I turn to my roommate to complain, but the figure under the blankets faces the wall, a miniature mountain range of sharp peaks and angles, unmoving, and so I lie down and stare at the ceiling and keep it to myself.

Mom

We've heard about Bodin a number of times, from the school, and from the bevy of therapists we have seen. They are educational consultants, and I soon learn that's a pretty polite term for what they actually do. We meet with Doug Bodin across his large, clean desk. He's a big guy, and he takes a moment to rearrange himself in his leather office chair before explaining his company and how it might help.

"We do psychological testing and advising, and match families with programs." He hones right in on the phone conversation he has had with Paul. "We often work on the spectrum between learning differences and behavioral issues. Sometimes our recommendations include sending your teen away, for recovery, rehabilitation, or to remove them from a destructive environment and help them to complete their education."

I shake my head at the notion that our home is a destructive environment. Maybe destructive environment means downtown, or school, but I don't want to ask.

Doug is still speaking. "Tell me, what are your objectives? That would give me a better idea about how we might be able to help you."

I state what seems obvious to us. "We want our daughter back. We want her home again." We ask him for help.

Hannah

Doug Bodin is big. He's big and ginger and pretty happy for a guy who makes his living talking to fucked up kids and their parents. He comes to the nuthouse, and we meet in a cheesy little conference room with a fake wood table and the same ugly orange chairs that they have in the crazy person section. The table is bolted to the ground, and I wonder if it's so I can't turn it over in a rage, or hang myself from the ceiling sprinklers by kicking it over. Anyway, this Bodin guy doesn't fuck around. He tells me that he is looking at educational alternatives, "in case you can't get along at home." He asks me if I know what that means, and I answer, "Fuck, no." So he explains about going to school in a controlled environment, how it some-times helps to get distance from the things that are getting me in trouble. I think this means a place they lock you up and remove fun until you are eighteen. I ask him for details, but he is vague. He's pretty clear when he talks about what is expected of me at home, though. I can't believe my parents have hired an enforcer. What wimps.

Mom

Bringing Hannah home again is wonderful and awful. She goes to her room wordlessly, and soon I hear music and the creak of her bed springs. I relax, thinking she has finally calmed down. Within twenty-four hours, she is asking to go out. We tell her that she can go out next weekend, as soon as she sees her new therapist. That night she sneaks out.

Hannah

They don't get it. I have been locked up with slobbering, vio-lent, confused, emotionally broken people for a whole week, locked in a little room at night and expected to eat green Jell-O every day. I listened to a bone-thin roommate cry herself to sleep every night, and watched her flush her dinner the way I flush my pills. I want to go out. I want to see my friends. I want to be free. Who the fuck do they think they are?

Mom

The next day we block the back doors of Hannah's bedroom with a heavy patio table, stacking the matching chairs on top of it, making a wall that will scrape and screech if she tries to push her doors open. Paul and I drag the heavy table together, and though he offers to sleep downstairs, in front of the other door to her room, I insist that it should be me.

"You have to be at work early in the morning," I tell him, bussing his cheek and moving off to get my bed pillow from our room, as though guarding our daughter was somehow deserving of a casual kiss and light conversation. I push the living room couch closer to her door, but don't make it up with sheets, preferring the discomfort of the leather to keep me on the edge of wakefulness. I pull the comforter up around my neck, trying to get comfortable on the cold leather of the too-narrow couch that we purchased to fit the long room just so. The furniture is now askew, a messy sentinel post in our living room, and I am a guard, dressed in sweats in case I have to chase after our escaped prisoner. I hug my pillow for comfort and resolve. If Hannah wants to go out, she has to see the therapist.

Hannah

Wow, this new therapist, this chick's got a doctor's degree? She looks about my age, and she can barely speak English. Not like an accent or anything, but bad grammar, and that bugs me. She's pretty stupid, too, even a drug-addled idiot like me can twist her into a pretzel. She pretends not to notice, her legs tucked under her in a sort of forced, casual pose. Is she trying to set me at ease?

She's wearing a little knit dress over black tights, and I can't keep my eyes off a run that's peeking out from under the hem.

I finally lose my patience with her, and tell her to stop speaking at me. "Do you have a fucking question? If you do, please try to use proper English. It will inspire more confidence in me." She is flustered. Good. I smile at her, knowing I have done my bad deed for the day.

Mom

This therapist is young and fashionable and upbeat, and I like her right away. She is so different from the others that I am hopeful it will be a good match. My hope falls away quickly, as Hannah brings her abusive A-game to bear. After less than thirty minutes, I am slouched in my chair chewing on my knuckles, Paul is standing next to me, and Hannah is grinning like a Cheshire cat. The doctor asks Hannah to excuse us, and my daughter pops out of her chair like a movie is over and flounces out to beat the crowd, smirking.

Hannah

That was fun. I wonder who they'll dig up next.

Mom

I don't expect that we will ever see this therapist again, and she confirms that for us in no uncertain terms. After her pronouncement, she walks Paul and me out to the empty lobby. She turns to us, her eyes compassionate.

"Please think about a residential treatment program," she says softly, adding "She's sixteen. You don't have much time." Then she is gone, another of Hannah's discards, another sign that our daughter needs something or someone we haven't yet found.

Hannah

Wow, I'm so fucked up, I did a bad combination of shit, and I can't remember exactly what I took. I'm getting that not-okay feeling again, not the kind that sent me to the wacky shack last time, but the spinny kind you get when you drink too much too fast or eat the worm out of the mezcal. I wouldn't have to party this hard if my fucking jailers just let me out more often instead of locking me in my fucking room and building a patio furniture wall around me. I feel sick, and I ask to get out of the car I'm in, and the car stops with a jerk, and someone pulls me out of the back seat and half carries me over to the sidewalk. Who was it? It's dark here, and I lean back and feel around my bag for my phone. I call Mom, cuz that what she tells me I should do. "Just call me," she always says, "I won't be mad if you call me." But that's a lie.

Mom

Hannah is very drunk and very high. She is calling from a side street downtown, where her friends have left her half lying in a hedge, a pool of vomit around her. Paul is out, and I have to bring Camilla with me. She sits in the car and watches as I pull Hannah to her feet and support her as she stumbles to the car. Camilla is silent as Hannah climbs into the back seat, the foul smell of vomit and smoke announcing her presence.

"Take me home," she groans, scrunching down in the seat so none of her buddies on the street will see her in the car. I consider taking her to the ER, but decide that I can take her home. She seems more drunk than anything, and without lithium this time. I drive home, keeping her in my rear-view mirror. After getting Hannah into the house, she staggers off to bed, and I upend her oddly heavy woven bag on the kitchen counter. Out spill an assortment of ways to get in trouble . . . cigarettes, a rolled joint, some pot in a small plastic box, and there, some old lithium tablets speckled with tobacco flakes and lint, more unidentified pills in a rainbow of colors, a kitchen knife, and a hammer.

That's the night we have the big fight. The night I dump her drugs down the toilet, thinking how much I would like to keep the pot and cigarettes even as I do it, longing for the pleasure of a buzz and the long slow inhale of nicotine to get me through this terrible night. She screams at me, flailing at my hands as they upturn her little boxes and bags into the john.

"That's my fucking property, you cunt, back off, leave me the fuck alone!" she screams, disjointed thoughts and ideas, all violent. She is going to beat the crap out of me. She is going to cut me, cut my thumbs off. She is going to kill me. I believe her, believe she could do it, but I'm too angry and too frustrated to be careful. Camilla is safe in her room, but I stand in the bathroom, listening to abuse, watching Hannah's hands for sudden movements. Paul comes home as she threatens me, his voice joining the fray. Wrapping his arms around her, he pulls her out of the bathroom and into her room, slamming her bedroom door so hard the frame breaks.

If we had neighbors, they would surely have called the police, but our woods buffer us from civilization, eliminating the need for control. That night Camilla cries in her room, hiding under her covers. That night Hannah tells us she wants to go away.

"Send me someplace, anyplace," she spits out. "Anything would be better than living here. I can't stand you fucking people. Let me go!"

We talk to Hannah in the calm of morning, light streaming into the living room, hot chocolate steaming between her shaking hands.

"Yes," she tells us. "I meant what I said last night." She sips, studying the swirls in her cup. "I want to go away. I don't want to live with you people anymore." Her words tear at me the way Paul has torn the remains of the broken door frame off the wall. I study the nail holes and the rough edges of the plasterboard that were revealed when the smooth wood was removed.

Bodin has prepared us, and we know what to say. Paul explains what happens next.

"Hannah, you have to be assessed before you can enroll in a residential program." She asks what kind of assessment. Paul answers her. "Either a hospital or a program that's designed specifically for that purpose. It could take us a few days to pull it all together."

"I prefer the hospital," she decides on the spot, her tapered finger pressed thoughtfully against her chin. "They're all fucked up crazy there, but at least they have a big screen TV."

Paul pulls out his cell phone and calls Bodin. "We've decided to go ahead with a placement." Their recommendation, when it comes later that day, does not include a big screen TV.

Hannah

I don't know what I expected, but I am surprised when Dad whips out his phone and starts making arrangements. Maybe I thought it was a bluff, like when you stick out your tongue and they tell you it will stick that way. But it isn't a bluff, and two days later Mom and Dad wake me up together. It's still dark outside, and I guess it's about 4:00 a.m.

"It's time to go," they say. "You have about an hour. You'll need to get up now if you'd like to shower before you leave."

What? Where am I going? They wouldn't wake me up this early for the hospital. I'm too groggy to ask a lot of questions, but when I get up to pee and see this big dude hanging out near our front door, I know this could have gone down a lot worse. I think about the kid in my school who was tackled in the hallway by goons. I get up and shower.

Mom

I want to give Hannah more notice, but the escort service is adamant. We have to negotiate hard with them to arrange enough time for Hannah to shower and have breakfast. We try to explain.

"This is voluntary. We want her treated respectfully." They say they understand, but when they arrive at our house they ask where the exits are, and put one person near the front door, and one on the back deck. I wonder what they've seen. What they've done.

Hannah isn't supposed to pack anything; our only instructions are to have her wear her glasses, not contacts. Paul and I pace heavily around the living room, waiting for the moment when Hannah leaves. I run my hands through my morning tangles, wondering if we are doing the right thing.

Hannah

The parents walk outside with me, but I don't say goodbye to them. Fuck them and their Nazi ways. My escorts have a green SUV that has boxes of binders on the back seat, and we all sit up front on the bench seat. I finally have a chance to get a good look at them. There are two, a guy and a girl. The guy is tall and a little burly with short hair that sticks up like he's been French kissing a socket. In his tight black T-shirt and leather jacket, he looks like a bouncer. I guess he's the muscle. The girl is pockmarked, like she worked her zits over pretty good when she was younger. She's wearing a cute pink T-shirt with a grey hoodie, and skinny jeans with Van kicks. She's so thin that she kind of looks like my bulimic roommate from the loony bin.

I can't get any information out of them, but it's pretty clear that I am flying somewhere when we pull into the airport, and my stomach flip flops at the idea. They park the car, and we all go through security, them waving some paperwork around, then to the gate, where the board says Salt Lake City. Shit, they are sending me to fucking Utah! I try to remember what I know about Utah, but the only thing I can think of is the TV show about the Mormon dude with three wives. Zit girl is cool and offers to buy me a magazine for the flight. I pick *Marie Claire*.

Oddly, it reminds me of Mother-person, and the magazines she used to send me at camp along with cheerful letters, decks of cards, and little gifts. I feel a stab of something, but it's time to board, and we all get on the plane.

It's bumpy, going over the mountains, and then we land, sailing between mountain ranges, the plane's wings waggling like they're signaling our arrival. My escorts walk me to the terminal and say goodbye, handing me off to a youngish chick with dreads and an old dude with grey hair and a grim face. They don't use my name when they say goodbye, and I wonder if they remember it.

"Wait!" I want to yell as they turn back into the gate area, "I'm scared to go with these strangers." Then I realize how ridiculous it is. They are all strangers, and I am on my own. Just like I want to be.

We get into a big white van, and I'm in the middle again, and it occurs to me that it wasn't the boxes that made my first escorts sit with me in the front of the green SUV. I wonder if anyone has ever actually tried to jump out of the car, and weirdly it makes me feel more sane to know I wouldn't do that. It's a long, quiet drive, the last part of it just long views with nothing to look at but distant mountains.

It takes about two hours before we finally get to a dumpy little town. Dreads tells me it's called Duchesne. Old Dude pulls the van into a small parking lot, and walks me into this little box of a building. The small sign on the door tells me I have arrived at Second Nature Wilderness Program. This is where I am going to be assessed? Fuck.

Mom

We feel it right away. A gaping hole in our family, and the feeling that we have failed our daughter. Her animosity lingers in the air, choking me. I throw open the French doors and rush out on the deck, gasping. Gripping the deck railing, I realize there is no place to go to get away from what just happened. Paul steps outside and stands at the railing next to me.

"I'll take Camilla to school today," he says. I wonder if he's trying to help me, or if he too needs to escape the oppressive air in our broken home.

"I'll go with you," I reply, not caring that I wasn't invited. There's no way to pretend that it's a normal morning, no way to reassure Camilla, and no way to rewind to the family that we were last year, or even last week. We would be something else now.

Chapter 4

Mom

We did it. We sent our child, our responsibility, one quarter of our family away to a place called Second Nature Wilderness Programs. We gave her over to strangers because we had failed to parent her enough, to love her enough, to discipline her enough. We had failed to see the bipolar disorder that separated her from the people she loved. We let others in some faraway place assign her to a group of strangers who would somehow provide better care than we did, and do so in the middle of a frozen wilderness. Up until that surreal moment when I watch her narrow back walk out the front door, I think "we are bluffing." I am sure that at the eleventh hour, Paul and I will have some kind of emotional "MacGyver moment" when we can find some magical way to keep Hannah with us. But we don't, and Hannah is gone.

Part of our anguish is about loss, but if I am really honest with myself, part of it is shame and embarrassment. We are not "one of those families," the ones with the problem kids, the ones who give up on each other to put their faith in—in what? The promises of strangers? It occurs to me then how little I actually know about these types of programs. My daughter–mother book group recently read a powerful book called *Jesusland* by Julia Scheeres that described all kinds of program abuses, so I know just enough to ask some basic questions before entrusting Hannah into their care. "What kind of population do you serve? What does discipline look like there? How often will Hannah have therapy? How exactly will she be assessed? What if she gets sick or hurt?" Later I find a complete list of questions recommended by the National Association of Therapeutic Schools and Programs, and realize that I hadn't asked nearly as many questions as I should have. Questions like "What kind of training is provided to your staff? How do you involve parents? What is your success rate?" And "Do you pay a finder's fee to the referring educational consultants?"

I spend my nights researching and reading, back in my own bed, leaning back on a pillow in the silent house. My phone, no longer a jailer's tool, now charges soundlessly on my dresser. As I read, my horror grows. I learn that there is a plethora of programs staffed with substandard, minimum wage employees, programs using starvation as a behavioral tool, programs that are therapeutically unsound, programs that are about growing profits at the expense of patients. I stare at the mute television screen vacantly and hope desperately that I haven't put my daughter in danger.

Hannah

The pillbox building that houses Second Nature looks like a car rental place, or a mechanic's garage, but without those big doors. Inside was gross—grayish speckled linoleum on the floor, a bunch of little offices lining a narrow hall that dead ends in a lounge with a couple of ratty couches.

My escorts hand me off like a fucking package, signing papers, and then waving to one of the office people as they leave. Just another day at the office. I watch them walk out the door and wonder where they're going next. I mean, nobody ever says, "When I grow up I want to catch errant drug addicts and deliver them to shitholes to be rehabbed." The office person, a young woman with greasy brown hair and a lumber-jacky kind of vest, is still fascinated by my paperwork, so I pass the time imagining Dread and Old Dude as kids. Did Dread round up her dolls into the Playschool sheep pen and tell them to stay put if they knew what was good for them? Maybe Old Dude used his toy gun to take plastic Indians from fort to fort. Whatever. I'm just glad to be out of the car. Until they strip-search me.

Mom

Second Nature tells us that Hannah's first evaluation will be a physical. They have to be sure she's not carrying any drugs, and they have to know that she is fit enough for the program. I imagine Hannah being checked out the way I had checked out my last rental car. Walking round and round the vehicle, noting the dents and scratches and making sure that I wouldn't be blamed for any damage that was previously incurred. And Hannah had plenty of dents and scratches. I imagine them marking some sort of ambiguous human line drawing—the self-inflicted cuts, the cigarette burns, the piercings and the home-made tattoos that had been done in the late hours of the night in her bathroom with an old electric toothbrush and a sewing needle. The large gauges in her ears would be hanging loose now, like pulled taffy. I touch my own earlobe, and fervently hope that Hannah and I can someday forgive each other for all of the indignities we have caused the other to suffer.

Hannah

"Better tuck those earlobes into your hat." That's what they tell me after forcing me to take out my gauges. I had worked so fucking hard to slowly increase the size of those gauges, until they were over an inch large. I had so much fun shopping for unusual pieces to put in the quarter-size holes. Beautiful stones, metal rings, and my favorite: flies encased in Lucite. I loved wearing those—it freaked my mom out so bad. She hates my gauges. She claims it's cuz I had "mutilated" myself, and done it secretly, wearing my hair over my ears and developing a sudden love of hats. But I think she hates them because it proves she wasn't really paying attention to what was happening to me. It's like, "These holes you didn't see in your kid's head demonstrate that you are blind to her needs." Well, what I need now is a TV, a smoke, and a nap. But instead I get more advice. "Those ear lobes will freeze and break off if you don't tuck them in." That's a joke, right?

Mom

As Hannah settles into the Wilderness Program, so do we. Second Nature requires Paul and I to complete an assignment every week, one similar to what Hannah is working on, and then we will eventually talk about it in therapy sessions that are going to be conducted over a satellite phone from the wastelands where Hannah's group wanders like nomads, continually searching—not for a location in the vast high desert, but for some calm, safe, inner oasis.

It is our job to write the first letter. We need to take responsibility for sending her away. Our new therapist from the program counsels us.

"Don't use terms like 'when you went away.' Take responsibility for what you have done, and make sure you tell her why you did it." His name is Jason, and he gives us careful instructions. He describes how specific the letter should be in some areas, and how vague it should be in others. In particular, he warns us not to make any promises about the timeline for her care, or where she will go next. "Those things are completely dependent on her," he states flatly. This letter is our only chance to reach out to Hannah, since we are not yet permitted to speak with her. Paul and I are expected to write this letter together, but we decide to each write a version alone, and then merge them.

I lie down in my bed, buffered by pillows, in the still part of the evening to write and to take inventory of myself. I still feel a deep sense of loss and grief, but something else too, as I soak in the quiet the way one soaks in a tub. It is the first warm, calm wave of relief I have had in over a year. An evening without stress and screaming and dread. Someone named Jason seems to have our back. I doodle his name in the corner, like a schoolgirl in love, and hope he won't break our hearts.

Camilla comes into the room like a prairie dog poking its nose out of the ground to sniff for safety. She settles next to me on the pillows, but says nothing. I notice her eyes are red-rimmed, and I reach out to touch her hand. Paul joins us, sitting heavily on his side of the bed, opening his laptop. Looking at each other through the hush of the house, we feel relief, but none of us admits it out loud. We write through our guilt.

It's time to compare our thoughts. Sitting in Paul's home office off the "family" room that is never used, we struggle to find words we both believe to be true. We agree that Hannah's behaviors have driven our decision, but we are both stunned to learn how far apart we are when it comes to specifics.

"I think that her heavy drug use is really frightening," I venture tentatively. He disagrees.

"Lots of kids experiment with drugs," he responds with a dismissive shrug. The conversation continues later as we undress for bed, spurred by the remnants of a bruise on my arm.

"She hits you." Paul says simply, pointing to the bruise as though its lingering presence is evidence enough of our need to send our daughter away.

"Don't put this on my relationship with her," I reply, the anger rising up just ahead of the denial. "You're the one who taught her to always question authority."

"At least I taught her something," he replies quickly, and though I know the response is more repartee than reality, it adds another layer of hurt to the growing pain of sending Hannah away.

We search for days for common ground. We argue on the phone, in bed, and in the bathroom—one of us sitting on the toilet, the other trapped in the shower stall. Finally, we realize that no one thing—even no few things—had led us to this point. No, it was everything. When I close my eyes, I can still hear the echoes of her screams, see her cuts, feel the hostility coming off her in thick waves.

Once Paul and I stop trying to place blame—at least out loud—we decide to base our letter not on her behaviors, but on the basic expectations she failed to meet, and our concern that she seemed out of control. Then, still reeling from the decision we made, we begin to write, our need to meet the deadline Jason had set acting as a tool for détente between us.

Dear Hannah,
We hope you are well. We made the decision last week to send you to Second Nature for the assessment you need before moving on to a boarding program.

So far so good. Paul and I work through the letter's introduction, sitting in his home office on the swiveling leather chairs he brought from his old workplace, my stocking feet on his desk while he sits at the keyboard and types the final version of our first letter to Hannah. I read him my next section.

> *For us, the decision was not because you indicated that you were ready to move out and away from us. It was because we have been concerned with your inability to take charge of your life. You were failing school, fighting the few rules and restrictions that we put on you, and making life here at home very difficult for all of us. You told us to "stay the fuck out of your business" when we asked even the most general questions about school. "I can handle it," you said. But you were not handling it.*

Paul lifts his hands off the keyboard. "Susan, it *is* partly because she was ready to move out that we made the decision," he says, picking at my words. "That's not truthful."

"But that's not the main reason, Paul," I respond impatiently. "There are larger issues, like what she wanted to do once she did move out. And how it was going at home and at school. And how she refused help." He grimaces, and types.

> *You could have earned our trust and more freedom by attending school, doing homework, raising your grades, and getting off of academic and behavioral probation at school.*

"Do we want to mention her friends, her embarrassment of us?" he asks. I think maybe we should, but not as a main focus. Lots of teens are embarrassed by their parents. But not a lot of them use a variety of heavy drugs, burn and cut themselves, and threaten violence. We agree to stay focused on Hannah.

You found our rules restrictive and refused to acknowledge any authority in your life. You spoke frequently about moving out. How you hated us. How we were making you sick. You were taking money from your sister, speaking threateningly to her and to me, smoking, drinking, and using a variety of drugs. You were failing school.

"Paul," I say, stopping my swiveling and lowering my feet to the floor. "We should remind her that we wanted her to stay home." He nods.

We tried to help you fix these problems at home. You would not work with a tutor. The outpatient strategies we tried did not work for you. You fired three therapists in the course of six months. You overdosed on lithium, and spent a week in a locked psychiatric facility. This, you told us, was our fault.

"Was it our fault?" I ask, and Paul is disgusted with me. "That's a bad attitude." He continues, without answering my question.

Hannah, we love you and want you to have a full, happy, and independent life. The Second Nature program will offer you qualified support to help you start on that path. We know that this program is a tough stepping stone, but we believe that you will grow and benefit from this experience. How long it lasts is completely up to you. When you are done with your work at Second Nature, you will move on to another level of care. This goal is achievable and completely in your hands.

"What about this next level of care? We haven't made any decisions yet." Paul has stopped typing again, his scowl pointing towards me.

I lose my patience. "Well," I snap, "the next level of care can be here at home. It's vague on purpose. Just let it go!" I want to be done with this project, with this confession to myself. It feels defensive, like we are trying to justify giving up. We struggle through the rest of the letter, until the end. The last line is easy.

> *We send you our love every single day; our thoughts*
> *are never far from you.*
> Mom and Dad

I look down at the single sheet of paper that represents the last long, ugly year with Hannah. It is a statement of our intent, but between the lines, the page contains some hard truths. I am disheartened at how distrustful Paul and I are of each other's parenting and how differently we think about Hannah's actions. We are off balance from the enormous decision we have just made to send her away, and in this moment, when I need Paul's support so desperately, I find that we may be adversaries.

Hannah

Well, fuck my life! I'm in a wasteland with a bunch of messed-up street urchins who are so bored that they want to fix me. I look at this bunch of hobos and whores and know they have nothing to teach me. They are dirty, they stink, and they are meaner than hell. At least they're mean to me. They seem to like each other just fine. They sit near the fire in the freezing Utah desert and chat away, like they're at some fucking Girl Scout Jamboree, watching me on the edge of camp with sideways glances, all smug like I am carrying Ebola, and they have the cure.

I'm not allowed to join the group until I write my life story, and they are making me live on the edge of camp until I do. I close my eyes and try to imagine Dylan, but for some reason the images that come are my mom's face when I was leaving, and my dogs trailing me out to the van like we were going for a ride. I tuck my earlobes up into my cap, and decided right then and there that I will have to go through the motions to get out of here as fast as possible. They are trying to get inside my head by knowing about my life, and if that's what it's going to take to get out of here, then fine. I can crap out some drama for them, let them stir it around, and get on the next flight home.

The therapist here, Jason, comes the next day, crunching over the scattered patches of new snow with his beat-up work boots and camo pants, and I am all good girl, telling him I'm ready to write my life story.

"That's good, Hannah," he rasps, in a look-through-you kind of way. "You can sit in on group session today, and then start the assignment during personal time."

Great, I have to let the bitches take me apart, and then I will have to take myself apart. Why? I'm fine just the way I am. I'm fine. But the fire looks warm, and my mother's sad face is waiting just behind my eyelids, and so I gather up my shit and join the group. Surprisingly, the bitches do not jump on me. Maybe it's a welcome gift. I listen to them, these girls who have been abused and raped, the alcoholics, and the drug addicts. I admit, mostly I think, "Get over yourselves, bitches." But who is this little girl, she couldn't be more than thirteen years old, why is she here? Who gave this girl heroin?

Mom

As November begins, the loneliness gathers around Hannah like the darkness of the shortening days, and she finally writes an abbreviated story of her life.

We receive it the way we will receive all of her communication. Letters and journal entries are collected in mailbags from the scraggly, filthy groups of kids living in the vast, cold, high desert, and processed by an office person at Second Nature—2N as they call it, then shared with us online.

The writing, when we finally see it, is a scrawl, and I picture Hannah, hunched over in the cold, layers of stained clothing like I see on the website pictures making writing awkward, maybe one glove off as she balances a notebook and a blunt pencil stub. The content itself is in as much disarray as the writer, out of order, confused, and rambling. The paper shows the grime and smears of rough living, and I can almost smell the campfire smoke wafting up from the pages I print out. I gather the pages up and walk softly down the stairs to her room, wanting to be alone with Hannah for a few minutes before sharing her writing with Paul. Curling up on her bed, still unmade and gritty, I push sketchbooks, dirty clothes, an empty cup, and a spool of thick wire out of the way with my foot and read her version of the family life that Paul and I have built around our children. I read her bitter complaints about her treatment at the private schools she attended, the deaths of her grandmothers, the tension with her little sister, and her over-identification with the troubled children at school. I am puzzled. Where, I ask, are all the good times we had as a family? There is not a word about the fun, the travel, her activities, or her friendships.

Hannah writes that our love for her is tied to her accomplishments. Do we really make her feel that way? Hannah complains about how strict we are as parents. Is she comparing us to the parents of the wild band of roving, underachieving teens who make up the downtown Santa Cruz scene? Her story shuns us, our life, our values, our love. I am confused—and yes, angry—to be painted in such a negative way to people who know us not at all, until I realize that this is her story, and she has a right to tell it her way. I suddenly remember a scene that took place in our kitchen the year before as she prepared to go out.

"Hannah," I had said, flipping through the pages of a cookbook at the kitchen table, "you might want to grab a sweater."

"You know how I hear that, Mom?" she replied, her lip slightly curled in the permanent sneer she seemed to wear during our conversations, "I hear you saying that I'm too stupid to know how to dress." No, Hannah's truth is her own, and I will have to accept it.

Once Hannah's life story is on paper, whether I think it complete or not, Jason asks her to reflect on the journey that has landed her in the program. For some reason, she takes this assignment on willingly, and as rough as I know the output is bound to be, I am buoyed by the fact that she is finally cooperating. The smudgy looking letter comes later that week, and I find myself in the middle of eight incoherent, scary, puzzling pages alternatively taking responsibility, blaming others, and musing about the impact her actions may have had on us.

The disjointed letter, full of scribbled out paragraphs, misspelled words, and frightening doodles, written by a young woman who has always loved language and writes beautiful, compelling poetry, is not recognizable as hers. Curling up in my now familiar spot on her disheveled bed, I search for chunks of letter that seem coherent. Hannah seems to be grappling with the choices she has made:

"I had to hide what and where I had done for no reason good enough to really hide it. I asked myself, what had I done? And why did I do that?"

And could this possibly be empathy?

"... I believe ... I am a liar, to myself and you, a selfish person, and that I don't recognize the consequences of my actions. I know that blaming it on you must have made you feel like a failure, and that the whole event made you feel inadequate as a protector. Let me tell you, though, that you shouldn't have to feel that way, and that it is awful and inhumane I ever made you feel that way."

When I start crying there on my daughter's bed, it might be from the pain of reliving the night she is describing, or it might be my relief that Hannah is finally taking at least some responsibility for her actions.

My relief is mixed with the fear that Hannah will never be the same again—my bright and talented daughter replaced by this drug-addled shell—a confused child with a broken pencil.

If I had thought of it, I might have cried too about the fact that Hannah may be manipulating me once again. I read the letters two more times through my tears, jot down some questions in a little brown notebook I've purchased, and put the letters in a drawer, asking Paul to print his own copy.

Soon after this first letter comes Hannah's first journal entry. Jason tries to prepare us for it in our weekly meeting.

"It can be rough," he says. "I mean, you know your kid is taking part in some dangerous behaviors, but this is the confirmation."

Jason is right. It is rough. Paul holds my hand as we sit on our bed and read the detailed list of her behaviors, a testament to bad judgment in Hannah's own hand, her scribbles acting as confirmation of the lingering effects of the damage she has visited upon herself. We read silently, together, Paul holding the pages with one steady hand and me worrying at a frayed place in the blanket as though trying to dig my way out of this situation.

The long list of drugs is vague; did she even know what she was taking? In some places she describes the drug by the way it looked, or what it felt like, not knowing what to call it. In contrast, her self-harm is described in vivid detail, the cutting, the burning, the tattoos, where she was, how she did it, what she used, how she felt. It is a methodical inventory of her misdeeds, a recipe for hastening death. Hannah has obtained a variety of drugs from friends, friends of friends, strangers, and our own medicine cabinet. She has smoked weed and cigarettes, and drunk alcohol. She has used a variety of amphetamines, hallucinogens, and narcotics. She has huffed paint and glue and gasoline. Her drug and alcohol use took place in parks, alleys, friends' houses, and sometimes here at our home. She has used drugs loosely and freely, not knowing or not caring that they would intensify the effects of the lithium she took to control her mood swings.

She has burned herself and allowed herself to be burned with cigarettes and lighters. And she has cut and cut and cut herself in an effort to relieve her pain when self-medicating did not help her. She has tattooed her self-worth on her stomach: one cent. I don't know how long we sit there, Paul and I. It probably isn't as long as I think it to be. I do know that we don't talk, and we don't move except for his grip on my hand, which tightens just before he releases it and slips off the bed.

"I'm going to feed the dogs," he says, his strained voice betraying the incongruity of doing something so mundane after reading Hannah's confession. He walks out of the room, leaving me with the damaged blanket and my guilt.

Hannah

It is weird to write it all down, and even weirder to read it out loud sitting in the dirt with these girls. You know what else is weird? They are strangers, but I know them, and they know me. They keep nodding, and saying, "Yeah," like I am talking about their life, not mine. They seem to know when I'm bullshitting too, so I mostly don't bother.

I breathe the smoke in from the fire, wishing I had a cig, and get to the rest of the story. The part about Dylan, and porn, and doing it on E with his buddy in the room. It seemed funny before, but now it seems grimier than the dirt I am sitting in. I tell them about tattooing myself, but none of them ask to see. I tell them about binging and purging with food, and how I dropped my goal by five pounds every time I reached my weight, but the only reaction is when one of them puts her hand to her own stomach and looks away. I tell them about sponging change off tourists who came to Santa Cruz, and how easy it was to get money to party with my friends, how they would laugh and tell me I was fucking awesome and how I loved to be out on the street with them, and how I wanted to live in a co-op there in that weird and wonderful little city.

It is hard to say these things, cuz I sort of feel like I'm talking about someone else, but also cuz I've started to stutter like a fucking moron whenever I get upset, and now I feel like a fucking moron too, for thinking that these things made me different or special. But they made me special to my friends in Santa Cruz, right?

Mom

Paul and I read a lot of "instruction manuals" when Hannah was born. That's what we used to call them, laughing as we planned the future for our little baby girl. She would be an overachiever, I was sure. A leader. A bright and happy girl who would share all her secrets and bake with me like I did with my mom. She would swim and run and read and have an insatiable curiosity. Her friends would love to come to our house, and we would be *that* house, the one with all the kids all the time.

Now we read another kind of instruction manual. This one is a set of guidelines for the Second Nature webinar we will participate in with the unlikely title of "Communicating without Judging." It seems like a tall order for a parent who suspects that maybe she has not judged her child quite enough.

Hannah

I guess while I am huddled around the fire with these bitches, my mom and dad are huddled with the bitches' parents, and they are probably all trying to figure out where they went wrong with all of us. I wonder why they bother. They all screwed up, so how can they be useful to each other?

Mom

Paul and I don't ask any questions at all in that first webinar. Instead, we listen to the program's head therapist talk about family dynamics, value systems, peer influence, and communication to the faceless, nameless group of parents who are in the same situation as we are. I don't get it at all. How can it be possible to love too much, to give too much, to care too much? It is as counterintuitive as anything I've ever heard. Paul listens intently, his mouth in a scowl, as though tasting something unappealing for the first time.

I ask Jason about it on our next call. "How," I ask with energy, "can we help her from here? Why can't we talk to her? Why can't we see her?" I argue that she has taken responsibility, and that she seems remorseful. I tell Jason that we need to respond, to listen.

Jason answers flatly, as though it is a script he has read from a hundred times. "It's important that you don't capitulate to her professed shame, Susan. She's playing you. She needs time to come around to the truth of what she is telling you. And then she needs the next level of care to make sure that she finds a better way to live after this experience."

I put my head down on the dining room table, next to the speakerphone, confused.

Paul puts his lips near my ear and whispers to me, "Let's give it a little time, Susan." And so, instead of welcoming Hannah home we write another letter—a masterpiece of understatement:

Dear Hannah,

Thank you for your letter. We think it's a powerful start to the work you'll do at Second Nature. We are very glad to hear that you are willing to work with a therapist and would like to fix things at home.

We didn't like a lot of what we read, but it helped us realize how differently we see and remember things from how you see and remember them. It also shocked us to know how much you held secret from us. We're sure that it's all important in ways that we'll figure out as we go along.

We want to reaffirm that the Wilderness Program has achieved excellent results with other students. We know it's tough, but you're strong and will be stronger than ever when you leave it. We are committed to giving this program its time, and allowing it to run its course. We really believe that you can do this.

Love,

Mom and Dad

Hannah

Well, my plan for a hasty exit didn't work. It looks like I'm going to be stuck here until I turn into a Popsicle. I keep going to group, cuz even though the good girl routine isn't getting me home, at least it gives me something to do, and it's warm near the fire, and you can only sit there if you're participating. And I like the way everyone listens to each other. I never felt like I was listened to at home. Mom would nod and smile but she wasn't listening. She was always thinking about something she wanted me to do, or like, or finish.

They make us write in our journals a lot here, so I think I can let her know about some stuff that she never seemed to pick up on at home. I write about being bullied at the lovely little Santa Cruz school they sent me too. Those girls made me feel so ugly and stupid. I was a good student in elementary school, and I learned to speak Hebrew and how to argue Torah, and how to write a killer poem, but that didn't mean squat at my new school. They studied a different math and science, and I felt dumb for the first time. It took me a long time to make new friends, and when I did, it was with the other newbie there, Ella. She was too tall and too quiet, but she was someone to eat lunch with. Our moms were both thrilled that we had connected, but I think that's mostly because they liked each other.

Before we knew what was happening the moms had schemed up a daughter–mother book club. Honestly, it didn't sound too bad to me, cuz I really did love to read, but then I found out that the other girls in the club were all a part of the group that gave us so much shit. I still wonder how Mom never noticed on the day Ella couldn't come to book group, me standing alone at the screen door watching her chat with the other moms in their lawn chairs, the girls upstairs buzzing to each other in low tones, like bees about to swarm.

I might be crazy, but she's fucking blind.

Mom

Hannah writes about being sad, about being bullied and ignored. She writes about her sexual adventures, her social anxiety, and her loneliness. All in all, Hannah sends us nearly thirty-four pages of scrawled, stained letters and journal entries that point sharply at our blindness as parents. It is truly a purge of epic proportions, and one that leaves all of us empty.

I try to fill the gaping hole by reading articles, books, and blogs about parenting, teen behavior, and bipolar disorder, curled up on Hannah's still unmade, rather ripe bed with my laptop propped against her tattered Mr. Bear, refusing to believe that my nearsightedness might have affected her future. I read on, searching for a path forward as Mr. Bear channels Hannah's accusations with his unblinking eyes. What have I done?

Chapter 5

Hannah

"The path out of the wilderness is carved by you, one day at a time." That's the kind of bullshit they tell us in therapy. They tell us that we have to take action to improve our own life. The other girls in Group 6 seem to believe it. They're pretty dramatic about it. After I write my life story and I'm finally allowed to officially join the group, they have this ceremony for me. One of the girls, Katie, actually makes a little speech. It's during our daily community meeting, which is another name for one of the two therapy sessions we have every day. She's been there the longest and is considered a community leader, but she's as much a filthy scarecrow as the rest of us, layers of woolen clothing hanging on her tiny frame, her yellow hair greasy and limp. She tells me that they all promise to be honest with me and that they will do their best to keep me safe. Then she hands me a stick and a stone; I guess it's a bow drill so that I can learn to make my own fire. It's part of the whole tough love thing going on here. If we want hot food we have to make it happen by learning to start our own fire. (They are very big on the whole metaphor thing out here.) I am touched, though, that they have given me one of their rocks. I am learning about how hard it is to find just the right one, with a depression shallow enough for the stick to turn smoothly and deep enough to keep your drill in place. It has a smooth top so my hand won't get hurt, and it's small enough to hold firmly while I spin the stick. When Katie drops that rock into my hand, I know that it's going to improve my life, if I can just learn how to use it. I just can't seem to get a fire going. I get a wisp, a hint of smoke, and then it goes out.

"Keep trying," Jason rasps.

"You have to work for it," the staff tells us, as they enjoy their warm meals on the other side of camp. I hunker down in the dirt with my cold tortillas and dream the pages of my mother's cookbooks, trying to ignore the metaphor of failure that's flavoring my meal.

Mom

I am in the kitchen making lunch when the phone rings. It's 2N's number on caller ID, and I put down the colander of spring greens and yell for Paul before picking up. It is a Wednesday, not our regular 2N therapy day, and we aren't expecting any communication until Friday. I swipe the panic aside and answer, relieved to hear Jason's cheerful voice on the other end. I put the phone on speaker and sit down at the table, just as Paul tops the stairs from his home office where he spends most of his time. As Paul sits down, Jason begins to speak, direct and to the point, as usual.

"I'm just out of a care plan meeting. There's general agreement among the Wilderness staff members and therapists that Hannah has been misdiagnosed. We're sure she's not bipolar."

"No," I say, shaking my head back and forth as though Jason can see me, "No, she is bipolar. The psychiatrist was sure." I speak slowly, as though to a child who is having trouble understanding. "He said she was the most textbook case of bipolar he has ever treated. That she's rapid cycling but can be controlled with lithium. That drugs can give her a more normal life."

Jason is unshakeable. "We've spent weeks with her, Susan, twenty-four/seven, and we simply don't find any evidence at all to support the diagnosis of bipolar, especially rapid cycling."

I look at Paul across the table; his eyes are wide, mouth grim, hands flat on the wood of the kitchen table as though holding down the implications of what we have just heard. Jason continues casually like he's ordering at a drive-through microphone. "Just because she's not bipolar doesn't mean she doesn't have serious issues to contend with. I think we should pull in an independent consultant to corroborate. I'd like your permission. It will cost about three thousand dollars."

Hannah

Jason has been asking me a lot of questions about the shrink that started me on lithium. He wants to know if I lied to him. Of course I lied to him. He was an idiot.

Mom

Clearly I am an idiot. And Hannah's therapist, the specialist in Watsonville, the one I believed so readily, is an idiot. And every therapist who followed him who blindly accepted his diagnosis and our money is an idiot as well. Here's the truth about the money, and addiction. We haven't had to worry about money for some time, but now as our daughter's illness takes center stage and the economy tanks, we stop doing all the things I have taken for granted. We stop eating out. My cooking becomes more careful, and our pantry stops overflowing. I stop casual shopping, and I stop using the dry cleaner. We talk about moving Camilla to a public school. We drop out of our temple community. They call and offer us membership for a token amount, but I am too mortified to accept. We root around and make decisions that will help us to pay the $500 per day that Wilderness costs, the $300 for local family therapy each week, the thousands of dollars in educational consultants, and the $18,000 in tuition for the private high school that Hannah attended for just two weeks before we sent her away. We will need to spend hundreds for flights and accommodations when we visit Utah, and for the new, more appropriate wardrobe that Hannah will need during her time away. If Hannah moves on to another facility we will continue to pay $10,000 a month. All in all, we realize that we could spend hundreds of thousands before this is all over. Our life savings are being consumed, decades of Paul's hard work eaten by the twin monsters of our family emergency and a deep recession that centers around the housing industry—Paul's business. I don't remember the exact moment when we realize that we are about to be in financial ruin, but the first time we speak about it is on one of our many pilgrimages to our latest therapist.

"I don't want to go any more," Paul says in an angry voice. "We're just shitting out money for nothing." I feel injured and defensive, and I ignore his rare profanity, replying quickly without thinking.

"Maybe if you participate more and remain open to change, we'll have a better chance."

"A chance at what?" He asks. "At going broke? At dredging up dissatisfaction with each other?" Paul is right. Our therapy is going poorly. It's only when I point out that Hannah needs to feel as though we are working with her that he capitulates. Anything for his daughter, even spending time with his wife.

We agree to have a Dr. Carl Smoot examine Hannah and set up an appointment for her in mid-December. Hope struggles with despair in my head. Hope that she is not mentally ill. Despair because if she is not bipolar, it means we have screwed up pretty badly. Hope that she can be whole again. Despair that we might not be able to afford the treatment she needs.

Paul spends most of his time in his office, working and worrying about money. Sometimes I step up to his door and find him staring out the sliding door at the rotting swing set and fort he built for his little girl all those years ago, or picking aimlessly at the unamplified strings of his electric guitar. He gives up his guitar lessons, the gardener, the pool guy, and his fascination with wine without discussing any of it with me. I wonder what is in his mind, but he is closed up around his feelings. Life savings for lifesaving. Still not the worst deal we could make. If it works.

Hannah

Thanksgiving is coming, and it's getting really cold here. I miss some things a lot, like hot water and hot food and a clean house and my friends. The whole wilderness thing is getting old. The good news is that they are going to start including me on the weekly calls to my family pretty soon. It's so remote out here that they have to use a special satellite phone, like in the movies. The good girl act doesn't work with Jason, but I'm pretty sure that I can talk my parents into bringing me home.

Mom

The care team decides they don't want to change Hannah's medication while she's in the wilderness, so she'll remain on Depakote until she's in a situation where she can be monitored while being taken off of her bipolar drugs. Depakote has some nasty side effects, but it's nothing like the lithium.

I punish myself for my mistakes by reading everything I can about what we did to Hannah when we agreed to put her on lithium. I find out that it is a very dangerous drug. It doesn't sound dangerous. The pricey psychiatrist who prescribed it smiled as he told us it is a naturally occurring chemical salt that decreases the chemicals in your brain that are caused by stress while it increases the feel-good chemical called serotonin.

I lie on my ruined child's bed and read that in the 1920s, lithium was actually used as a hangover cure. In 1929 it was marketed under the catchy name of "Bib-Label Lithiated Lemon-Lime Soda"—7 UP. (Of course lithium is no longer used in their formula.) As a drug, lithium has been used to effectively treat bipolar disorder for over fifty years.

Hannah

When they give me my drugs here, I have to line up with the other tattered girls in my group and open my mouth like I'm taking some kind of communion, and the staff person puts the pill on my tongue and then I have to drink from my water bottle and swallow it. I can't cheek the drugs here, cuz they check my mouth. Tongue up, down and side to side like a genuflection to modern medicine, while they peer in my mouth like the answer to all their questions are in there. It doesn't matter. The Depakote they give me now instead of lithium doesn't make me feel any different anyway.

Mom

Once you get past the fact that a naturally occurring salt can alter brain chemistry, lithium doesn't seem that scary. But there are two great big problems with lithium. First, in order for lithium to work therapeutically, it has to be taken at levels that bump right up against toxic. If you go past that therapeutic level by even a little bit, it can harm or kill you. Second, it's easy to accidentally take too much because it interacts with many common recreational and over-the-counter drugs and can even be affected by something as simple as how much water you drink. Lithium can also cause dehydration, and dehydration can then cause dangerous increases in lithium levels, starting a downward spiral that can lead to overdose, coma, or even death.

We had willingly supplied this poison to our daughter for six months before she overdosed. Now I know she never needed to take it, and I don't know how I can live with that.

Hannah

It's funny how I can feel better out here, even stinking, hungry, and cold. The girls huddle close to me sometimes at personal time while we do our writing, and I feel like we are all crowded into some kind of wild carnival ride together. It's less scary like that, and I don't feel alone any more.

Mom

The psychiatrist we saw with Hannah asked her if she was taking recreational drugs. Hannah told him no. That gave him the confidence to put her on lithium. Because troubled teenagers taking recreational drugs never lie, do they? The psychiatrist and our pharmacist also didn't take the time to mention that alcohol, caffeine, and even Ibuprofen can interact with the drug, dangerously affecting blood levels, though I'm sure the paperwork you get with your prescriptions covered it all, if I had just taken the time to study it. Hannah was not limiting herself to beers and Starbucks though. Like 10 percent of all teens in the year she overdosed, Hannah was regularly using Ecstasy, and also drugs like oxycontin, and psychedelics. The serotonin that was being produced by the lithium was being employed by the Ecstasy like some supersonic roller coaster ride gone wrong. The other drugs intensified her lows, and her confusion.

Hannah

I still have ups and downs here, but they seem less crazy. I guess I'm feeling . . . well, stable. That scares me, cuz I have no highs or lows for my art. I try to find my edge in the drawings I make in my journal, dredging up the anger at my parents and the sadness I feel from being here. I border my journal with sketches, and the figures I draw feel like old friends, keeping me company.

Mom

Ecstasy, a drug Hannah used even more frequently than the opioids she favored, works by massively releasing serotonin— the feel-good chemical in your brain—producing an extremely pleasurable rush. A teenager on Ecstasy will feel fantastic, and appear to be manic for as long as their serotonin production can keep up with their drug use. Lithium provides the extra serotonin to intensify the effect. But the brain is so depleted of serotonin after the use of Ecstasy that it can take weeks before brain levels come back to normal, inducing a chemically created depression. It looks a lot like bipolar disorder.

Hannah

I like the therapists on staff. So I don't want to complain too much or give them a bad time. But some weird shit is going on with me, and it seems to be getting worse. First off, I start having this moronic stutter when I speak. Then my eyes start twitching like they want to look somewhere else. Sometimes I can't remember shit, even from the beginning of my sentences to the end. I think maybe it's the smoke from the campfire in my eyes, or the fact that I'm not sleeping too well. Sometimes when I'm drawing, my hands will seem to move and shake on their own, and my work looks like it did in grade school, choppy and unformed.

Mom

When a person like Hannah overdoses on lithium, brain toxicity leads to nerve damage, tremors, and a lack of coordination. It can cause speech disorders, eye twitching, kidney failure, confusion, drowsiness, impaired memory, seizures, coma, and even death. Though lithium toxicity is usually reversible, persistent neurological problems can follow. So we wait, to see if the "cure" the psychiatrist prescribed to our daughter, the unnecessary lithium, will scar her permanently.

I pore through Hannah's journal entries, tracing the ugly sketches with my fingers, looking for coherence in her writing, for some sign that she is recovering—but there is none. I read them over and over again, trying to convince myself that I am missing something, that I am the one who is confused. But the writing remains tangled knots, fragments of ideas, accusations, and apologies.

Hannah

I never had therapists like the ones I have out here. They aren't afraid of me. They look for those pills in my mouth, and they check my smelly feet to make sure they aren't rotting. They made sure I eat the crappy food, and then they made sure I don't run off and barf it out. They are really tough on us, but they do everything they ask us to do. They make their own fire and break down their camp, they hike with us, they make sure we all keep warm and organized, and they listen to us whine and complain and confess. They stay calm when we are sick, and somehow know when we are pretending to be sick. They watch us and care for us every hour of the day and night. It should be stifling, but it isn't. It's comforting to know that out here in bum fuck Utah, someone is still watching out for me.

Mom

Hannah is now fully integrated into her group, Group 6, a collection of troubled teens who had challenges dealing with "normal" life. When we first considered the Wilderness Program, I was skeptical about placing our coddled and over-protected teen with a bunch of "bad girls." It seemed to be a recipe for disaster. After all, isn't that how young juveniles became hardened criminals? By associating with criminals who have done far worse things than they? I was later to find out that some girls and boys who go to wilderness programs do have drug problems and behavioral problems, but that others go to try to wash away the scars from neglect, promiscuity, violence, abuse, eating disorders, self-harm, and a full spectrum of the traumas that life offers.

This group, these damaged children, were to be Hannah's touchstone. They welcomed her with ceremony and a promise to keep her safe. They formed a family, a community, a hard, sharp mirror for her self-reflection. We would eventually meet these girls, and looking back, I want to hold each one of them, each of these beautiful girls who struggled so hard to define their individual truths, and who helped Hannah start on her path home.

Hannah

Fuck, it's cold. We're not allowed to set up a tent unless it gets below ten degrees, so we're sleeping right on the ground like frozen slabs of meat in our sleeping bag shrink wrap. I have to hug old fuel bottles filled with hot water from the staff fire just to stay warm enough to sleep, and I pull the top of the mummy bag tight to keep out the cold air.

It would help if I could start my own fire. They call it "bustin' a flame" here, but I'm just bustin' my hands, which are all red and scraped from using the bow drill. I spend so much time kneeling in front of my little pile of kindling that I get a tiny patch of what looks like frostbite on my knee. Fucking frostbite!

The only thing that makes it bearable is my group. None of them can bust anything but smoke either, but they keep trying for fire, and we gather around any sign of smoke and cheer like demented, filthy, crazy cheerleaders. Bustin' is something to do in between the chores and the hiking. They make us get up at eight (though by eight I'm usually awake, hugging my cold, hard fuel bottles like they're my Mr. Bear), and then we break down camp, sifting hot coals from the staff fire, rolling up our double sleeping bags, and reorganizing the few pieces of clothes we took off for sleeping. Then we load up camp into the giant frame packs we carry like we're Santa Cruz hobos carrying our life's belongings on our backs. If we don't pack up fast enough to "make time," the staff makes us unpack and then pack up again, for no fucking reason. This irritates me. Once we achieve the dizzying speed required to move on, it's time for our meds, a foot check, breakfast, and then the sound of constant hollering as girls go off to dig their latrines and poop out the lousy food we eat.

I don't get to go right away—me and the other eating disorder bitches have to wait a half hour so we don't sneak off and spew our breakfast. Finally they tell us we can go, and we take our turn, disappearing behind rises and bushes with our trowels, yelling or singing to let the staff know we haven't hightailed it out of there.

By 10 a.m. we're hiking, then therapy until lunch, which is cold, bagged meat or beans unless our keepers let us use their fire to cook. Then we can make our glop—butter, rice, beans, and tomatoes stirred up in an old coffee can over the fire. Gross. Pathetic, too, how we glom it all down off our blue-speckled plates that look just like the ones I used at camp when I was little. You'd think they would want us eating disorder gals to gorge, but we have to be careful how much we eat, since they only supply us once a week. That freaks me out, because at home the cupboards are always full. I remember one time my friend Selina came over and opened the cupboard and asked me how many families lived there.

Mom
Every day starts the same. I wake up at about 6:30 and stare at the ceiling for a while, until it's time to get Camilla up.

She looks sad in the morning, but gets out of bed and dresses, always jeans and a T-shirt. She scrapes her curls into a ponytail, not allowing me to help, and stuffs her homework into her backpack. The drive to school is silent. Camilla is sensitive to noise, and she doesn't appreciate conversation in the morning. Usually she pulls the hood of her sweatshirt over her face and closes her eyes for the twenty-five minute drive. She gets out of the car quickly once we're there. Sometimes she says, "Bye."

I don't get out of the car or linger. My anger at the school and their awful handling of Hannah's situation leads me to withdraw from all of my volunteer activities. My shame over our family's trouble prevents me from socializing, too, skipping the once regular morning walks that the moms take along the ocean—walks I had once helped to organize.

I head home, stopping to run errands along the way. Post office, supermarket, maybe the library, anything I can think of to avoid being home in the silence with myself. By the time I'm home, Paul is already in his office, door closed, muffled sounds of the Grateful Dead playing on the computer. I might do dishes then, standing in silence at the sink, the muted tones of our kitchen matching my mood. Maybe laundry too, before sitting down to hunt for a job or find project work. I don't have an office any more, since I gave Hannah my room, so I work in the little windowed alcove upstairs, distracted by the view of our neglected pool and yard, dead leaves floating aimlessly in the water.

Hannah

After lunch comes P-Time. Personal time. We can write letters, but I stick to assignments and journal entries and sketching. I don't really have anything to say to the people who sent me here. What were they thinking? How is this supposed to help? Was this just a trick, a way to get rid of me?

Mom

Sometimes Paul joins me for lunch at the dining room table, the elbows we prop on our mismatched placemats betraying the fact that we care little about all the things that so recently brought us pleasure. Most of the news we have to share is bad, so we keep it to ourselves, pushing it down with our sandwiches.

After lunch it's time to write. I write to Hannah every day, sitting in her room, either at her vandalized desk, or on her bed, in the company of the stoic Mr. Bear. Sometimes I even send the letters. Afterwards I take a long hot shower or bath, trying to wash off the guilt and remorse churned up by my writing.

Hannah

They make us wash twice a week. We use cold water out of an old military billy can, and it's ass-up crazy how cold water in cold air can burn so much. I do it fast, splashing water where I think it might help the most. I try to wash my hair sometimes, my fingers getting stuck in the dreads that are forming. Once when it was super cold outside, my hair froze before I could get from the wash area to the campfire. My. Hair. Froze.

Mom

In the evening, Paul and I read. We read a wide range of books on addiction, parenting, emotional dysfunction, brain development, religion, and teen programs. We don't talk about the books, but when we finish one, we add it to the pile on each other's nightstand. We read every night, but the pile never seems to go down. When I feel my eyes closing, I turn away from Paul, pull the down comforter up around my ears, and wonder what Hannah is doing.

Hannah

Every night after our crap dinner that looks just like our crap lunch, they put us in this circle that's therapy disguised as a community meeting. We all know it's therapy, but we don't care, since it means we can sit near the fire. Mostly they want us to talk about talking—how we are communicating. The girls pick on each other sometimes, throwing it down over people not being honest, or "checking in" with their feelings. Really, we have nothing more to lose, and eventually all our shit comes out. It's okay, I guess, cuz honesty is another thing that breaks up the boredom. I hate it when the meetings end. It means we have to go off to our sleeping bags, with only those warm fuel bottles for company.

Mom

I tell myself that I am writing to prepare examples and questions for our weekly therapy sessions with Jason. But I think it's more about reminding myself how the child I miss so much terrorized our household.

Hannah threatened to rip her sister's homework in half. When I told her to stop, she called me an ugly hag and told me to shut the hole on my face. Then she smiled.

When Camilla refused to give Hannah money, Hannah cut the heads off Camilla's favorite stuffed animals. This scares me. Is she a psycho?

I try to imagine the roots of Hannah's dysfunction, looking for ingredients that Jason can mix into some kind of cure, writing in my little brown notebook.

Hannah cried all the time at school. It started in second grade. Mrs. J. told her she would never be good at math. How could a teacher hurt a kid that way? She cried when we took her to school. She cried when she had a big project. She cried when we took her to the

Center for Talented Youth Awards. She was receiving a special commendation for scoring in the top 1 percent of talented students. How could all of this be true at the same time?

I ask Hannah's therapist Jason to explain. I put my face near the phone's speaker on the dining room table and softly ask, "Why does she think she's okay? How can she believe that her lifestyle choices are working?" Jason listens, and he gives us feedback.

"Sometimes depression is anger turned inward," he says.

I look away from Paul, sensing the truth of Jason's words, knowing that Hannah isn't the only angry person in our family. Jason continues.

"Hannah has trouble regulating her emotions. She thinks very negatively."

Ah, I think, looking at Paul's grim face and knowing that my expression mirrors his completely. Jason has more to say.

"Hannah accepts her own negativity because she has been led to believe that she's not responsible for how she feels. She doesn't think she can change things to make herself happy."

Jason lets that one hang in the air, but neither Paul nor I choose to touch it.

Hannah

Jason is always talking about how we can control our lives and understand our feelings, but if I were in control of my life, I'd be at Fall Creek Park with my toes in the river tokin' on a big fat joint. I try to tell him that I can't control the bully Barbies at my school, or the teacher who decides to make me her target, or my parents who don't let me go or do or be. Nobody understands me, is it the stuttering? I draw my anger in the pages of my journal and it feels good to let the pain out, like cutting but with no blood.

Mom

Jason works hard to find Hannah, digging beneath her flip answers, her screams of frustration, her denials about drugs and self-harm, and her history of wandering the moonscape of Santa Cruz in bizarre community with others like herself. All the while, through her talking and writing, her personal time and group time, she sketches. Monsters, screaming women, and headless torsos line the sheets of her journal. The roughly rendered, frightening images express her feelings more than words ever could. We still haven't spoken to Hannah, and Jason is loath to take that step before Hannah is ready to communicate.

"I want to try something drastic," he announces one day in our weekly phone call.

I sit upright in alarm. Isn't living in the frozen Utah wilderness drastic enough? Jason continues.

"I want to take her art away." I actually gasp. Take away her art? Why not just carve out a hole in her? Art is her solace, her lifelong companion.

"Jason, how can you possibly think that's a good idea? Isn't that the primary way she's communicating? Isn't that why art therapy exists? To help kids like Hannah open up and let us see them?"

Paul grips my arm to control the panic bleeding out of me. "Let Jason answer," he says.

I hate his calm.

Hannah

I just let it go through my hand and it comes out on paper. Sometimes it even surprises me. Then I say to myself, yeah, that's just right. That's how I feel.

Mom

Jason has decided that Hannah is reinforcing her most negative feelings with her art.

"It's not a window for her, Susan. It's a wall. I have to take away the place where she hides."

Hannah

"No, no, nonononono. God damned mother-fucking asshole crud-faced shrink!"

This can't be right, it's like cutting off a piece of me. Art is the only thing I have left here. Now I'm losing that too? Jason's face doesn't move, it doesn't change, he doesn't hear me, and so I scream louder. I have to make him hear me. I try to reason then, but he shakes his head. I cry, and he just watches. Finally I have no choice, I have to show him what this means, that taking my art isn't moving forward, it's moving backward. He's not listening, so I show him in the only way I have left.

Mom

I can hardly breathe thinking of what I have agreed to. Hannah reacts predictably, trying to cut herself with her jacket zipper in front of Jason.

"You have to give me a way," she screams, "to let it out!"

And he does. He listens to her scream and cry. He talks until she is worn down enough to talk back. Then he starts asking for her participation. Not just listing her crimes, and considering the impact of her behaviors on her family, but examining whether her behaviors and her value system match. He asks her to write it all down, and she does. She writes about valuing friends, but confesses to hurting those who did not support her life choices by dropping them from her life.

As Hannah writes, her deepest feelings, ideas, and actions come under scrutiny, and when magnified under Jason's lens, reveal the gaps between her actions and her words. She is forced to discuss her lying, begging, and stealing, her self-harm, her drug use, her disrespect for her own body. Jason pushes her hard, pointing out that she has used twisted logic to justify her lifestyle. He writes syllogisms with her. Some of them are easy:

> *People who use drugs get their brains fucked up.*
> *I used drugs.*
> *I got my brain fucked up.*

Other efforts fall short, as Hannah grapples with building a future that looks nothing like her past:

> *People should not do things to fuck themselves up.*
> *Drugs fucked me up.*
> *I will probably continue to do drugs.*

I read it over and over bitterly. I taught her this game; it's one I play in the classroom, using my students' daily lives to demonstrate reasoning forms to them. I remember some of her more playful examples:

> *People should not eat worms.*
> *Fast food burgers are made of worms.*
> *People should not eat fast food burgers.*

"So," I had challenged my then twelve-year-old daughter, "Why do people still eat fast food?"

"Well, Mom," Hannah had explained proudly, "the minor premise is wrong so the whole thing is wrong."

So, I think, rereading her current efforts again, either she believes that it's actually okay to fuck one's self up, or she is confessing to the inconsistency of her beliefs. I want to ball up her efforts and throw them away in frustration, but instead I crease the paper neatly in half and add it to the growing pile of her writing.

As Hannah struggles to make sense out of her values, ideas, and actions, Jason asks her if she thinks she can share her thinking with us through letters. She takes a long time to answer him—days of nail biting for me, a new habit that keeps me from running out and buying a pack of cigarettes or a pint of ice cream. Finally, she agrees to write to us. The first letter we receive from Hannah that is not an assignment is fairly friendly, if a bit flippant.

> Dear Mom and Dad,
> Hello. How's your day going? I'm not angry at you, and I'm going to try to take this opportunity to get my shit together . . . They want me to write to you, and at first I was reluctant, but I do want to know how you are and how my friends are and what you all have to say. Oh, one of the girls who has been here a long time wants to know if people are walking around in silver space suits and driving hover cars. I told her it was probably like that SNL skit where bears take over the world, but she is persistent in her vision. Mark of an addict. Can you tell that I'm writing before my session? It's hard having insights into your own problems, and surprisingly that's the hardest part here. I guess it was pretty helpful growing up in the woods. The Bev Hills bitches have it the hardest here, dealing with therapy and also dirt for the first time. Anyway, you can write what you want back, that is if you are not a bear.
> Hannah

Funny, how one line can stick. I sit outside on my dirty lawn chair, wearing a sweater against the coolness of the California November, wanting a few last breaths of fresh air before the rains start in earnest. I turn Hannah's page round and round in my hands, as though trying to find north on a map. The line that chills me is "how my friends are," and though I know this letter is another step towards bringing her home, I am suddenly alarmed at what will happen when she gets here. I complain to Paul.

"Will she run into the arms of these so-called friends, the ones who left her in a pool of vomit on a dark side street?" He shakes his head at my outburst, glancing up at Camilla's open door.

"Just ignore it, Susan."

Ignore it? I scrawl a note in my little notebook about that, wanting to ask Jason if we should answer all her questions when we have our next session. He tells us we can, and I tense up before I relax, realizing that I don't have any idea of how her friends are.

Hannah

Writing is like talking made easy, and I'm kind of surprised that I like to do it. I can say as much or as little as I want. Jason says I don't have to write therapy shit, or about what I'm working on in group, but if I want I can try out some of the shit they're teaching us, and see how it feels in real life. Pretty soon I'm writing to the parent people every chance I get, and they write back a lot too. I write to them about how they made me feel smothered, how I used them, and how I feel like I wasn't ever good enough for them. I really don't like some of the shit they write back, but I guess that's part of the deal. I do like getting the mail, and I picture Mom sitting at her glass desk with her little laptop open, agonizing about punctuation or some such crap. Sometimes she sends pictures and I like to show them to my girls here. They pass them around the fire during our coffee can dinners and remind me of what a jerk I am. Mom reminds me of what a jerk I am too.

Dear Hannah,

You are right in saying that I always feel manipulated by you. I would like to trust you, but part of me wonders if you are manipulating me right now! I ask myself, "Why would she stop?" I also ask myself, "What now?" I can't tell from your letters if you care enough to fix things. If you do want to fix things, I would like to ask you another question: "What do you think has to happen?" I'm asking you because I can't do this alone, and I shouldn't try to do it if it's not something you want. Finally, I see in your letters that you are thinking about some of our good times. I want you to know that I am too, and that I miss you.

Love,

Mom

P.S. I told Dad about your friend's idea about silver space suits and hover cars on our way to the molecular food generator, and he laughed so hard he almost fell out of his jet-pack.

Dear Mom & Dad,

I'm actually doing pretty good here. I bet you keep up on the daily log on the Wilderness web site, so you probably have a pretty good idea of how my days are. I myself have been on separates for four days now, and am not allowed to talk to the other girls. I have been letting my thinking and my behaviors contradict each other again, and I am sending mixed messages to people, including you. I guess I can see how those mixed messages can damage and destroy relationships. I know you think I'm not too remorseful for being such an asshole, but please let me clarify. I strongly regret hurting you. And me. But I learned a lot of lessons that I wouldn't give up.

I believe that those two ideas can work together.
Anyway, on a lighter note what are you doing for
Hanukkah? One of the staff here said they would
help me carve a menorah, and that maybe we can
make latkes. That's all I have to say about that.
See you later.
Hannah

Mom

Finally, after a long month of hard work in the wilderness, it's time for our letters to turn into weekly phone calls, and I am scared. I spend so much time with each letter I draft, rewriting again and again to make sure that I am really saying what I want, what I mean. The spoken word will be much more difficult. One try is all you get. I prepare for our first phone conversation as though I'm going on a first date. I use my weekly Santa Cruz therapy session with Paul to try to calm down, and to find my balance. "What if I screw up?"

It is weirdly helpful that just days before our call, I receive a disturbing journal entry from Hannah. Jason asks Hannah to rework her life-story assignment, the one that she wrote in her first days in Utah. The disappointment I feel as I read it is a cold splash of reality in advance of our first conversation.

The revised life story is four pages long, Hannah's tiny, cramped writing pushing as much unhappiness onto each page as possible. It is a masterpiece of self-pity, sibling rivalry, and confused revisionist history. She writes sweetly about her relationship with her father, but then calls him boorish. She writes that by third grade she was embarrassed by my lovey-dovey affection. She writes about violence in our family, but then asserts that we are all gentle and peace-loving. She reminisces about how special our holidays are, but then provides examples of how badly behaved some of our relatives are. By the time I reach one bright note, it is entirely unexpected. Hannah details a Fourth of July celebration from years ago, using a half page of precious space in her life story to vividly paint a moment I had entirely forgotten.

> The best great holiday I remember was Fourth of July with my Aunt Darlene and Uncle Mino. It was Darlene's birthday, so during the day we made her a cake and set off firecrackers. At night we drove my Dad's truck to a field, and him and me and my mom, and Mino and Darlene watched the fireworks. The grownups sat in camp chairs near the truck, and Camilla and I put aside our differences and squeezed into the truck bed, sharing a blanket and eating Chinese takeout. There were lots of people there, and it felt like a party.

After this brief, bright peak, Hannah falls back into negative memories until she chronicles the way her friends make her feel, and how angry she is at the limits we place on her seeing them, her chosen family.

> My friends brought me happiness without the fighting. I stopped talking to Camilla except to ask her for money to see my friends. I stopped eating dinner with my parents every night because I didn't like answering their questions. I pushed them away, but needed them more too, cuz I needed rides and money to go out. I told them a lot of stuff about my life but on my terms. I refused to recognize them as authorities and would not talk to them for days.

Were we really the twisted reality show that Hannah was scripting?

Hannah

It feels good and bad to write everything down, and it feels like it isn't complete. Mostly it's a chance to leave stuff on paper so I don't have to carry it around with me anymore. I want to make that life story into a paper airplane and shoot it out over the desert when I'm done. But Jason collects it, and I know that Mom and Dad will be reading it pretty soon, and I'm feeling sad knowing that it will hurt them, and happy that I can tell them these things, and I hope they can understand that maybe I didn't write more good stuff because I'm keeping it, not letting it go.

Hannah

The first phone conversation in a month that I have with my parents is totally weird and awkward. Jason comes lumbering over the ridge from where he parked, carrying a black bag, sort of like a camera bag, and asks me to join him. We walk a little ways away from camp, and he sits down on a rock and unzips the bag. It's a phone, but it looks more like a walkie-talkie, and before he calls my parents he spends some time with me reviewing the rules. Mostly it's about shit like staying calm and accepting that there are more viewpoints than just mine. It's funny, I planned on making a case for going home, but once the phone starts ringing I feel like my throat is closing up and none of that stuff can get out. Mostly I just say idiot things to fill the spaces where I'm supposed to talk, and Jason lets there be spaces where nobody has to talk, and it seems okay for now to just be quiet. They're pretty quiet too, and I wondered how it's possible that people who live together their whole lives can be so strange to each other, and I wonder if that's good or bad.

Mom

A non-event. That's how I think about that first awkward conversation. Paul and I sit at our usual places at the dining room table, staring at the phone. Hannah is with Jason, sitting outside somewhere in the vast Utah desert. I don't know it for a fact, but I picture the satellite phone perched on a rock, Hannah and Jason kneeling in the dirt. I'm afraid of showing my feelings or saying something wrong, so I choose not to say too much. I'm pretty sure Paul will be quick to point out my flaws after the conversation, or use my words for therapy fodder, so it seems easier to be quiet and let Jason guide us. The conversation is quick and utilitarian, the communication equivalent of a first handshake. Pleased to meet you. Will I ever get to know you?

Chapter 6

Hannah

Jason gives us a book to read called *Man's Search for Meaning* by a dude named Viktor Frankl. He's a guy who survived being in a Nazi concentration camp. I wonder if Jason wants me to read it cuz he knows my Grandma Bubbe was in a concentration camp, or cuz he thinks that somehow being out in the desert is like being in a concentration camp. I guess I'll find out.

Mom

I turn the pages of the book gingerly, knowing what's about to happen through my mother's stories detailing her experiences in the same concentration camp, dreading the account but wanting to know more about it. Frankl wrote about how some people survived—and even thrived under—the most extreme hardship, while others lay down to die. He observed these behaviors and outcomes in the concentration camp where he acted as a doctor . . . passing out aspirin to people who were dying of typhoid.

Hannah

Frankl said that "caring is the last human freedom." I like how he talks about choosing your own attitude towards suffering. We are all suffering out here in the wilderness, but sometimes we laugh too, and it feels good to know we are stronger than our situation. Jason wants to talk about Frankl a lot (I think he has a man crush), but I don't mind.

Mom

I read what Frankl said about meaning being in every moment of every life. I read about how important it is to have hope for a future. I think about this as I write to Hannah, as I take Camilla to therapy, as I search for something to say to Paul.

Hannah

So this Frankl dude says that it's hard to leave bad places. His language is complicated, but the way I understand it is that after the wilderness we'll go a little crazy for the physical stuff we haven't had out here, and we have to avoid turning into greedy hogs or going loopy and turning into haters because of what we had to go through. Then we have to find something to work towards to give our life meaning. I know that's not exactly the way Frankl describes it, since he wasn't in a wilderness program, but it works for me to think about it like the stuff I'm going through, because even though my grandma was in the same concentration camp (!) as him, I just can't get my mind around what they went through. It makes me too sad.

Mom

Our reading has given us something to talk about on our calls, which are getting longer and tougher. We're all looking back and talking about our choices, how we got here, and what we want to change moving forward. Hannah still doesn't seem too sure about what she needs to change, but she's pretty sure about what Paul and I have to change. She wants more freedom, she wants trust, she wants privacy. We want respect, responsibility, and a peaceful home. I don't think we're all going to get what we want. I flash on a dusty memory of a lecture I once attended. "Consensus means that everyone is equally unhappy."

Hannah

So I make lists about pros and cons of change in my journal. But when I put the lists next to each other, it's confusing. Like, I know that changing my evil ways might get me some new friends. But I would definitely lose friends too, at least the ones I partied with. I know that I would get along better with my parents, but I would lose a lot of personal power in the house and have to give up freedom. Most important, I know I would feel better, but I'm afraid I would lose my edge and my art.

Mom

We try to make the most of our calls, and our letters, which we are now writing almost daily.

Dear Hannah,

I see that you are struggling with understanding your history and planning your future. For a person as social as you are, starting the list with friends seems pretty natural. But what kind of friends would leave you because you have decided to be sober? Not real ones, I think. Also, I don't think that personal power comes from negative behavior. What kind of power are you looking for? We should talk about this. Finally, I know you are concerned about your art. I am compelled to remind you that you were a fine artist, and an edgy one before you ever started using. Why would that change?

Hannah answers all my questions, the ones in my letters and the ones in therapy. She doesn't always answer them right away, and sometimes she answers them to herself through the writing in her journal. She writes endlessly during the long, cold Utah afternoons that she spends with herself, remembering things through the filter of drug use and anger, sometimes reaching deep enough to remember what she has lost.

Hannah

I do remember good times. I remember that I loved to laugh with Mom, and go to janky restaurants with Dad, especially on our trips to Mexico. I remember that I had freedom but wanted more, I always wanted more, but I didn't treat my freedom very responsibly. So now I have no freedom at all. I pushed myself right over the freedom cliff, and here I am, at the bottom, sitting on a crusty foam mat so dirty that you can hardly see where it ends and the ground begins, using this stupid pencil stub to reveal my "innermost self," but honestly I'm cold, so my outermost self is getting all the attention right now.

Mom

We are all learning to listen and to respect each other's feelings. Hannah writes a lot in her journals about her resentment at how we judged her friends, about our blindness at the struggles she had at school, and then, surprisingly, about her goals for the future:

> I think that my decisions affected the way that you respect me, and yes, feel about me.

> I feel my choice of peers has little significance. You as a parent might not like them or even know them, but mostly they are honest and well-meaning people.

Going to school in Santa Cruz does have something to do with my drug use I guess. Santa Cruz has a very high drug culture (ha... . . . pun), so I probably had access to drugs at will, but I guess I shouldn't blame where I live and go to school for my own bad decisions.

College is an important part of my life. Even if it might not show in my current academic standings, education has always stood at the forefront of my concerns. Mom, I know you think this too. I feel that if I don't graduate high school with a good portfolio and get into an art school, I will have failed you and myself.

How do you reply to a profound truth, when you don't want it to be true? I sit at her scarred desk with my laptop, wondering how honest I can be with her, tracing the foul, angry language she had gouged into her desk with my index finger.

Dear Hannah,
I believe that I wanted you to have a life without struggle,
but struggle is life sometimes, so I'm sorry.

Hannah

I know she's sorry, but I don't think she knows what she's sorry for, and I don't know exactly what I'm sorry for either, and it seems stupid to try to figure it out on our own. We could probably do this a lot easier if we were in the same fucking place, and by same place, I don't mean Utah.

Mom

Hannah writes a lot about the things she gave up—freedom, friendship, art, and of course a warm bed and good food. She begins a concerted campaign to come home, working hard to craft rational arguments in her journal, then repeating them in her letters and in our weekly phone calls. Jason warns us that these pleas will come, and they do, tempting us the way Hannah was tempted by drugs. Jason is adamant about how we should respond.

"She's going to keep asking, and then she's going to get angry and accusatory. You have got to remain calm, and tell her that the length of her stay here depends entirely on her, and how focused she is on the work she's doing." Jason is right, but even his preparation does not help, and I cover my mouth with my hand during our call that week, pressing hard to keep the words from coming out, from shouting, "Send her home." Hannah is undaunted by our silence, writing beseeching letters that seemed to make perfect sense to me.

> Dear Mom and Dad,
> I want things to be better with our family. I think it's time to come home so that we can work things out face to face. Putting other people between us will just make the problems harder to solve. I think it was okay to send me here, I'm not really mad at you, because I can see how it calmed me down and got me thinking about things, but I think I have done all I can here. Really, there's no point continuing. I would really like to come home.

I would really like her to come home too. Like the pain of childbirth, the memory of the havoc she has wreaked on our lives is fading. I begin to wonder if, at the rate we are paying for her wilderness experience, we are now simply being milked for money. I sit in her filthy room, reading our impact letters over and over again, studying the art on the wall of her room and the way she has vandalized her own paintings, the spray paint dripping like tears down the beautiful faces underneath, and I come to my decision. She will stay.

Hannah

They are leaving me here to rot, and the only people who understand how I feel are the other girls. It's like they are me, and I don't even have to say anything. I guess it's because we are sharing this experience together, it's sort of a bond. What a fucked up way to be connected to someone. But I am connected, and now when I am punished by being put on separates for not participating or cooperating, I really feel lonely. I am writing to pass the time, and to let my anger out in a way that won't freak Jason out. I mean, that will just leave me here for longer, right?

Mom

Once she knows our decision, everything changes. Hannah's writing turns raw and angry, revealing feelings and thoughts that have been dormant for years. She accuses us of loving her sister Camilla more than her, of listening without hearing, of focusing only on our own vision of what family should be and trying to force her to adapt. She also moves towards her group, reaching out from the fringes of camp, where she's so often isolated for minor infractions like eating too slowly or not sharing her thoughts with others. She is required to write requests to rejoin the group:

> I want to be a member of this group because I want to grow in this program. You can't grow with only yourself to reflect back. The group, aside from helping me through this shit box of a place, has helped me to gain insight into my own life by being able to relate to their personal stories, like

Julie's control issues and Katherine's body image problems and Katie's problems at home.

Hannah

I'm doing good in group, and I feel like I'm actually helping some people. It's sure a lot easier to see solutions when it's someone else's shit. But then I realize that I *am* them, and that it is my shit, and that the solution could work for me too. Bam.

Jason wants me to write about my art. He wants to know if I understand why it was taken from me. I don't really understand it until I write about it, starting with his words but then finding my own, and then I have one of those cartoon light bulb moments. Here is what I wrote:

> I would like to see my art. The reason I'm not allowed to see it or draw it is because it has the possibility of reinforcing my negative attitude, not releasing it. I want to see my art because I want to see the progression of my art as I got older and hid my emotions more and only let them come out on my canvasses . . . but I also really want other people to look at my art and be reminded of something, anything in their own lives, not in mine. It's like being here I've learned that I can relate to someone I thought had nothing in the world to do with me in twenty different ways. Even though I don't like the flowers that I painted when I was little, I also don't like the angry faces. The difference is that even though the flower art is crappy, people can relate to it more, instead of being disturbed or scared off and hiding from what I do. I want to find a middle path where I can express myself, and people can relate and find something for themselves.

Mom

Jason's voice seems to boom out of the little speaker, and as is so often the case I felt like he is right there with us.

"Okay, guys. I think it's almost time to give Hannah her art back. She's earned it. But I think she needs to realize what she's channeling with her hands, so before I allow her to sketch, I want her to share her work with the group. Not the doodles. The real stuff."

I choose some of Hannah's work, layering her young self (penguins and sunsets, lakes and swans, cattails and barns) with her middle school self (icy streams, pensive people in every shape and size looking away, off the canvas, never meeting your gaze) and finally her high school self (these I touch squeamishly, the screaming faces, the limbless, headless bodies, and the grotesquely malformed human-like creatures).

I spread the body of work out on the living room floor to photograph, watching the bright blues and oranges of her childhood turn to muted colors and then to angry reds and blacks like a spectrum of deteriorating mental health. The introduction of drugs is apparent, I realize, looking at these paintings. I could have known everything about her, had I just paid attention. Fantasy themes, unfinished canvases, foul language scrawled in marker—twisted, screaming, desperate drawings in a frightening tableau of need. I sat down on the wood floor for a long time, thinking about my blindness, her talent, and her troubles.

Hannah

I wonder if it's like this in art school. I'm really nervous to do my little art show for the bitches and Jason. If I had to name this show it would be something like "Crumble" or "Progression of Fucked-up-ness" or maybe "An Illustrated History of Losing My Shit." It's really weird seeing my art in order like this, getting weirder and wilder, and I have to admit I still really like some of the sick pieces, and I like that some of the girls make little sounds, even when they say things like "Ew," because that means that I touch them in some way, and that's really what art is all about. But I don't like some of the other pieces; they feel hot and wrong and pissed off and not very good at all. If I'm about the art, and I don't like my art anymore, does that mean that I'm not that person anymore? Who am I now?

Mom

Jason uses Hannah's art to talk to her about her emotions, and starts working with her to recognize what she is feeling in the moment. He explains to us in our weekly phone call, "I'm setting the stage for Dialectic Behavioral Therapy—DBT. It will give Hannah a way to recognize what's happening to her emotionally, and a toolbox to address her feelings." Of course I research DBT right away, filling my new dearth of trust with information.

I read that DBT centers on building a patient's tolerance to living with uncomfortable emotions and thoughts, instead of fighting them. It is simple yet profound, and I picture Hannah whipping out some of the DBT "tools" in her toughest moments. It might be a way for her to accept her darkest thoughts without acting upon them, and could give her a way to manage and even change her mental state. I am engrossed in my reading, and suddenly, newly hopeful.

Hannah

Jason tells me that I do the same things every time I get pissed off. I ask him "like what" but he says the next time I get pissed off or upset, he wants me to notice and write it all down. Dude, really?

It doesn't take long to get upset. We're all sitting around the fire that afternoon when staff, I think it's Laurie, announces that Katie is leaving us. She's been in the woods for about eight weeks, and lots of us rely on her. I almost forget to watch myself, but then I realize that my hands are in fists and my shoulders are all up around my ears. What else do I do with my body? It's weird but interesting to be the lab rat and the researcher too.

———

Mom

Thanksgiving comes. It will be the first family holiday without Hannah, and I hide in the pages of my books. After I read *Man's Search for Meaning*, I turn back to *Primal Teen* by Barbara Strauch, so I can understand what Hannah might be able to control and what she cannot. I scour the Internet for parenting articles, for clues on what happened, on where I went wrong. When that weighs too heavily on me, I comfort myself by reading commentary from the Zohar, writings that explore the nature of our existence. One passage seemed to be written for me and my errant girl:

> *"I have already punished you and you have not heeded. I have brought fearsome warriors and flaming forces to strike at you and you have not obeyed. If I expel you from the land alone, I fear that packs of wolves and bears will attack you and you will be no more. But what can I do with you? The only solution is that I and you together leave the land and both of us go into exile. As it is written, "I will discipline you, forcing you into exile; but if you think I will abandon you, Myself too [shall go] along with you."*

"I and you together," I say out loud. I write the passage out by hand and tuck it under my pillow.

Hannah

I can't believe it's been a year since last Thanksgiving. So much has happened this past year, most of it bad. I'm searching for something I can be grateful for, and I decide it should be that I didn't lose my family or die due to being a moron.

Mom

I sit at the simply set table with Paul and Camilla, and all of the big, ornate Thanksgiving dinners we have hosted over the years go rolling through my head like a family movie. There I am, complaining about the centerpieces (too small), the guests (too late), the food (too dry), then moving on to complain about the work (too much) and the mess (too little help). Oh, what I would give to have all of it back again.

We practice our Thanks-Giving tradition, moving around our little trio, to reflect on our good fortune. I fight tears as I pronounce my gratefulness that we are together, Hannah's empty chair making my words a lie. Paul, keeper of the accounts, notes that we are fortunate to be able to get the support we need to help Hannah. But it is Camilla who expresses what we are all thinking, and it comes out as a wish. "I hope that Hannah comes back soon and can be my sister again." We eat in silence.

Hannah

Thanksgiving comes, and we have bagged turkey that I don't eat, and then it's gone, and then suddenly it's December, and it makes my stomach lurch to realize that I might not be going home for Hanukkah, Christmas, or New Year either. I wonder if Mom will decorate the house in blue and silver, if Camilla will light the menorah without me, if she will make a potato candle to honor what our bubbe did during the war, if Dad will drive everyone over to visit the Christmas part of the family, if Camilla will have to wear that stupid elf hat the cousins are always sticking on her head, and if on the way home they will stop to see the lights at Vasona Park. Memories crowd into my head and fight for attention, but I am focused on my body and how it is telling me that I am upset.

Mom

The Jewish holidays use a lunar calendar, and this year Hanukkah follows Thanksgiving closely. Nobody feels too festive, but we do huddle around the menorah each night to light the candles—candles that represent an ancient fight for freedom—and every time we do, I try to picture Hannah with her bow drill, trying to turn smoke into flame and earn her own freedom.

Hannah

What I would do for a match right now is fucking scary.

Mom

We speak to Jason about a holiday gift for Hannah. Can we put together some type of package? Can we send her something warm? A treat to eat? Buy something to show we are thinking of her and missing her? The answer is an unequivocal, "No." Instead, he suggests that we make something for her.

"Susan," he suggests, more gently than usual, "she'll get the idea more if a present—a thing—doesn't get in the way."

Hannah

Getting mail here makes me think about what it must be like to get mail in the army. I mean here we are, marching around like soldiers, and then one day a pickup truck pulls up, and all the supplies for the week are tossed out of the back by an old guy in an olive-colored parka—I think he's named Jake, though he's never talked to us, and he doesn't do much more than grunt at the staff. Sometimes there's a mail bag. All of us hover around like dorks waiting for our ration of fruit loops and bagged beans, but we keep our eyes on the canvas bag that might have mail. I have to say, I get mail a lot, and sometimes I feel bad about it, seeing the other girls turn away and try to pretend it's no big deal. Sometimes I even take shit for it.

"Did your mommy and daddy write to you again, Hannah? Are they afraid you'll forget about them?" I'm not mad when they tease me. But I also don't want to tell them how much I'm thinking about my parents, and how getting letters makes me know they're thinking about me too.

Mom

Every time I speak to a family member, they ask me what they can do. Now I have an answer for them.

"Write something to Hannah," I tell each one of them. "A positive thought, a wish, a memory, or a hope. I'm going to make her a little book for Hanukkah."

I laugh and cry my way through the project. I pair my brother's "I love you thiiiiiiiis much" message with a picture I find of him with his arms spread wide and his signature grin on his face. Aunt Cory writes to remind Hannah of how brave she is, Aunt Connie tells her to trust in God, Aunt Sandy sends her their favorite song lyrics, and her best friend from childhood writes such a long note that it takes up a whole page. Of course Paul and Camilla write too, hovering over me as I select pictures of her time with each one of them. I include pictures of her Mr. Bear, of our dogs, of her grandmas in her birthday bounce house. I scan and Photoshop everything together in a happy collage of our best memories, and turn everyone's efforts into a sixteen-page scrapbook of loving moments and messages. I tuck the little book into an envelope and address it to her at Group 6, hoping to remind her that she is part of a much larger group as well.

Hannah

I have to explain every single picture to the girls; they want to know who everyone is, and what they're like, and why I thought they picked the quote or message they sent, and when and where the picture was taken. Nobody teases me about the pictures of the father–daughter dance at my bat mitzvah or being hugged so hard by my Auntie Robin that my face is squished in like a cartoon character. Dani, my little heroin girl, cries a little, and I hug her hard and share some of the love that I've been mailed.

Mom

Mid-December now, and it is time for Hannah to meet with Dr. Carl Smoot, an independent psychologist who will assess her diagnosis of bipolar disorder. The possibilities tumble around my brain. If she's bipolar that's okay, we'll deal with it. If not, then, well then I don't know. It means we have to figure out what's really wrong, and that seems more frightening than hopeful. It also means we have failed Hannah in a very fundamental way, and that's the most frightening diagnosis of all.

Hannah

I guess being a smart-ass just comes naturally to me, cuz as soon as Smoot starts talking to me, sitting there in his nice warm SUV with heated seats, I start giving him crap, scratching at myself and talking like a doofus. After a while, he just sort of looks at me through these smart guy glasses and gets all quiet, and I start feeling pretty uncomfortable. Then he says, "This could matter. Are you going to stop fucking around so we can figure out what's going on with you, or would you like to get out of the car?" Well, the jeep is warm, and it's the first time I'm sitting on something soft in weeks, so I decide that assessment might be a good idea after all. I tell him that I'm willing to try, and he smiles and says, "Well, I guess you're not crazy then." I kind of like him.

Mom

I hit the "end" button on the phone and sit down hard. It's corroborated. Hannah does not have bipolar disorder. That overpriced, undereducated asshole in Watsonville misdiagnosed our daughter, fed her toxic psychotropic drugs, and told her she would never recover. And we let him. I let him. I let that fuckhead shrink poison my daughter. I sought him out, I drove her there so he could do it. I can't hang up from Jason's call fast enough, and I dodge Paul's offer of comfort, instead opting to walk outside, to let the fine December drizzle wash away my stupidity, my horror.

Hannah

What do ya know? I guess I'm not bipolar, just an oppositional idiot with run-of-the-mill mental disorders. Is that better or worse?

Mom

Now Jason tells us, "It's time to start thinking about the next step. I know it's hard in lots of different ways, but I want you to consider moving Hannah to residential treatment so that she can work on life skills." I am not convinced that Hannah should go to another program far away from home, but even as I shake my head no at the phone, I agree to at least think about it. I do think about it, wondering if my protests are about my shame at not being able to teach my own daughter "life skills," or that maybe it's the money it will take to send her to another program, or just my missing her. Finally I decide that it was all of those things, and that all of those things were about my needs. Finally I think the way I ought to. What is best for Hannah?

Hannah

I watch some of the other girls go out on solo. At first I think it's pretty hokey. "Go—find yourself, little one. Come back after your animal totem is revealed," or some such shit like that. But the ones who go actually seem different somehow, when they come back. I know my night is coming, and I'm a little freaked out. I check in with the group about it, but the girls who went don't really say much.

Mom

Hannah's letter tells us that she's going out on solo. I'm worried, and ask Jason about her safety when we have our weekly call. "She'll be fine," he reassures us. "The solo experience is very rich. It teaches the kids a lot about themselves, and how to question the barriers in their lives. I think it will be especially good for Hannah, who needs to get to know herself."

Hannah

They are giving me lots of rules about being out by myself. Eat. Drink. Stay warm. I can't bust a flame yet, so I probably won't have fire. I have to figure out what I need and how much I can carry. I'll be out of sight and really, truly alone with only myself to rely on. I'm scared because I don't even like being at home alone, listening to our house creak and watching the redwood branches make creepy shadows on the walls of my room. I want to cry, but the other bitches are watching me, and I think that I have to act like I'm okay or little Dani will be scared when it's her turn to go. I heft my pack and start walking.

Mom

Jason is talking about how Hannah over-identifies with others, and how that's one of the reasons she picked up so many destructive behaviors. I want to disagree, but instead I listen, knowing it's true. I scratch my pen back and forth in my little notebook until the paper rips. I know that her actions are far more than simple peer pressure. She took on smoking, drugs, alcohol, drug use, shoplifting, burning and cutting herself, watching porn, skipping school, leaving the house in the middle of the night, violence, and other high-risk behaviors one at a time in some kind of silent solidarity with her out-of-control community. I realize now that there was very little of Hannah in those actions; instead it was a compilation of characters that she was trying on for size and acceptance. I love her for her empathy, but wonder why she didn't see what we see. That she was enough—interesting and exciting and beautiful enough as Hannah. I touch my tear-moistened finger to the inky wound I have made on the page, and watch the ink dilute and smear.

Hannah

I can't see too well. I'm not allowed to wear contacts out here, and my glasses want to keep fogging up because of my big fur parka head. It makes me want to cry again, this time from not being able to see. I stumble around, tripping over myself, finally putting enough distance between me and the group that I can't see them or hear them at all. Then I go a little farther. Eventually, after a long time, I stop to wonder if there is anyone in the world who can see me. I drop my pack in the snow, stretch my arms out to the sides, and turn slowly all the way around like some ballerina turned homeless woman in rags.

I know that the staff has a rough idea of where I am, but I don't know if they will check on me, or if they would know if I were in trouble. It's so beautiful that I want to sketch it, but then I remember that I still don't have my art, and I decide to just be in it and a part of it. I make camp after a while, clearing some of the snow with my gloved hands, and foraging for some kindling before it gets too dark. I make a little pile of the mossy bark that we use to start our fires, and feeling optimistic, I gather a few sticks to feed a flame. I dig my bow drill out of my pack, and kneel on the cold ground, my knee hurting from the cold even through the insulated wool over-pants. I thread a stick through the twine of my bow, and place the bottom part of the wood in the base that I had made weeks ago, the grooves deeper and smoother each day that I work to bust a flame. My capstone, a welcome gift from my group, holds my stick securely in place under my left hand, as my right hand rolls the bow back and forth, spinning the stick faster and faster, trying to magically make something out of nothing.

Mom

The thought of Hannah alone makes me push Jason.

"Jason, tell me when she'll move on. Does the solo signify her readiness to get out?"

Jason replies calmly. "She needs to work hard for herself, not to get out of here. She needs to know when she leaves that it's because she made things happen through her own actions."

I am insistent. "When will that be, Jason?"

"Let's let Hannah show us when she's ready. Meanwhile it would be a good idea for us all to talk to Bodin, and have some possibilities in place for her next step."

Hannah

No fire again tonight, and I'm too tired to eat, so I make a brief entry in my journal about that, about my failure and what I learned from it. Then I pull my ratty olive sleeping bag off the frame of my pack and unroll it, doubling it up with the water-proof outer bag and spreading it on the snow. I keep most of my clothes on until I get in the bag, then shimmy and roll until I have enough clothes off to sleep. I kick the outer layer of clothes to the bottom of my bag so that it they won't freeze overnight, and add my water bottle so that it won't turn to a block of ice.

I spend some time playing with a bag of M&Ms they gave me as I was leaving camp. A test to see if I'm strong. I am brave enough to spill the candy into my palm, and I slowly count the pieces. Shit, they accidentally gave me extra. I'm hungry, and it's been forever since I had candy, so I think about eating the two extra pieces, and then quickly spill them back into the baggie, pulling myself halfway out of my bag in the cold night air to dig a shallow hole in the snow beneath me. I know if I start eating, I won't stop. I don't know why it matters to me, but it does. I snuggle back into my bag, rolling on top of the baggie, and try not to think about food.

I study the sky, beautiful as it changes from blue to pink to fire to black, watching my breath cloud and then clear in the freezing air, and think about my own fucked up, ugly little world at home. I think about what I just did, and let myself be proud at being alone and being okay. I take a last look at the clear night sky before closing the mummy top of the sleeping bag, sealing myself in with just me for company.

Mom

My brother calls me, asking about Hannah. His number is one of the few I still pick up. He is impatient.

"How long will she be there, Sue?"

"I don't know. It's usually about six to eight weeks, but she's been there for nine weeks already, and nothing seems to be happening."

"Do you think they're just emptying your bank account?"

"Maybe. How would I know?"

"Maybe you should go and see for yourself."

"Maybe you're right." I hang up and call Bodin to set up an appointment, thinking about what my brother said.

Hannah

I did it. When I wake up in the morning, that's the first thought that comes into my head. I spent the night in the middle of the fucking wilderness all alone, without turning into a Popsicle or being eaten by wild animals. I use my toes to pull my clothes out of the bottom of the bag, and then dress quickly, body half in and half out of the warmth I created for myself.

Mom

I am desperate to see my daughter. I want to see how she is living, and who she is living with. I want to meet the mysterious Jason. I want to see if she is okay without us there to take care of her. Hannah's daily journal tells us that she is learning to judge her actions against her values, to identify her emotions, and to respect herself and her abilities. But they don't tell us how she is.

Hannah

I'm pretty good at packing up camp, and my little circle takes no time at all. I roll my bags and get my pack together. I smile at the benefit of my big failure at fire-making . . . no coals to crush! Funny thing is, I'm not in a hurry to get back to the group. Don't get me wrong. The group is great. I care about them, and I think that they care about me too. And I'm learning a lot about myself in therapy. But maybe not as much as I learned last night. I'm strong. I'm okay, even when I'm scared and alone. And, oh yeah, I still suck at making fire.

Mom

It's time for Paul and I to go see Bodin again, though this time we don't see the big, ginger-haired Doug Bodin, but rather a small dark-haired woman named Alicia. She greets us in the lobby, says "Hi" to a couple of unhappy looking, pimply teens sitting in chairs as though waiting for the dentist, and then invites us into her office. There she waves her hand towards a small round table with four matching chairs, and we sit down silently on the nubby black upholstery. I look around at the pale blue walls and idly note that blue is supposed to be a calming color. Not so much, I decide, pressing my hands together tightly in my lap so they won't shake.

Alicia picks up a neat stack of brightly colored packets from her desk and joins us, smoothing her gray tweed pencil skirt as she sits. "I'm so happy to hear that Hannah is doing well," she begins. I wonder how she knows, and why we would believe that she is happy about a person she's never met. I decide to give her the benefit of the doubt, because mistrusting everyone is becoming exhausting, and because her niceties will not affect the decision we are making. Luckily Alicia has no clue about my skeptical inner dialogue, and continues smoothly, "I've reviewed all of Doug's notes, and I've spoken to Jason and Carl. We all agree that a residential treatment setting would be the best choice for Hannah."

My anger rises like mercury in a thermometer that's been dipped in boiling water. "You all agree?" I grip the smooth edge of the wood table and lean forward, glaring at her over my glasses. She has the good grace to retreat.

"Of course this is a recommendation," she amends, "and we've provided a number of choices as far as programs go." I am instantly ashamed, realizing how defensive my reaction is. Sitting back, I take my glasses off, so I won't have to meet her gaze. There is no reason to panic, I tell myself. We haven't given up our parental rights. Bodin is just doing the job we are paying them to do. They are trying to help us make a tough decision.

Hannah

Everyone here has lightened up because of the holidays, or maybe because our group knows what it's doing now, and how to do it. We're pretty quick with breaking down and setting up camp, and cooking gets easier once you figure out the tricks. I like the hiking cuz it keeps us warm and busy—plus anything is better than therapy or community meetings. That when I wear myself down to a nub trying to be honest with my group of bitches here. Noticing the way I talk, how my body acts when I'm stressed, and trying to control myself is a lot harder than hiking. It's still the hardest thing we do here. Well, that and bustin' a flame. When I get home, I might turn to arson, just for the chance to use matches again.

Mom

The three slick pocket folders Alicia hands us contain information on schools. Not schools exactly, because for at least two of them, schooling seems to be a sidebar. They are Residential Treatment Programs, or RTPs, the highest level of care available. My anger rushes back in, with its good friend denial, who is still hanging around after all these weeks.

"Hannah's not sick." I am adamant, turning first to Alicia and then to Paul, who sits quietly. "I thought we just proved that. She's a normal teenager who fell in with the wrong crowd, was misdiagnosed bipolar, and then overdosed on prescription drugs that she shouldn't have been given in the first place."

My voice rises above the level appropriate for the serene blue office. Alicia stands, clearly dismissing us, urging us to review the schools and then check in with Jason. With a tight smile, she invites us to call her with any questions we have. Paul practically pulls me out of the chair and out the door. He is equally angry, but at me.

"We need to hear all the information available, not attack people. How can we make good decisions if we don't know all our options?"

He marches me to the car, slamming his door hard, the crack of the locks and the zip of his seatbelt pulled too quickly expressing his feelings without words. I hang my head, knowing he's right but not wanting him to be.

Hannah

Today we hike over to some foothills, and crunch over the snow to a little cave to see some petroglyphs that are painted with some kind of dye. The first thing that comes into my head is that some ancient scamp had taken up tagging. Dani is pretty sure it's a billboard for twig toothbrushes or leaf toilet paper, but Maggie decides it's a declaration of love. She's such a romantic. It's good to know I can still laugh. At the same time, it's pretty scary how normal all of this seems to be getting. Sleeping on the ground, having therapy in the snow, cooking over a fire. It should be weird, but somehow it seems more real than the freaky life I was living at home. I'm filthy, but I feel clean. There's order here, and I know what's expected. I still have sad days, but the angry days come less and less. I think I would like to take some of the shit I'm learning home with me. And I'd like to do that pretty soon.

Mom

I talk to Jason, and he defends his recommendation, reviewing what we all know.

"Susan, it's true that Hannah presents very well when she wants to, but she was misdiagnosed in the first place because she already had a serious drug problem. Part of the reason for her drug use is the way she over-identifies with peers."

I listen as Jason summarizes our pain and suffering, seeing Hannah in my mind, staggering into the house at night, dressing, speaking, acting like her friends, picking up their mannerisms.

Jason continues, "Plus, Hannah has had long-term problems dealing with emotions, and I really think she will benefit from continuing the DBT training we started here. She'll have a chance to master the tools at a residential program, and that could ultimately get her to the point where she won't need to self-medicate."

Now I think back to second grade, to third, her crying over assignments, to fifth, her clutching at me to avoid walking up to the stage to accept an award. I scowl at the speaker on the phone, but agree to at least read the school folders. I disconnect the call, and as Paul submerges to his home office, I sit and think about our last year—the school, the therapists, the consultants, the wilderness, and now residential treatment. I feel as though I am watching a pattern of dominoes, each one falling and leading to the next in line, out of control, unstoppable until they reach the final piece. I just can't see the end of the pattern. I lower my forehead to the cool wood of the table. Then I pick up a folder and start reading.

Chapter 7

Hannah

Did I mention we got a new girl? We all start calling her the poopster because she sits on the edge of camp and shits her pants on purpose. All that she accomplished is shitty pants, so now she's holding it in. I guess she's pretty desperate to control something in her life. I totally get that. I still don't like to think of myself as being compliant. I choose to participate because I don't want to be lonely. I choose to hike for warmth and to get rid of some of the weight I've gained on my rice-on-rice diet. I choose to let the staff look at my feet and give me meds because I know they are looking out for me in this hard place. I choose to cooperate in therapy because I want to go home.

Mom

The three schools are all different, except for the fact that they are all in Utah, probably because that state allows the private incarceration of teens in treatment programs until the age of eighteen. Isla Vista is the largest of the three, with both open and secure areas, and seems to have a focus on peer group support. Vista is a locked facility with a highly structured regimen.

The third catches my eye right away. L'Arts, a fine-arts-based program. Two of the schools are in Salt Lake City, and Paul and I decide we should see both, though he's just as excited about the arts program as I am. Bodin has provided us with basic information about each facility. Paul and I meet at the dining room table and draw up a list of other specifics we would like to know before committing to any program. How often will therapy be offered? What are the credentials of the staff who will be interacting with my daughter? How is schooling accomplished? The list fills a page, and each question reflects our concerns about letting others parent our child.

Hannah

Poopzilla, as I've taken to calling her, has not pooped in days, and has now been picked up by the mysterious Jake and taken to the hospital. I know I should care but I just look at her and think she's an asshole. Oh, that's a pun! Or is it an ironic reference? No matter what I call it, it's a relief not to have someone with blocked bowels lurking on the edge of camp. It was creepy, and we talk about it a lot, wondering how long a human can go without pooping, and making lots of "full of shit" jokes. That's how desperate we are for amusement. Nothing different ever happens here, and I settle into my sleeping bags, shimmying around to dig my body into the snow and gravel, and close my eyes thinking about how good it's going to feel getting into my own bed.

Mom

Before booking our tickets, Paul and I make a special request of Jason. "We would like to visit Hannah, Jason. Is it possible, and if so, how is it done?" We expect resistance, but Jason is completely agreeable, as though the request is unremarkable in every way. He even gives us the name of a lodge that's perched between Salt Lake City and Duchesne, suggesting that we visit schools in the city and then drive halfway to Second

Nature so that we can arrive early the following morning. He also instructs us to rent a four-wheel drive vehicle. "Corolla's not going to cut it," he warns. I'm confused, and he explains that we'll be driving over some difficult terrain. "I can't give you the details of where you'll see her because the groups move constantly." I think of my daughter, a nomad, making camp wherever she stops for the day, the staff radioing base to report their position. Sighing, I wonder again if this is all necessary. Jason works through the long list of steps we'll have to take to catch up with her and wraps up with, "Come to the main headquarters in the morning. You'll get further instructions here."

After feeling so helpless, it's good to have something concrete to do, and Paul and I swing into action, booking tickets and room reservations, calling treatment centers for appointments, arranging for Camilla to stay with a friend for a few days, and trying to find a four-wheel drive rental during the Utah Christmas ski season.

I wander through Big 5 and Outdoor World with Paul, studying how fashion has changed since the last time we went to the snow. The last time we went, it was to ski, and I had been shamed by my size, whispering my weight to the man at the ski shop and selecting ski pants that were more Spanx than sportswear. Now, another two sizes larger, I am back, opting for clothes that serve as camouflage for my curves. It is good to have a distraction.

The longer Hannah is away, and the more therapy we have, the more confused I feel. I long for the days when we had no idea how messed up we were. When Hannah was just a typical screwed-up teenager instead of an emotionally dysregulated, misdiagnosed, over-identifying, high-risk youth. I feel defeated. And alone. I hold up a black puffy jacket and decide that it will conceal just about everything.

In the end, we manage it all except for the car rental, and we end up renting a truck from some "Crazy Eddie" type place near the airport. I'm caught up with excitement and maybe even happiness for the first time in many months.

Hannah

I don't really know what it's like to get an enema, but it sure doesn't look like it feels good. Poopzilla is sitting at the edge of camp, more surly than ever, and I guess I don't blame her. We're still not allowed to talk to her, so tracking her bowel movements continues to be a spectator sport. She's done a complete 180, and instead of holding it in she insists on pooping in her pants again, like she has typhoid or something. I ask the staff to place her downwind, but they don't think it's funny, and I guess I do respect that they are professionals and that it would be nasty and wrong for them to laugh. I hate to admit it but I'll miss them, and my group of bitches here too, when I go.

Mom

I check Camilla's bag, which she has packed by herself. Pajamas, toothpaste and toothbrush, extra clothes and underwear, and her favorite beanie baby, a horse named Oats, its head carefully sutured back on after Hannah's cruel decapitation. She also packs her Gameboy, a copy of Homer's *Odyssey*, and a sketchbook. "Good job," I tell her, realizing how self-sufficient she has become. I'm watching Hannah so closely that I haven't been watching Camilla at all. I watch now, as her hunched shoulders disappear into her friend Ruby's house, and I hug Ruby's mom with a mixture of guilt and gratitude, and sadness too that we have to rely on the kindness of people we don't know very well.

Hannah

Someone should really tell Poopzilla that she's going to have to live in that sleeping bag for a long time, and that she really shouldn't let it get gamey this soon, but we're not allowed to speak with her until after she does her life story. It occurs to me that I took a long time to write my story too, and even minus the excrement, I must have looked pretty moronic to the group. I wonder if they were rooting for me the way I'm secretly rooting for her. *Write*, I tell her telepathically, *we'll help you with the other stuff.* Maybe she receives my message, because she starts writing that same day. I would share my newfound telepathic powers with the staff, but honestly, they already suspect we're all nuts, and they might think I believe my own malarkey.

Mom

Paul and I do an accounting right before we leave for Utah. I don't usually get involved in finances. I'm not good at it. Paul, on the other hand, has a knack for financial stuff. I asked him about it one time and he shared that his parents had urged him to find a trade job, telling him, "You'll never amount to anything." He proved them wrong by becoming successful at an early age, hitchhiking across country to California at twenty-two, and starting a small jobs publication that was quickly eaten by a larger career services provider. There his little magazine grew into a chain of career-related publications and an Internet jobs board. That's when I met him. I worked for an advertising agency, and our argumentative beginning turned into admiration and finally flirtation and marriage. I am angry at him all the time now, but it doesn't blunt the love I have for him, stoically emptying our accounts to pay for Hannah's treatment, never complaining, never considering denying her help.

We don't talk about it on the way to the airport. The Delta flight is smooth, and I gasp at the snowy "V" of the Wasatch Mountains as we fly into Salt Lake City. We cab over to the tiny, no-name rental agency to pick up our vehicle, probably the last four-wheel drive rental left in Utah during the height of Christmas ski season. It's a long, dented Dodge 2000 with a broken windshield and the thick scent of stale cigarette smoke and dirt inside. The guy at the counter gives us a used map and his good wishes in a hurry, rushing away to the warmth of the little back office.

As usual, Paul doesn't linger for me to figure out the map, starting the truck and injecting himself onto the busy beltway that runs around the city. "Which exit?" he demands. He'll soon be screaming at me as I turn the map around and around, fighting off nausea and trying to find our first stop, L'Arts. Sounds like a spa, I think, raising my eyebrows at the beautiful building featured on the front of the glossy packet in my hand.

Hannah

I find out about the money after I ask Jason how my parents can send me away like this, shifting their responsibility for me onto someone else. He asks me why I think it's easier for them to send me here. He tells me to make a list of what's easier for them and what's harder for them. Easier? Not having me around, I guess. Harder? Maybe how they write to me so often. It must take a lot of time. They also do everything I do here except shit in the woods, and that's probably a pain in the ass for them. Mom's probably pretty embarrassed too, since she always tries to be super mom. The money though, I guess it's a lot, it sounds like a lot, but honestly doesn't it just mean that they have enough money to send their demented kid away? It did start me thinking about the other kids here though. Most of them are white, and from the stories they tell it seems like they were pretty well-off. We have a Bev Hills bitch here, her Daddy is a Hollywood mucky-muck, and she makes sure we know it. The other girls talk about their trips, their cars, and their private schools. I can pretty much tell the size of their allowances from the kind of drugs they bought when they were using. So I guess I'm one of the poorer kids here. I wonder what people do when they really are too poor to pay for a place like this.

Mom

As we careen down the unfamiliar, snowy Salt Lake City high-way, it isn't money on my mind, but death. Not my own, though that certainly appears to be a possibility with Paul's aggressive driving. I am thinking about the reading I have done on teen depression and suicide, which could be the cost of bringing Hannah home without treatment, and which puts the whole money thing into perspective. The most disturbing figures I read come from the Center for Disease Control. Every day thousands of teens and young adults attempt suicide—it's the third leading cause of death in those age groups. Four out of five of them will have given clear warnings about their mental state. Over five thousand of them will succeed each year. I sit fiddling with the map corners, ignoring Paul's rude remarks, and think about parents, including us, who ignore warning signs. Now I realize how hard it is to see what is clear to others. I wrestle with the new knowledge that you can love too much, give too much, and get too close. Denial can blur your vision. Our own good intentions can blind us to our child's needs. Paul is not attuned to my pensive mood, swinging our big pickup truck around a slow moving car and then swerving over two lanes to the exit, which he has found with no help from me.

Hannah

I keep scanning the ground this morning, looking for a gift for Poopzilla, whose real name is Penny, which is unfortunate because it goes so well with all of our nicknames for her. It's little Dani who spots the rock first, smooth, gray, and palm-sized with a small depression in the middle.

"I'd feel better about giving her a fire kit if any of us could actually bust a flame," she says, squinting at the rock like it's at fault for our lame efforts.

"We'll do it, Dani." I try to say it like I believe it. But the bad patch on my knee from kneeling in front of my kindling, and my raw hands definitely reduce my enthusiasm for making fire. Fuck these fire analogies anyway. Why can't they just say, "Overcome hurdles and be persistent," and be done with it? Why do we have to bust a flame? I'm tired of cold food and sore knees. I know this program is costing a bucket of money, and I'm beginning to think they charge by the analogy.

The staff and Jason really want me to say that I've kicked the habit, but I'm the only one in the group who says I'll probably use again when I get out. I look around the circle sometimes, and know I'm the only one here brave enough or stupid enough to admit it. They say here that they want us to be honest, but they really don't. I guess they probably feel like failures if they send us home before we are "cured," especially since the cure costs so much. I don't really see the harm in using sometimes, but Jason tells me that's addictive thinking. Then he gives me a book called *Addictive Thinking*! Sometimes he's really in my head, but other times he's a million miles away from understanding me. I can't get him to understand the sadness or the loneliness or how a little bit of artificial happy helps get me through the day.

Mom

By the time we arrive at L'Arts Academy, the map is shaking in my hands from fear and anger. If you haven't been to Salt Lake City before, you cannot imagine the challenges of navigating the city streets there. "It's a simple grid," residents say, smiling sadistically. So we look for Vine Street, but we have to navigate West North Street to get there, and that takes us the long way through streets that seem to have nonsensical names like West or North Northwest, or South Northwest.

As usual, Paul speeds down the unfamiliar roads, yelling at me to find the turns, while I swivel the map this way and that, pleading with him to slow down or pull over before I get car sick. I am relieved to finally be at a full stop, and I look away from Paul as I struggle to fold the well-worn map that the truck rental place gave us.

The brochure was accurate, but I'm still surprised to see that the residential treatment center is a large home, not quite a mansion, with graceful pillars and a lovely wood-and-beveled glass door fitted with brass. I don't know what I was expecting—snarling guard dogs? Electrified chain link? Certainly not this Beverly Hills façade in the middle of Salt Lake City. I give up on folding the map and shove it between the seats, running my fingers through my hair and pulling the visor down to check myself in the dust-covered mirror of our rented truck. The film of dust makes my image look like a washed-out, old photo of the person I once was. Sighing, I snap the visor back into place and slide my ample rear out of the truck.

Hannah

I forget how dirty I am until I look at the other girls. It's weird, cuz I feel clean here. The air is clean, and the snow is clean. I think that what we say to each other is clean too, even when the words are angry, because it's mostly honest, and honest is clean. The way we live is clean too. Simple. There's nothing here to get in the way of noticing yourself and how you act. If I don't notice, one of the staff will notice for me.

"You seem upset, Hannah. What is your body doing? Would you like to check in with the group?"

I check in. I talk. I breathe deeply in and out and lean back against my frame pack, letting my body tell me that I am okay.

Mom

I take a deep breath and knock, Paul standing just behind me as though to keep me from running away. The door is answered by a youngish woman with a page boy haircut, looking more like a curator than a keeper. She smiles pleasantly and invites us in. Immediately to our right is a small group of girls lounging on a big couch. Two of the three girls say hello; the third looks uninterested but not unfriendly.

The room itself is tastefully furnished, with muted oriental rugs, casual but elegant furniture, and what seem likely to be acrylic paintings in many styles hanging on the walls. Walking into the room, I realize that it's enormous, and that there is not only another equally large grouping of plush sectional couches, but a long, heavy, oak table with carved chairs stretching the length of the hall.

"For our girls," says page boy. "Our program is based on the healing power of the fine arts," she continues, smiling graciously and pivoting her slim, well-dressed frame. She gestures us into the oaken dining area with a well-manicured hand. I turn after her, tugging at the rolls of my thick jacket and then hiding my square fingers in my pockets. Page boy continues, "We are, temporarily, a home for these young ladies, but also a haven." I catch my breath at the idea that my daughter might need a haven from me, from us.

From the dining area, which is large enough to seat all twenty-six girls, ages thirteen to seventeen, we step into a spotless commercial kitchen. There we meet Cook. She nods at us, pulling her broad shoulders back, tipping her chin upward and declaring, "I cook for whatever special needs these girls have." She taps her ample bosom with meaty palms, clearly proud of the job she does. "I cook gluten free, vegan, kosher . . . you name it." Her enthusiasm is impossible to resist, and I catch myself smiling at Paul before remembering that I am angry with him. Smiling back, he wraps his arm loosely around my waist and steers me out of the kitchen to the area we have especially come to see—the art studio, with rooms for painting, pottery, and a separate small crafts cottage across the garden.

Page boy describes the art program in detail, but the work on the walls doesn't really need much explanation. Cheerful canvasses crowd every corner, lighting up the room with their colorful bouquets of flowers and bowls of fruit. I bend to look closely at some of the work, lacing my fingers together and smiling inwardly as I recall how Hannah always struggled not to touch the canvasses at the museums we visited over the years. Sometimes she would grip my hand to keep herself in check, her free hand fluttering, the guards glaring a tacit warning.

Hannah's work is typically darker and more intense than the pieces I am studying now. I wonder if the girls' art changes much as they themselves change through therapy. Paul helps me up from my none-too-graceful squat, and I ask page boy about that, but she doesn't know. Mentally, I give her credit for not making up bullshit, and move on.

After a quick stroll through the classroom, with its bank of computers and an impressive variety of shelved literature and reference books, we circle back to the main house. We're given a peek into the girls' dormitory, colorful bits of clothes and makeup evident on the beds and dressers, just like you would expect in any teenager's room.

After the tour, we are introduced briefly to the staff, a young and rather eager group who hold forth in the corridor about art and healing, family involvement, and helping young people reconnect with their best selves, sometimes speaking over each other in their enthusiasm for the work they are doing.

Paul joins right in. "Oh, yeah, Hannah's been painting for years. She wins every art show she's in. Except one time when she was nine and the judge accused her teacher of doing the painting."

Everyone expresses polite outrage. I can't believe he is standing in the hallway of a residential treatment center bragging about his daughter. Am I supposed to be warmed by his great and undaunted pride in his daughter, or floored by his denial of the trouble she is in?

As usual I am the wet blanket. "Are the girls competitive in their painting here? What percentage of time is spent on art, and what percentage is spent on school work? How directed is the subject matter? Are they working on portfolios?"

Paul sidesteps away from me, making me feel like an overeager soccer mother questioning the referee. Is he embarrassed? We are about to empty our bank account into this program, and I feel I have the right and responsibility to ask these questions. I shoot him my best evil eye, which he studiously avoids. Sensing the sudden tension, the staff quickly disbands, promising me that the director will be able to answer all of my questions.

The center's new director is a young man with neatly combed hair and earnest eyes above his dress shirt and tie.

"Tell me about your program," I say, keeping the question as general as possible. I listen hard and nod dutifully, taking lots of notes in my little brown notebook as he speaks passionately about art and healing. He also outlines the costs and the billing procedures. We already know that it will be expensive—Bodin has prepared us for the roughly $10,000 per month we will be expected to pay at any residential program. The director takes a breath and gives us the bad news about what we can expect most insurance companies to cover. Very little, it turns out. We are forced to board Hannah out of state because our home state of California requires her consent, even as a minor. In Utah, we have stewardship of her until she is eighteen. But sending her to Utah for treatment lessens the insurance benefits. Bottom line, our insurance will pay for twenty therapy sessions. That's less than two weeks of treatment. They won't help with the room and board at all. Paul and I look at each other grimly. We know what this means. I close my eyes and let the jumble of canvasses and their bright images crowd out the objections in my mind.

Hannah

They tell us about how much it costs here. I guess they want us to know that our parents make sacrifices so that we can shit in the woods and eat out of a nasty, burnt coffee can. I think back to my talk with Jason, and admit to myself that this might be hard for them. I study my body to see how I feel about this but I can't tell. It just fucks me up to be mad at them for sending me away and at the same time know that they are giving stuff up too. How should I feel?

Mom

Finally, we meet the L'Arts girls. We sit at one end of the long, heavy dining table with the three pretty teens from the living room, my stomach rumbling from the delicious cooking smells now drifting out of the kitchen. "How is it here?" I ask, again starting with a general question. They trip over each other in their enthusiasm to answer.

"It's great, we have lots of art and music time," answers one girl, her face animated, and her midriff peeking out under her Juicy Couture tee.

"The teachers here are so cool, they understand if we need extensions and work with us a lot to get things done," the second girl adds.

"I just earned makeup and jewelry," adds another kohl-eyed resident gleefully, lifting her thin arm and pointing to her face with the jangle of shiny bracelets.

By the time Paul and I leave, I feel I can breathe again for the first time in months. It turns out that residential treatment centers are nothing at all like I expected. Paul reaches out to squeeze my hand before starting the truck, and I squeeze back, sorry for all of the morning's anger. I close my eyes and picture Hannah here, her clothes smudged with paint, and her long, slender fingers once again curled around a brush, canvasses alive with color. To hell with the money.

Hannah

I still don't have art privileges, and it's still hard to be, to just be without it, though now I guess I understand why it is that Jason took it away from me. Art has been a part of me for so long that I don't know what to do with my hands or my mind when I don't have it. Sometimes, when I'm trying to explain something to Jason or my group of bitches here, my hand moves by itself, like I'm drawing it, but my hand is empty, so my words have to fill the emptiness. It makes me feel naked and exposed, and I guess I am. I guess I'm supposed to be.

Mom

We like L'Arts so much that we nearly decide not to go to our other appointment at Vista Residential Treatment Center and High School, but since we are in Utah, it seems silly not to keep the commitment. The map leads us to a rather barren area west of Salt Lake City called Magna. The streets here are a bit easier to navigate, and we find the facility easily. The contrast is clear, even before we turn into the short driveway that leads to the simple iron gate. The low ranch buildings sit discreetly behind a high stone wall. It's neat without being manicured, three separate buildings in a U-shape, set apart from other modest homes by about a half-acre of empty lawn and a small parking lot that Paul struggles to fit our oversized vehicle into.

Once again I feel self-conscious getting out of the truck, this time realizing that there are cameras mounted over what appears to be the office door. I smooth my puffy black jacket and try to look competent as I tumble out of the filthy, battered truck onto the shoveled walkway.

The staffer in the small, utilitarian office greets us with a reserved smile, and asks us to sign in while our visitor's badges are prepared. After adding my name to the log, I pass the cheap plastic pen to Paul and glance around the small, square office. The furniture is simple light wood and metal, and French doors adjoin what appears to be a music room, with a dozen guitars hanging on the walls. A second set of glass doors face an average sized dining room table and kitchen.

"We don't eat here," says the staffer, noting the direction of my gaze. "We mostly do tutoring at that table. The kitchen is left over from the original house, and the staff and residents use it mostly for light snacks."

Now I can see the row of cereals in dispensers, like the ones you get at "breakfast included" hotel chains. I continue my inspection, ending at a bank of video screens hanging from high on the office wall, angled down towards the desk. Again, an explanation comes, unbidden.

"We have closed circuit cameras in all of the common areas, especially the living rooms, where our new admits spend their first twenty-four hours."

The medical language brings back the days of Hannah's stay at the behavioral hospital, of my begging Hannah to please see us, to just talk to us. I can make out an image on the screen now, the mattress on the floor, a girl in scrubs on the mattress, matted hair covering her eyes, her mouth defiant. Panic rises in me at the bizarre sight, imagining that we have stumbled into a setting where kids are jailed and beaten into submission as a matter of policy. I chew on my knuckle, my obvious anxiety prompting the staffer to add a gently-voiced explanation.

"It's for their safety. The first twenty-four hours can be difficult, and we want to keep an eye on them. Once they've had their first night here, we get them settled into their rooms."

Here at Vista, our tour is given by a student, her mane of black hair pulled back with the kind of pink plastic clips you would expect on a toddler, her face bare above a simple long-sleeved T-shirt and jeans. She walks us to the girls' dormitory first, and I peek into the open bedroom doors, beds made up neatly, clothes hung in closets.

"We earn points by keeping our personal and common

areas neat," the resident informs us in front of an open door that features a large corkboard. "This is my room, and this is my family," she shares, pointing in turn to the white room with its brightly covered twin beds and small connecting bathroom, and then to the corkboard, on the door, festooned with pictures of what I imagine to be her brothers and sisters, father, mother and family pets. She smiles at us. "We'll go see the living room next. It's where we have therapy and community meetings."

The living room is smaller than the massive space of L'Arts, and filled with a circle of oversized couches in soft brown leather. Plunked down in the middle of the room is the mattress we had seen on the closed-circuit camera, the subject of the staffer's scrutiny no longer present. Instead, there is a small group of conservatively dressed girls filing in from a field trip of some kind.

"Pockets please," the teacher states in a polite but no-nonsense voice, and the girls proceed to pull their pockets inside out.

"Contraband check" is the two-word explanation from our young guide. The girls ignore us as we file past them, on our way now to the cafeteria, walking through spotless hallways and a shiny foyer. One flight of steps takes us downstairs to a small cafeteria, complete with sneeze guards and tray rails, the half dozen tables looking much like a Sizzler restaurant—salt, pepper, a metal napkin holder on each table's gleaming wood surface. I admire the housekeeping, letting my hands drift across surfaces, thinking that they must have an excellent cleaning service. After quick stops at a large, traditionally furnished classroom and a small, high-ceilinged gym where a basketball game is underway, we cross back over the lawn area to the office.

A tall man in a dark blue sports coat is waiting for us there.

"Hello," he says, extending his hand to each of us in turn. "I'm the school principal here."

I smile at him, in familiar territory now, the involved

mother chatting with an educator. We follow him out of the office to the second floor of the main building and settle into a second living room. This one is furnished a bit more formally, with a large velvet couch and armless floral chairs in a soft salmon color. Again, I stick to my plan and start broadly.

"Tell me about your students."

"Well," he replies, settling into the chair he has chosen for himself, "most of the kids here have had trouble in their own schools. We encourage them to work at their own pace." He frowns. "Within reason." He crosses one khaki leg over the opposite knee before continuing. "That allows them to slow down when they need to concentrate on their therapeutic issues, and accelerate when they are better able to focus. We work closely with the therapy team to know when to do that. They do a good job of catching up, in general. We support them with tutoring."

Hannah

Jason and I talk a lot about how I have used my art as an escape, and I decide to think about that. I guess there's a difference between expressing yourself and hiding yourself with art. How do you tell the difference? Is my art just another way for me to be oppositional? Jason makes me think that shocking people might be the point of my art. I think that he understands art as much as he understands vegetarianism, which is not at all, but it turns out he might understand me. I think about all the bad days in school that I hid out in the art studio. I think about that feeling I like when I make people gasp at the gruesome stuff. I don't want my art to be about shock. Or revenge. I don't want my art to be just about me when I finally get to do it again.

Mom

Once again, we are permitted to meet the students, settling in at the tutoring table near the office. Our tour guide rejoins us with two other girls who are similarly dressed in solid colored T-shirts, pulled back hair, and no makeup or jewelry. I start the conversation as I had at L'Arts. "So, how is it here?"

"It's hard." Our guide speaks first, the others nodding as she explains. "It's harder than the wilderness. In the wilderness there are lots of rules that are mostly to keep you safe, but here I think they are more interested in keeping us honest, and that's harder."

"I think they do it with love, though," adds the smallest girl softly, and again all three girls nod in unison. The girls are serious, plain-spoken, and thorough in their description of their well-ordered life at Vista, talking about the schedule, the expectations, and the consequences meted out for disruptive behaviors.

"Is it okay if I ask you why you're here?" I finally venture, curiosity getting the best of me.

"Our stories are probably the same as your daughter's story," our guide answers simply, making me feel like a clumsy voyeur. I look away, relieved when a woman in gray silk appears, heels tapping decisively on the wood floor.

"Hello, my name is Bobbi." She holds out a silver-braceleted hand in greeting, a faint wisp of floral scent reaching me just as our fingers make contact. She thanks the girls and asks Paul and me to follow her to her office so she can discuss the treatment center's therapeutic approach. We cross the courtyard again, through the shining foyer, this time turning left into Bobbi's small office and settling into the tweed arms of a loveseat. She wastes no time with small talk. "We believe that self-destructive behavior in teens is a symptom. We acknowledge and treat those symptoms while we identify and address the root causes. Most importantly, we work to provide our residents with tools to move forward in a healthy way."

I look up from my little brown notebook and ask her about the girls we met, and the lifestyle at Vista. "Our girls adhere to strict dress and behavioral codes," she responds pleasantly. "It's important that they all meet on common ground as equals. I'll give you a list of the house rules to read."

She asks us lots of questions then, about Hannah, our family, and our experiences. And though she asks many more questions than we did, I feel I have a good idea of what it might be like for Hannah at Vista. We leave, suddenly unsure of what would be best for our daughter. The colorful disarray at L'Arts wrestles in my mind with the calm, focused order of Vista.

Hannah

Jason is the person who took my art away, and I guess I should be mad at him, but I'm not really, because it makes me notice everything, and I kind of wonder now how I could even *do* art if I wasn't noticing everything. Jason wants me to keep noticing *myself* now, and my feelings and what my body does. It's weird how you can live in your body for sixteen years and never notice how it connects to your feelings. Even freezing, dirty, and frostbitten, it seems that my body has a mind of its own, and sometimes I am surprised to feel my fists clenching or my shoulders bunching up, and then I have to ask it, "What's up, dude?"

Mom

School visits complete, we climb back into our truck for the drive out of Salt Lake City to a place called Daniel's Summit Lodge, about an hour east of the city on Highway 40. Paul doesn't want to stop, seeming to need to put distance between us and our day as quickly as possible, but I insist, urging him to stop at a shopping center just past Park City, where I purchase a large tin box of cookies at Mrs. Fields. "It's not a dinner party," observes Paul dryly, but I cannot be dissuaded, wanting to bring a treat to the girls we will be meeting in the wilderness, and not knowing if there will be another opportunity to stop along the way.

With Jason's input, we have decided to drive about half-way that evening, and then drive the last hour to Duchesne early the next morning to see our daughter for the first time in two months. I close my eyes and picture her slight body walking away from me, that last day. Then I close them tighter to keep the tears from coming. I look out the side window of the truck, watching a light snow begin to fall.

Hannah

I'm so tired of the snow. I know this because my body tells me so with its new connection to my brain. It clearly notifies me, "Crap, it's fucking freezing." I used to like to go to the snow when I was a kid. Some of the girls here giggle when I say, "go to the snow." They think it's so funny because they come from places with snow, but I swear when I get out of here I never, ever want to see snow again. We walk in it, we sit in it, we cook in it, and we sleep in it. When it gets to be ten degrees, we are allowed to put up a big tent at night and crowd our stinky selves into it for warmth, and we've done that twice in the last week. It's supposed to be for safety. I guess the staff would have a hard time explaining to parents that they made frozen burritos out of their kids.

Mom

The snow is beautiful, blanketing the Uinta Basin wilderness as far as the eye can see. There isn't much else to look at between Park City and our next stop at Hebron, and Paul drives the well-cleared mountain road to the Summit Lodge in good time, ignoring my cringing and gasping as huge, double-long semis blow past us at eighty miles per hour in an attempt to make it up the steep hills to the oil and gas fields of Duchesne. Exiting Route 40, we arrive at the lodge, crunching over salt and ice to park in front of the main building, a sturdy wood and stone structure with a large portico and steps that are still covered with ice, despite the evidence of recent shoveling.

The lodge is completely unexpected—a mecca of comfort. We check in quickly, and passing a massive stone fireplace and roaring fire, climb up stairs to a well-appointed room. I don't much like the antler coat hooks, or the deer hide coverlet on the bed, but I like the soft sheets and quiet surroundings, so soothing after our emotional trip. Shuddering, I pull the poor dead deer off our bed and fall onto the pillows for a brief rest before heading down to dinner with Paul. Images of the two programs we've visited are warring in my head, and I toss and turn with the discomfort of the decision that has to be made. Maybe Paul is feeling the same way, or maybe my tossing is keeping him awake, but he lies next to me, silent, eyes wide open in spite of his exhaustion. Restless, we decide to walk over to the lodge restaurant.

We pass a little general store on the way, and I stop to buy Camilla a horseshoe puzzle, a sudden surge of guilt tugging at me for leaving her once again in order to serve Hannah's needs. I grip the clever toy, knowing that it will take a lot more than a souvenir to make up for our neglect. We are just hours away from Hannah, but that night, back in our room after a tasteless dinner, I can only see Camilla's face when I close my eyes.

Hannah

It's another stinky tent night here at the basin, and we crowd in towards each other and away from the outer walls of the tent, watching them flap in and out like a big white mouth sucking up the cold from outside. We put Poopzilla on the perimeter of the group, in case she relapses, and the rest of us try to settle down on the hard ground to sleep.

Chapter 8

Mom

We wake up early, before it's light, but both of us jump out of bed without our usual complaining. It feels like the first day of school, a first kiss, and a trip to the dentist all wrapped up into one package. We are checked out and in the truck before 7:00, agreeing to have breakfast in Duchesne if there is time.

Hannah

Hi ho, hi ho, off we go. Another day of community meetings, writing, trying to make fire, and hiking, hateful even though it keeps me warm. I am adding hiking to my never-do-again-after-the-wilderness list, along with snow. And eating beans. It's hard crawling out of my sleeping bag sometimes—hard, cold ground and rocks are still more comfortable than therapy. But at least I'm in a group of people who are just like me in a lot of ways. I mean we all went through our own shit, and we all fucked up, but at least I know when I talk and they are nodding it's not just manners—no, they *know* what I'm saying. Now that I'm not allowed to sketch during session, I can really look at them and see their expressions and if their faces match their words. We aren't supposed to talk in a way that glorifies our behaviors, but I think there is still some of that going on. "Oh, you did E? I did heroin. Oh, you were arrested for lewd behavior? I got caught shoplifting condoms." Whatever, bitches, we're all morons. This should be called Mount Moron.

Mom

The Uintas are a chain of mountains, a sub-range of the Rocky Mountains, really, and the highest range in mainland United States. The area is full of rises and basins carved out during the ice age, including the Uinta Basin where Hannah is spending her winter outdoors, at approximately 5500 feet of elevation. Driving over the peaks, we can see the basin stretching out across the three-thousand-plus square miles of Duchesne County, dotted with the squat cottonwoods, sage, and rabbit brush that's the only vegetation hardy enough to survive the harsh environment. I can't stop myself from looking for specks of movement, for a sign of life in the vast white sea, but there is no clue in the rolling landscape that anyone is there. The temperature that December ranges from an average low of zero degrees, to a balmy high of thirty-three. Today is on the low end. I shiver from the desolation, as much as from the cold.

Our next stop will be to check in at the Second Nature headquarters in Duchesne. Duchesne itself is a utilitarian little town of about 1,500 people, situated at the junction of the Strawberry and Duchesne rivers in the Uinta Basin. Sounds pretty, but it's not. It's about 2.3 square miles of businesses serving the oil, natural gas, and livestock industries that sustain the area. Though there are supposed to be pronghorn antelopes, elk, moose, bighorn sheep, mountain goats, black bears, and mountain lions in this region, we see nothing on our drive in but empty snowdrifts stretching to the horizon. The emptiness matches my mood, like a gaping hole where family used to be.

Hannah

It doesn't take a rocket scientist to figure out that we are well and truly stuck here. Even the dumbest girl in the group (I shall not name her) can see that there is just nowhere to go. I don't know why they bother to make us holler or sing when we are out of sight digging our latrines and doing our business. Probably so they don't have to bother to chase us down. Still, sometimes at night, I close my eyes and dream of hiking out of here. I amuse myself by trying to remember those survival shows Camilla used to watch, and I imagine how I could snare rabbits and build snow caves after I sneak off. I try to decide if that would be easier or harder than the honesty they're asking for here. I have found out from being here that I lie automatically, and it's pretty disturbing. It's sort of a habit, like playing with my nose ring or chewing on my nails. It's always little lies, not important stuff, except that I don't want to tell them anymore because it's blocking my way out of here.

Mom

Driving through areas with names like "Starvation" and "Desolation Canyon" finally brings us into Duchesne proper. The nasty rental truck seemed to finally fit just right here, and Paul parks and jumps out of the driver's seat as though we have arrived late to a sporting event. "Come on," he says impatiently, as if I want to linger in the frigid outdoors. We crunch over the snow and ice to the front doors of the squat little building that is Second Nature's headquarters. Entering, we find ourselves in an institutional-looking ring of small offices with gray metal desks and pin-sprinkled topographical maps taped to the walls—marking the places, I guess, where we would find the roving groups of teens that the program shepherds through the basin. Paul pokes his head into one of the occupied offices.

"Hi. We're the Burrowes. We have an appointment to see our daughter today."

An appointment. To see our daughter. The tears well up before I even realize I am upset, and I turn away, embarrassed. The rugged-looking staffer in the office pretends not to notice, leading us to a lounge containing a sagging checked couch and some institutional-looking stacking chairs against a back wall.

"Help yourself to coffee. I'll collect Jake and we'll get you going."

I sit tentatively on the nasty looking couch, the smell of wet dog drifting up as I lower myself onto the cushions.

Hannah

Our hike is shorter than usual today, and the staff keeps stepping away to use the radio. I imagine to myself that World War III has happened, and before they inform us of the apocalypse, they need to make a plan to deal with the Zombies so we don't panic. I may need those rabbit snaring skills after all.

Mom

The staffer isn't gone long. Paul and I don't even have a chance to finish our bitter, burned coffee from the old Bunn coffee maker in the corner of the linoleum-covered lounge.

We receive instructions. "Jake's going to meet us outside, he's loading his truck. Meanwhile, let me see what you guys have on." We stand and he takes his time looking us over. I wonder what he sees. I'm pretty sure we look ridiculous—out of place and uncomfortable in the stiff new clothes we have purchased in sunny California. "You'll be okay, I think. I can get you some wool over-pants if you're cold." He rushes off to get a pair for Paul, checks our gas gauge to make sure we have a full tank, inspects the big truck, and finally introduces us to a gnarled, wiry guy named Jake, who grunts at us before climbing into his own battered truck.

The staffer gives us some final directions: "Just follow Jake out to the site. If you lose him, just stay in his tire tracks. If you don't feel comfortable finding your way back out, or if it snows over the tracks, have the staff radio us, and we'll send him back out." Jake has already pulled out of the small parking lot, and we scramble to get into the truck, turning onto the deserted Main Street in pursuit of his tail lights.

Hannah

Something is up. Jason is here, and I'm pretty certain it's not a Jason day. Jason waves at all of us and then steps over to the staff. More radio conversation, and then we all sit down near the fire to get our daily foot check for rot or frostbite or something while Jason pulls his little canvas camp chair out of his truck.

Mom

I can hardly breathe. I tell myself it is the cold, or Paul's driving but who am I kidding? I am going to see Hannah for the first time in months, and I am petrified. The only contact we have had with her is a few brief, emotionally charged conversations over a SAT phone with Jason moderating. Per Second Nature's policy, Hannah doesn't know we're coming. Paul seems relaxed, almost cheerful, whistling as he turns off the main road onto a narrow, paved track that soon begins to weave through the oil fields, the rise and dip of the black oil rigs looking like vultures feeding on the dead land. *Hannah is here?* It is ugly, forlorn, and empty. I wonder where all the people are, the ones who work the fields. Finally, about twenty minutes into the fields, we see three heavily bundled men in hard hats and orange vests near a utility truck, bent over blueprints of some kind. They are the last people we will see for the next forty minutes, as the little road seems to end in a sparkling snow bank. I gasp as Jake forges straight ahead into the glittering snow, white plumes spraying up around his truck, and looking ahead I can see faint tracks that make up a route visible only to the people who know it is there.

Hannah

Looks like we're having session today. Jason unfolds his low little chair, and we unroll our scruffy, ripped mats in a circle around the staff fire. He always takes his time, unlacing and taking off his big boots and stretching his legs out in front of him like he's in his living room. He wags his wool-covered toes around a little and then looks at each of us dirty little urchins with his big smile and an invitation to share.

Mom

Paul is having fun, fishtailing the big four-wheel-drive truck through the giant drifts of snow. I can see the pleasure on his face, and it's making me mad. There was a time when I might have enjoyed this adventure too, and it makes me more upset thinking about what a dried-up prune of a woman I have become. How long has it been since I have laughed out loud? Will I ever find my joy again? Why is he okay? It makes me feel alone.

Hannah

The sound of a truck. We all lose interest in Maggie's check-in; I mean, we're all together twenty-four/seven, so how stunning can it be? As a single unit we crane our heads towards the edge of the plateau we're on. The terrain keeps us from seeing the approach, but the sound of an engine is clear, and that means Jake is here. And Fruit Loops. And mail. Jason calls us to order, and Maggie continues, distracted, but determined to complete her report to the group. We all suck it up and turn back to our work. There is no rushing Jason. Or Jake.

Mom

About an hour out of Duchesne, we finally come to a hill that seems to lead to a plateau at the top. Jake pulls over, and we stop behind him. As he unloads some canvas sacks from the back of his truck, he motions for us to go ahead, up a steep rise with no path. Paul and I look at each other, doubtful, and then we hear it—the faint sound of girls' voices. Paul and I turn towards the voices and start climbing up the hill, struggling against the new snow, and our emotions. I grab my tin of cookies, hugging it hard to my puffy-coated midriff like a life preserver. As we top the final rise I stop to catch my breath, not believing my eyes. There are six ragtag girls there, an unkempt human dot in the middle of a pristine snowy wilderness. Their backs are to us, facing a stocky man in glasses and (could this be right?) no shoes. The man seems very relaxed, his feet stretched towards a small fire, the girls arranged around it on filthy pieces of foam, the dirt on the ground blending with the dirt on the mats and the dirt covering their clothes, and as they turn we can see that it covers their faces as well. My heart is pounding out of my chest, and I freeze in place, realizing that I cannot identify my own child in the group, they are all so uniformly dirty and bundled in matching Second Nature–issued clothing. But Hannah recognizes us, suddenly standing and staring at us, not seeming to comprehend what she is looking at.

Hannah

Holy fucking shit! Is that Mom and Dad? What the fuck are they doing here? Part of me wants to run to them and throw my arms around them; they look so good to me, like home. But my feet don't want to move, and so I end up doing some sort of Frankenstein shuffle over to where they are standing.

Mom

Hannah looks shocked; she doesn't seem to know what to do. We take a chance then, Paul and I, and open our arms. Maybe the scariest moment in my life, waiting to see if she will love us back. She comes towards us slowly, tears tracking through the grime on her face, filthy dreadlocks peeking out from under her watch cap. Finally, she steps into our arms and Paul and I enclose her in our circle, the metal of the cookie tin forming a chilly barrier between us. She holds us for the briefest of moments and then catches herself, stepping back and wiping the emotion off her face with her sleeve, leaving only a streaky clue of how she was feeling.

Hannah

I ask them what they are doing out here, and they say they miss me and want to see me. So they're not here to take me home. They're here to see what they are spending all their money on, I guess.

Mom

The man near the fire pulls his boots on and stands up, laces trailing behind him as he approaches. "Hello," is all he has to say before we recognize the gravelly voice. It is Jason, the man who has brokered our relationship with our daughter for the past two months, and who has gotten to know her well enough to question her diagnosis. Paul shakes his hand, but I hug him.

Hannah

Jason asks them to join the circle, and then he has all of us introduce ourselves the way we have been taught—like the addicts and alcoholics we are.

"Hello. I'm Hannah. I'm an alcoholic and a drug addict, and a cold bitch (double entendre)! Pleased to meet-cha."

Mom

The girls seem at home under their protective layers of rugged, worn clothing. As we sit, they share stories and observations about abuse, about drug use, alcoholism, rape, and more.

"He wouldn't stop, and nobody would believe me."

"My parents were in Europe when I overdosed."

"I always put vodka in my water bottle. It helped get me through the school day."

Every story cuts me, and I clutch at my arms as though to stop the bleeding, but the girls seem armored against the horror of their words. I can't help but see Hannah in each account, remembering the girl at Vista telling us that their stories were all the same. It wounds me to know that so much had happened to Hannah while we weren't looking. She is very quiet, and so are we, but Jason lets us be. Our turn will come.

Hannah

I wonder what the parents think about all these stories. They look so out of place and upset. Dad's mouth is turned down hard, and he's rolling a rock around in his hand like he wants to throw it at someone. Mom looks like she wants to jump over the campfire and hug everyone, every time they share. Ease on back there, Mom . . . this is what you signed me up for. Thugs, not hugs. Group is winding down, and I don't know what's coming next, so I ask Jason to be excused to go to the bathroom. He nods at me, and I uncurl myself from the mat, using my circle mates' shoulders to help me up. I choose a distant bush; the snow-covered branches with leaves somehow still hanging on. I do have to pee, but what I really need is a minute to myself.

Mom

Hannah gets up to go to the bathroom, the girls on either side of her helping her up off her shredded mat. Hannah had chosen to sit across the fire from us, the flames and smoke obscuring her from our view. Paul and I sit with a gap between us, the place we had left for her.

Hannah

I kind of feel bad, I admit it. I should have sat with them. After all they did come out to bum fuck Egypt to see me, and they are the only parents who ever did. Even if they aren't going to rescue me, that's still a pretty cool thing to do. They are the first outsiders we've seen in over two months, and I use that as my excuse not to act right.

I do my thing, ducking out of sight on the other side of the dead bush I pick out, and step downhill a bit, calling out the way we do to let the staff know where we are.

"A B C . . ." I sing loudly, squatting towards the downhill side to pee, a trick I learned the hard way. After two months, peeing behind a bush while singing seems normal to me, but seeing it through my parents' eyes, I wonder if I will be permanently scarred from this toilet ritual. Will I yell and sing every time I have to pee for the rest of my life? That could be awkward.

Mom

As Hannah ducks out of sight she starts yelling the alphabet song. Nobody reacts, and I realize that it's normal—a way to let the staff know where they are. Paul and I look over at each other with raised eyebrows, and I quell a sudden urge to laugh, she sounds so silly. Hannah appears over the ridge a few moments later. Too cold to hang her bottom out for very long, I guess. As she comes back, Jason dismisses the circle for lunch.

Hannah

I hurry back cuz it's not cool to ditch therapy when your group is depending on you. I think maybe I can make up for my bitchy greeting by joining the parent people in the space they left between them. It was awkward looking across the circle at the space where I should be. But right before I get to the circle everybody scatters, and I kind of stand there not knowing what to do. Jason saves me.

"Hannah, take an ember from the fire and set up a spot for you and your parents. You can make lunch." Okay, I can do that. I know how to do that.

Mom

Paul and I just stand there like idiots, our arms dangling by our sides, as Hannah swings into action. She runs over to the far side of camp and using her hands, sweeps most of the snow off the ground, creating a rocky circle about the size of a child's swimming pool, and then motions for us to come over. Walking around the perimeter of camp, she bends to pick up bits of mossy looking bark, knocking off the snow before making a small pile of kindling in the middle of the circle. Then she makes a little pile of larger sticks off to the side. Finally, she picks up an empty coffee can from near the main fire, and using one of her sticks, drags an ember out of the fire and over the lip of the can.

Hurrying back to our little clearing, she kneels on one knee, carefully spilling the ember out of the old red can onto the fluffy moss and bark. Putting her sweet face close to the ember, she gently blows, cherub lips coaxing a small lick of flame, which she feeds with more kindling and then sticks. Her face glows with the sudden warmth of the flames, or from the effort, or maybe from pride in her accomplishment. She is a far cry from the privileged princess we sent off, and once again I have the unsettling feeling that I might not know her at all anymore, even with all the journal entries, letters, and weekly calls. I sit on the cold ground, feeling like a Big 5 ad in my stiff new clothes, trying to figure out some way to help. But she doesn't seem to need me.

Hannah

Making camp goes pretty easy, especially since Jason said I could take an ember. I am relieved that he doesn't make me try to bust a flame in front of my parents. I guess he knows I've failed them enough without making them watch me working the bow drill, getting nothing but sweaty and frustrated, not to mention the little patch of dead skin that has developed on my knee from kneeling in front of kindling for so long. I have come close to success a couple of times. I get smoke. But I just can't seem to get to flames. I'm not sure what I'm doing wrong, but until I figure it out, I have to rely on other people to help me get fire going. In some ways, I like that the program doesn't reward you for trying. Trying isn't enough. You have to have success through your own hard work. It's not easy, but I know it's going to feel great when I finally get there. Hey! Maybe this metaphor shit works!

Mom

Hannah drags a giant frame pack over to our little camp and leans into it, the upper half of her body disappearing from sight until finally she pops up with an armful of food. I smile at her enthusiasm, and she smiles back, but for just a moment.

Hannah

I mentally do inventory—do I have enough food for all of us? —and then I remember that Jake just delivered supplies. We shall feast!

Mom

Hannah makes one more trip to the main camp for supplies, and then sets to work. Unwrapping a full stick of butter, she drops it into the well-worn coffee can, without first wiping it out. I cringe, but manage to stay silent. As the quarter pound of butter melts over the fire, she tears open individual packets of tomatoes, beans, and then rice, stirring it all into a gloppy mess. The thick mixture is soon bubbling in the coffee can. Hannah uses her hand to sweep most of the remaining snow off the dirt and rocks near the fire, and throws three tortillas down on the ground. Using her scarf as a potholder, she pours the bean mix over the tortillas, and wraps them snuggly into burritos. I am a picky eater, but even I know this is not the right time to comment on her recipes or hygiene. I thank her and eat.

Hannah

Ha! Mom looks a little green, but she's eating. Dad eats gross shit all the time, so he's okay.

Mom

Hannah watches us until we take our first bites, then picks up her burrito and digs in. She seems a little more relaxed after her success, and talks as she chews.

"They keep trying to make me eat meat, you know. Didn't you tell them I was a vegetarian?"

We both nod in unison as she continues.

"They don't let me go pee or anything until at least thirty minutes after I eat, cuz they think I'm gonna go barf it up."

After we decline her offer of more food, she uses the remaining mix to make herself a second burrito.

"No place to store it," she explains. I wonder if Hannah will get extra rations to make up for feeding us, or if she will be hungry because of our visit. I want to ask her, but I am afraid to know.

Hannah

I know them so well. I know they are here for a reason and so I ask them again. They look at each other like Nixon and Kissinger and then tell me the big secret. They are in Utah looking at schools. Schools in Utah! What the fuck! Why can't I go home? I am clean and sober, and I work and play well with others. I'm not bipolar. I am cold. I miss my friends. I want my life back.

I feel my shoulders hunching up and my fingers pulling at each other, so I take a deep breath. I should use reason here, I figure. They like reason. It always works, because Mom teaches reasoning and Dad likes a good sales pitch. I wind up and start working on them. I tell them the M&M story, but I don't tell them how much I wanted to eat them. I just talk about how I passed the test. How I'm strong and ready to come home.

Mom

Jason told us it was okay to give Hannah a general idea of our plans but no details. It comes as no surprise that she's upset when we talk to her about the next step. I want to persuade her that we are right, to show her that this is for her own good, but I keep quiet. Am I learning to communicate more effectively, or am I just not sure about leaving her here? I busy myself with the dusty, buttery burrito, listening as Hannah turns on the charm and starts working us over. I think of all the times my lovely girl has manipulated me over the past years. She is good at it. This time though, her words harden me, and I make myself remember all of the times she has gotten what she wants from us, and then turned on us with no remorse.

Jason joins us. It is surreal to be sitting here, in Utah, in the snow with my daughter and her therapist. That day we talk about her friends, a topic she has been writing about in her journal and in her letters. Hannah has always denied that her friends encouraged her to use drugs, but now she seems resigned to the fact that Jason knows, that we all know that she was pushed.

"Yeah," she says looking down at her torn gloves, "I guess that was pretty fucked up."

As our session starts winding down, Jason asks the question for which I have been selfishly waiting.

"How is it seeing your parents, Hannah?" He studies her as she closes her eyes and thinks about her answer. I hold my breath, running my hands up and down my stiff new cargo pants while she carefully chooses her words. Finally, she is ready to speak.

"I'm happy that they're here, and that they're seeing how I'm living."

I wonder exactly what that means, and if it's supposed to be confusing. She continues, "I feel like I've grown a lot, and I'm ready to go home. I don't understand why I have to go to school out here. I hate the snow." I listen to the edge in her voice, and look around at the icy shelf we are on, the snow stretching to the horizon, thinking irreverently that hell has frozen over. In some part of my mind I realize that Jason is explaining to Hannah why she is moving on, to what they in the troubled teen industry called "after care." Hannah's lips are fixed in a pout, but she says nothing. I say nothing either, struggling to stick with the decision we have made. I look down, so I won't have to look at my daughter. I feel Paul's hand gently on the small of my back, in tacit support.

Hannah

I want to go home. Please let me go home. I don't want to be away, to be here anymore. I want to scream, so I stay quiet, because I'm not sure about what I'll say or do, and the only one talking now is Jason.

Mom

I miss her so much. I want to hold her, but she's distant again, and so I wrap my arms around myself instead. I sit as though frozen to the icy ground, as Jason asks Hannah to participate in our decision.

"I want you to write it down, Hannah. What you want and need in a school." Hannah nods, and with that Jason stands up.

Hannah

The staff comes up with a challenge so we can earn the cookies the parents brought, and the girls in the group are all whooping it up like idiots on the other side of camp. Jason starts walking over there, and my parents and I line up like little baby ducklings behind him, all of us just looking at the back of the person in front, not talking, which suits me just fine. It's easy not to talk to them when we get to the group, cuz the staff gives us a water drinking challenge. The staff is always after us to drink more water. I think we each slug down about sixteen ounces from our metal water bottles, and then the cookie tin comes out, and the girls make lots of R-rated noises while they glom them down. Everyone thanks my parents, everyone but me. I don't feel too grateful at the moment. Truth is, I just want them gone.

Mom

It gets dark early in December, and so our visit is winding up. We still have an hour's drive back to headquarters, and then two hours to the airport. We walk Jason to the edge of camp, and I tell him how impressed I am with Hannah's composure. I guess I am hoping for enthusiasm or at least acknowledgement. Instead I get an unwelcome assessment.

"Susan, Hannah knows she's close to leaving, and she's putting on the face she thinks we want to see."

He asks us about our school visits, and then urges us to choose a school that utilizes Dialectic Behavioral Therapy, and to make sure they employ experienced therapists.

"Bobbi at Vista is good," he rasps. "I trust her completely."

I tell him that we liked her too, and that Vista and L'Arts were both possibilities.

"Oh," he adds as an afterthought, "in the interest of full disclosure, I should tell you that Bobbi is my wife."

I am taken aback, trying to picture this stocky man in army boots with the lovely, silk-covered Bobbi.

"Yeah," he responds, seeing our surprise, "I married up."

With a grin he makes his way over the rise, and as we walk back to camp, we hear his truck start up and pull away.

Hannah

I make a final pitch, but they just say they'll wait for my letter about schools before making any final decisions. I am their fucking prisoner.

Mom

Time to go now, and Paul and I step towards Hannah. She takes a step back as I reach for her, but then falls forward into my hug. I grip her tightly, and Paul encircles us both in his long arms. "I love you, Hannah," I sob, and her silence slices my heart in half. "I love you," I say, softer this time, mumbling it into her filthy hair, and though she tightens her arms around me for a moment, she keeps her silence.

Hannah

I catch shit after the parents finally leave. The bitches in my group say I am wrong not to tell them I love them. "You do love them," says Maggie. Dani just shakes her head and turns away. Later I have to sit through the community meeting, and guess what everyone wants to check in about? Me! They are harsh too. I tell them that they were all bought off by a handful of cookies, and they could go fuck themselves. Then suddenly I'm on separates for disrespecting the group. Shit.

Mom

It is a pensive silence on the way back to Duchesne headquarters. Paul drives our long truck in Jason's tracks, letting his spectral presence guide us out of the wilderness. Paul is done with fishtailing and playing in the snow. Now, he seems to want to move forward towards our next stop as fast as possible. Once, I ask him to stop so I can take a picture of the sunset for Camilla, and he does, uncharacteristically compliant. We drop off his wool over-pants at the small, squat 2N building, but don't see the staffer or Jake. I study the topographical map on the wall while Paul changes, realizing now that the cluster of pins to the south is our daughter's group, and wondering where on this map she will end up next.

On our way to Salt Lake City, we decide that we will once again do the same thing that Hannah is doing. We will each write down what we think is the most important thing for Hannah's next placement. All we are sure about is that it won't be home.

Hannah

I sit on the edge of camp trying to figure out how I feel. The parents travelled here to see me, only to tell me that they didn't want me anymore. I guess deep down I can't blame them. I sit in the freezing cold on the edge of the camp and review all the bad shit that makes them not want me.

Mom

Nine long hours after leaving Hannah in her desolate camp, we walk into our dark, empty California home. It's well after midnight, and the dogs and Camilla are at their respective sleepovers until the following morning. Paul and I dump our bags in the living room and drag up the stairs to our room. We have come to an agreement about what we are looking for in a school, and I have jotted it down in my little brown notebook on the plane.

We decide that the program should be well-established, that the therapists should be experienced, and that catching up in school matters. Our sticking point is art. It's so confusing. We have supported her art for so many years, only to see her greatest therapeutic leap happen when her art is taken away.

Too tired to talk anymore, Paul brushes his teeth and climbs into bed, and I follow, moving into his outstretched arms and lying still against his long body, listening to his steady breathing turn to snores and then to soft, guttural cries as whatever feelings he has hidden on our trip try to sneak to the surface. He shivers, and I get up and add a blanket to the bed, to chase away the Utah cold that has followed us home, then settle onto my half of the bed to sleep, leaving him alone to deal with his demons.

Hannah

We have personal time right after the community meeting, and since I am on separates anyway for my cold and unfeeling behavior towards the parents, I decide to write the letter Jason wants for my educational consultant person. I remember that I liked him when he visited me in the loony bin, and so I think he might be able to help me get to someplace "not Utah."

"I'm Hannah, I'm sixteen, and I'm in wilderness because I lie, cheat, steal, pierce, burn, cut, have sex, drink, and do drugs." I decide that looks pretty bad, so I think about what might help my case and write, "I have made many mistakes; however, I have also learned a lot in my life, especially here." I use the top of my pencil to make shapes in the snow, and then remember that I'm not allowed to have art and wipe them away. This sucks. I turn back to my note and make my pitch. "I suppose my future is in your hands. I hope that you and I can work together successfully so that I don't have to live in some crazy shit hole like Utah." I read it over, sign it "Sincerely" and then decide I left something important off: "P.S. I would like to find some sort of art program if possible. I find it hurtful that through my actions, I have made it so much harder to accomplish my goals in art. I don't know if this is possible; however, I am hoping that it is." I read it one more time, fold it in half and give it to the staff.

Mom

We measure school choices against our criteria and Hannah's letter. After a lot of heartache we pick Vista. Though Vista has art class as part of their school program, their main focus will not be art, because we realize that our focus is not art either. Our focus is finding experienced, compassionate professionals who can help our daughter find her health and happiness. We measure the steady, structured life of Vista against the vivid, colorful backdrop of L'Arts, and decide that Bobbi's years of experience with DBT, the measured tones of the principal, the simple statements of the residents, and the long success of their program should count for more than a well-meaning cook and an enthusiastic, youthful staff. I wonder if we'll ever have the courage to tell her we passed up an art program, in spite of her request.

Hannah

Jason asks me what I want to "take with me" to my next place. I think about it and decide that I have learned to value myself and that I should try to hold on to that. I'm pretty proud of the stuff I have learned to do here. I think I'm better at communicating than I used to be. I am an honest person. I am genuinely odd, and that's okay.

Mom

Making the decision to go to Vista is different than making it happen. Alicia explains the process as I grip the phone hard, picturing her in the calm blue sea of her office.

"Vista runs full. It always has. I can't tell you for sure how long the wait will be, but let me get the process started for you." She explains that unlike the wilderness, residential programs typically have students for several months to a year, and so it is difficult to predict when an opening will come available. I bite back my anger at how we have struggled with this decision, only to have Hannah wait in the woods for an opening, not wanting a repeat performance of my temper tantrum the last time we were in Alicia's office.

Hannah

Jason asks me what I think I need to work on at my next place. I look over at the main camp, at the other lost girls who are trying to make things right for each other, and see Maggie and Penny working together to repack Penny's frame pack. I decide that I should work on my family values, or at least at valuing my family. I also believe that I should not spend my time and energy seeking approval from people. I shouldn't take stupid risks to impress my friends. I think if I put the same effort into growing that I put into deceiving myself, I could be okay.

Mom

It's Jason who tells us that Vista is expecting an opening in early January. That means two more weeks in the wilderness. Jason also explains to us the process of transitioning Hannah to Vista.

"We'd like you to come here and spend the night, to share the experience with Hannah." Share the experience? To me, camping is a hotel without room service. I haven't spent the night in a sleeping bag in thirty years, since a Girl Scout camp debacle involving a daddy long-legs spider and a trashed tent.

I confess, I try to play my way out of it, shamelessly using Camilla's welfare as my chip.

"Paul, it's so soon to leave Camilla again. Maybe you should go and have a father-daughter experience."

He smiles at me. "You'll be okay. It's too cold for bugs."

Hannah

Jason tells me to spend some time figuring out how to stay sober and alive once I leave. I tell him that I will probably have to avoid some of the people I know in Santa Cruz. He nods and looks up at the sky while I try to think of more ways to survive.

Chapter 9

Mom

Jason sets the transition date so that we can attend a seminar at a Salt Lake City hotel that's being given by the organization's head therapist before heading to 2N headquarters. After attending the afternoon seminar, we'll drive all the way to Duchesne, passing by the comfy Summit Lodge this time for the close-in digs of a rental cottage right in town. As we lean close to the speaker, Jason tells us that there is another woman and her daughter transitioning out on the same night. We'll meet her at the seminar, but she wants to drive over to Second Nature Headquarters in her own car.

Flights and a four-wheel drive rental are a lot easier to find in January than December, and we reserve a two-bedroom suite in Salt Lake City for after the transition, hoping we'll be able to spend the night with Hannah at the hotel before taking her to her new program. My stomach has butterflies at the idea of spending family time with Hannah. Is it joy? Is it fear? I smile across the dining room table at Paul, who smiles back and reaches for my hand. Jason's voice over the phone is less optimistic. "We'll see how it goes."

Hannah

Jason tells me a joke: "How many therapists does it take to change a light bulb?" I don't know, so he tells me the answer with his cute gap-toothed grin. "None. The light bulb has to want to change." I groan, but I do want to change. I want to find a way to accept myself, to cope with stress and depression, to find a way to communicate with my family. I want to live.

Hannah

We've been hiking for hours, two staff and me and McKenna, a girl from the group, and finally the scenery changes from the white on white of Utah winter, to the ugly as fuck industrial wasteland of the oil fields. The oil rigs look somehow different than they did when I got here. Maybe I'm just sober and clear-headed now, or maybe it's cuz I'm coming at them from a different angle. Anyway, when I first got here, I thought they looked like science fiction creatures, dipping their beaks in the ground to sip earth's blood. Now the rigs represent people and civilization. Still ugly as fuck though, after looking at snow-covered dunes into infinity for the last three months.

As usual, they don't tell us much about what's going on, but obviously this must be transition. They give us a few minutes to say goodbye to the group, and I pass out hugs and advice. Poops, it's time to get regular. Maggie, I'm sorry, but there is no Santa Claus. Dani, call me, tell me you'll call me one day so that you can tell me how fucking good you're doing. I am surprised at how sad I am to leave these girls, my bitches, and how important they are to me. Would I have been able to change or grow without them?

It's hard hiking through the snow, and just when I think I can't go on, we get to a place where a big bank of snow gives way to the road. I see faint tire tracks and wonder if that's the road that Jake and the parents took to our campsite. I wonder if they will be here at transition, and what it will be like. I imagine some sort of sorority hazing, with McKenna and me forced to wear blindfolds and swallow live goldfish.

"McKenna," I ask nonchalantly, "do you like sushi?" Busy with her own thoughts, she doesn't bother to answer.

It isn't long before a big van pulls up and we are handed over, staffer to staffer. I don't know this dude, but he's kind of cute, with long dreads and a big smile. He tells us he'll be transporting us to our transition site. Transporting sort of makes me think of Nazi death camps, and I have a sudden need to pee, but I decide to wait it out.

Mom

Yuck. That's the word that comes to mind as we pull into the snowy driveway of the little Duchesne cottage we have rented for the night before transition. It is too close to the road, and the gray spray of snow from the street pollutes the white clapboard exterior. The door is red, the cracked and peeling paint revealing black underneath. We have been instructed to use the back door, and we kick through the snow to the three uneven concrete steps that lead to a storm door. The key is under the mat, as promised, and we clumsily maneuver our way into a tiny mudroom that contains a washer and drier, a line of coat hooks on the wall, and a low bench squatting on multicolored, flecked linoleum. It is still light outside, but dim and cold in the cottage. Paul is all business.

"Find some light switches, and I'll grab our bags from the car."

I fumble around, the light switches forming a trail that leads me into a dilapidated kitchen with a 1950s refrigerator and metal-edged Formica counters, then into a small living/dining room. My horror grows as I scan the room. There is a scratched maple table with two chairs just outside the kitchen. An old television set with rabbit ears stands off in the far corner, a threadbare armchair and checked sofa the only other furniture in the room. Catching my courage, I move across brown shag carpet to the doorway that must lead to the bedroom and flip the light switch. The bed is centered in the room, one nightstand standing sentry to the faded garden of the bedspread. The tiny bathroom, with its once-white shower cubicle and chipped pedestal sink, smells vaguely of vomit. I fight back the tears as Paul, carrying our little bags, steps into the room.

"Paul, I think you'd better put the bags on the dining room table out there. I don't really want to put them on the floor in here."

He grimaces and turns back to the living room, taking a moment to acknowledge the dismal state of the cottage.

"It's just one night, Susan."

Hannah

The new camp is awesome! There are actual campsites, there is cut wood and—wait for it—porta potties! They give me a ground cloth to use under my sleeping bag, and a big tarp too, and I think it's sort of the wilderness equivalent of my mom taking out the good dishes when company comes. McKenna and I weren't that close at regular camp, but here we decide to double our ground cover, and use our tarps to make shelter. There is better kindling here, and I go to town sawing on my bow drill, but as usual, all I get is smoke and a sore knee. McKenna gives up too, and we dig into our bagged food for a cold dinner in the little tent we made. It's a nasty meal of cold beans but nothing can ruin our mood. We sing all the songs we remember, and then a staffer pops into our tent to explain that our parents will be here tomorrow, and that we will have closing ceremonies. That's what she says. Closing ceremonies. I picture myself on a podium—in first place, of course—with the parents approaching, carrying a velvet pillow with gold BIC lighter perched upon it, and a piece of bark kindling. I generously share my vision with McKenna but, of course, she is irritated that in my vision she comes in second place.

Mom

It has been a long day of travel, and we are exhausted. Paul stands on one side of the sagging bed, and I stand on the other as we pull down the bedspread. As we tug, rumpled, unwashed sheets come into view, complete with an assortment of hairs. I don't have to say anything to Paul. We look across the bed at each other, and then pull the bedspread back into place. Paul gets a blanket out of the little closet and lies down on top of the bedspread, but I go into the mud room to retrieve my black puffy coat, spreading it out across as much of the bed and pillow as I can, and putting on most of the clothes I have brought, including gloves, I lie down and try to sleep.

Hannah

Doing all the regular morning stuff surprises me, cuz I'm over it. We still have to deal with our meds, a foot check, and a hike. But at least breakfast is warm, oatmeal heated over the staff fire. Suddenly, Jason is there, and I know this is it, transition, and I feel like throwing up a little thinking that he won't be there for me anymore. As usual, he knows what I am thinking, and we talk about change and how scary it is.

Mom

I can't get out of that cottage fast enough, and after a greasy breakfast at the diner next to the Second Nature Headquarters, we stop in the little building for a map. Thirty minutes later we are driving our shiny rented jeep into a pull-out area on a tiny dirt road, where a staff member stands signaling to us.

After about a half-mile walk down the dirt and gravel fire road, punctuated with stunted trees and granite boulders, we come across a circle of porta potties standing like some kind of wilderness Stonehenge. This is our signal to turn up the hill, and minutes later we see a small campfire, with a group of people clustered in conversation. I can make out Jason, and the woman we met at the hotel seminar the day before. There are two girls there, too similar in dress and posture for me to make out. But Hannah sees us and stands, and this time she bounces over to us and gives us each a hug in turn. I hug back hard, her arms around me squeezing out any exhaustion from the long night we have just endured.

Hannah

The parents arrive, and I am surprised at how happy I am to see them. I want to make up for being so shitty to them last time they visited, so I make sure to go bounding down the hill and pass out hugs. They already met McKenna's mom, so we get right down to the business of getting the hell out of Dodge.

Mom

The day is surprisingly structured. We have a series of debriefs about Hannah's time in the wilderness, our concerns, our hopes for the future, and the plans we have made. McKenna and her mother will be leaving for the airport, and McKenna will be continuing at a boarding school in Georgia, near her home. We share that Hannah will be continuing in Utah, and I catch the glimpse between McKenna and her mom with a stab of remorse. Hannah will still be so far away. We all have lunch together, and afterwards Jason asks the girls if they have any heroes.

"My mom," answers McKenna sweetly. "She's a single mom, and my dad doesn't help out, and she had to do everything, and she never gave up on me up even when I was terrible to her."

McKenna's mom starts crying and holds her daughter close. Jason waits a minute, then turns to Hannah.

"What about you, Hannah? Do you have any heroes?" Hannah takes time to think, chewing on her lip, and I know it isn't going to be us.

Hannah

My heroes? A hero is someone you respect and admire. Maybe a person who saves you. I guess that could be my parents. But that's sort of one step removed, so I say, "The staff are my heroes. It's so hard here, but they do every single thing they tell us to do, even if they don't have to."

I don't mean to hurt anyone, and I'm relieved that the parents seem okay with my answer.

Mom

Did I mention how much I love Hannah's honesty? Even when she is screaming mad or out of her mind on drugs, you can count on the truth. I mean her truth. I look over at the staffer who is a short way off, unpacking bagged food from a crate, and wonder about her. I rub dirt between my fingers and consider how it must be to make a living outside in the dirt and snow, tending to teens who do not want you. I nod at Hannah and acknowledge the truth in what she is saying. I look over at Paul, and he is nodding too.

Hannah

My mom used to do training gigs using this experiential crap, and I always thought it was hokey when she told me about it, but today when I take off and unroll my neckerchief and let it flutter in the wind, I can just imagine my failures and my sadness floating away over the hills. After letting go of those things, I tie the little scarf to a tree, adding it to the bloom of dozens of other neckerchiefs from past transitions, and it reminds me of the magnolia trees that my bubbe loved, that my mom loves, that I love, and I feel the unbroken line I have damaged but can maybe now repair.

Mom

It is electrifying to watch Hannah turn away from the tree, and away from her past. Her eyes are clear, her back is straight. She takes a step towards me and reaches out, a little leather pouch in her hands.

"This is for you," she says in a ceremonial voice. "The stone inside is from the wilderness here. It stands for me bringing my learning with me, and my commitment to a better future."

She gives one to Paul as well, and he takes it silently, at a loss for words. We three stand on the windy hill, close together but not touching, the gnarled tree like nature's clergy, officiating over us while McKenna and her mother take their turn, and then we two little families separate until morning, the girls charged with caring for us until then.

Hannah

I can tell they are impressed, and I am proud. I never even imagined feeling so in control, emotionally and physically. It must be all the positive thinking—but when I kneel in the camp circle and roll my bow drill, I watch smoke and then, for the first time, flame! Flame! Wow! This shit is like a made for a fucking TV movie! That chick from *Girl Interrupted* can play me. Oh wait, she's probably a grandma by now. I smile to myself and feed the fire. Maybe they'll see how good I'm doing. Maybe they'll change their mind about this school in Utah shit.

Mom

Hannah makes a fire and cooks us up some of her specialty glop. She seems to be everywhere at once, smiling and chatting as she brings extra firewood up the hill with Paul, and showing me how to "ghost" the corners of her tarp so the bungee cords will grip the vinyl securely and allow her to make a shelter for us, for this transition night. Paul and I set our sleeping bags inside the newly made tent, and Hannah squeezes her bag in between us, a sweet memory of how she would wriggle between us when she was a small child. She hands me an old fuel bottle tucked into a rather stinky sock.

"I brought you some hot water to keep you warm, Momma." I try not to notice the "Momma," afraid that it will disappear like a hummingbird given too much attention.

Hannah

I make sure they tuck their clothes into the bottom of their bags so that they will be warm enough to put on in the morning. It's weird taking care of them. I wonder if this is what it's like for them, worrying that I will be uncomfortable or hurt if they don't show me what to do.

Mom

We three sleep in a heap of sleeping bags, the small stones under our ground cloth seeming to grow sharp points as the night passes. Paul is tired, and it will take more than hard ground to keep him awake. He is snoring happily after a few minutes, looking like a long black sausage in his sleeping bag casing, mummy top pulled tight against the cold. Hannah seems immune to the noise, cuddling up close to me and breathing steadily. She always tells me that I sleep like a crime-scene tape outline, and I fight the urge to twist and turn in the bag. Exhausted, but sleepless, I lie still until I can't anymore, and try to gently disengage and slip out of my double bag to go to the bathroom.

"Ma," the sleepy whisper comes from nearby, "pee downhill."

Good advice, I think, as I pull up my pants and hurry back to the relative warmth of the tarp.

Hannah

Poor Momma. People are always pushing her out of her comfort zone. Dad found her in the city, but he made her live in the woods. She likes the theater and ballet, but he made her go to football games and learn to golf. I asked her about it one time, why she was with Dad. She told me he made her life bigger. I like that.

Mom

Morning comes, and I wake up with stiff fingers, having somehow fallen asleep with one hand partially out of my mummy bag as though signaling passers by for help. We dress and take down our little camp quickly, Paul whistling like he is at some Boy Scout jamboree. Thirsty and hungry, I pick up my water bottle, but it is a solid chunk of ice. Hannah gives me some of her water, and a handful of her gorp, a sort of trail mix. It isn't long before Jason comes lumbering up the hill, McKenna and her mother in tow. We all set out on a short hike, and I am relieved that even though I am chunky, I am more than fit enough for the trek. Finally, it is time for our closing circle. It is there that disaster strikes.

Hannah

Things change fast. Jason is spouting off about continuing the work we have started here in the woods, and I just pop my top. I. Am. Done. I ask them, "Why can't I just go home? I don't want to go to aftercare. I want my art and my friends and my bed. I want to be with my family."

Why can't they hear me? What do I have to do to make them hear me? My frustration bursts in my head, and I open my mouth and let it come out before it explodes me.

Mom

Hannah is crying now, suddenly, unexpectedly hysterical, snot running down her face, untended. McKenna's head is down, and she is looking at Hannah with an empty stare, impatient with the drama. Jason asks McKenna to take her mother to their campsite and then turns to us.

"Hannah," he tells her, gently but firmly, "you need to go and calm yourself down before we can talk about this."

Stunned, I watch Hannah turn away and walk a short distance before crumbling into a fetal position on the cold ground, mumbling disjointedly. My sea of doubt evaporates like waters after a flood, leaving me stranded with the undeniable truth that Hannah still needs support, and that the strong and confident young woman who has cared for us over the past two days shares space with this distraught child curled up in the dirt. Jason uses the same gentle but firm voice on us.

"Paul, Susan, I'm concerned about unstructured time between two structured programs, especially given Hannah's emotional state right now. I don't think you should take Hannah for an overnight. It could get very tense or even angry."

I cover my eyes with my hands, not wanting to see the truth of it. Jason continues, "We have escorts who can take her to Vista, and that's what I recommend." I look over at Hannah, still rolled into a ball, clutching herself as though in pain, and ignore Jason's advice for the first time.

"We told her we would take her, Jason. We want to take her ourselves. We can skip the overnight, but we want to take her."

Paul puts his arm around me, agreeing. "We told her we would, Jason."

Jason nods, and Paul and I sit down on the ground to wait for Hannah while he moves away to send off McKenna and her mother. I think the fetal position Hannah is in looks like a pretty good choice at the moment, but I remain seated somehow, my puffy black jacket firmly pressed into Paul's side, my gaze fixed on Hannah as she gathers herself together.

Hannah

Aw shit. I guess I fucked up again. I look over at the parents, and they look back. They probably can't wait to dump me on someone else and hightail it out of here. I feel just like you do right before the dentist pulls your tooth. You know you probably need it but just can't stand the pain that's coming. Dad is impatient as usual and he calls out, "Come on, Hannah, let's get out of here."

So I stand up, walk over to my big pack, and shrug it onto my shoulders. I look at Jason, and he looks at me, and I want one more gap tooth grin from him, but there are no jokes today. Instead, he nods, and I wonder what he's thinking.

Mom

We say goodbye to Jason, somehow thanking him through our shock, and drive over to 2N headquarters, Hannah sitting silently in the back of the jeep. When we get there, her big pack is boxed up to send directly to California. Next, a staffer comes in with a white banker's box filled during Hannah's check-in to the program.

Hannah

Wow, the stuff in the box seems to belong to some other person. There are my flies in resin—the gauges I wore when I was transported to Utah—and some other bits of feather and leather jewelry, artifacts of my past. They give me my old clothes and tell me I can shower before we drive to Salt Lake City. That's about it, except for a Polaroid they took right when I got there and I'm glad that it was a pretty good picture cuz, well, cuz there's a cute staffer holding the photo and looking at it, and it is more attractive than the "raised in the wilderness by wolves" look that I am currently sporting.

Mom

We wait in the wet-dog-smell lounge while Hannah showers, a staffer standing outside the door. When she comes out, my mouth is faster than my brain: "You're still dirty." It is undeniable. There is still dirt in the cracks of her neck, her ears, and under her nails. Her dreadlocks drip water like grass after a good rain, but her hair seems no cleaner for the effort.

She shrugs. "I washed twice."

The staffer at the shower door chimes in with a smile, "It will take a few good washes. The first shower is top layer only." Paul is already putting on his coat, uninterested in Hannah's hygiene and eager to get on the road.

Hannah

It feels wrong to be in my old clothes. They don't really fit me too well anymore. I guess my shoulders are wider from carrying my big pack, and my middle is larger from my rice diet and the meds they give me. I squirm around trying to get comfortable in my old Hannah costume, and then climb into the shiny jeep, a red color that screams, "Look at me," and finally we are driving away from the hills and my life for the last three months. I want to turn around and look, but force myself to face forward. The parents have a surprise for me, but I am tired of surprises unless it's a plane ticket to California, so I'm not really interested, and I unbutton the top button on my pants and try to sleep, the soft blanket of warm air in the jeep comforting after being cold for so long.

Mom

We let Hannah sleep, as we use the rented GPS to help us find the destination we are looking for. It is a vegetarian restaurant in Salt Lake City that Hannah has written about, a recommendation from one of the staffers.

Hannah

Okay, that is pretty cool. They find this place from one letter where I kind of, sort of got the name right. It's pretty much a dive, but definitely a step up from eating gorp on the ground. I go pee, and turn the water on and off a few times for fun. I am pretty surprised at how bad I look, and I turn away from the mirror, trying to convince myself it's the lighting. When I go back to the table, the server is there, and I order quickly, fake chicken in curry sauce and some noodles. No, no rice, thank you.

Mom

I smile at Hannah across the table, happy to be with her, and relieved that her crisis seems to have passed.

"It must be great to have a regular bathroom again, Hannah," I say.

With raised eyebrows she replies, "It's feels great to sit on a chair again."

Another pang of guilt assaults me, realizing that even with my best intentions, I can't imagine what she has been through for the past three months. I dare to ask her if she wants to talk about what happened at transition.

"Naw," she replies decisively. "I don't want to waste our time."

We talk about other things over lunch, snippets about her group, their friendships, and the lessons they learned. It feels almost normal, but the moment she finishes her food, she pushes her plate away.

"Let's go."

Hannah

I just can't sit around and yuck it up with them. I need to see what's next. I don't want to ask them about it, because they'll just quote crap from some brochure. I need to see it for myself. It's dentist time.

Mom

Hannah's welcome at Vista is courteous, if a little cold. We have shipped a box of clothes ahead, but they aren't available yet; Hannah isn't expected until the following day, so they haven't been checked yet for dress code or contraband. She can put scrubs on after her shower, she is told. She goes off with a Vista staffer then, while we finish the endless medical and insurance paperwork that seems to be our life now. When we are done, we are taken to the upstairs living room, the one where we met the principal on our first visit. After waiting for what seems like a long time, Hannah and the staffer finally appear.

"I washed two more times, but look"—she holds out her arms—"still dirty!"

The staffer, clearly experienced at intake of wilderness kids, nods. "It'll take a while."

Hannah

I sort of stand there with my arms at my sides then, all dorky and not knowing what to do next. The girl who took me to the shower saves me. "You can say goodbye to your parents now, Hannah, then I'll take you over to the girls' dorm."

Mom

I am suddenly swept back to Hannah's first day at kindergarten. She is independent even then, running into the brightly colored room, standing in the middle, and throwing her arms up in joy at the confusion of toys and children. The teacher, a veteran of twenty years, has started herding the parents out of the room, and I back away with the others until Hannah whips around and shouts, "Bye, Mommy," running to me for a last sweet hug. That day she broke away from me before I was ready, to turn to her new world.

"Bye, sweetie," I had whispered, holding back the tears until I was safely in my car.

"Bye, sweetie," I whisper now, all these years later, holding tears back once again as my now sixteen-year-old daughter walks away.

Suddenly, like her five-year-old self, she turns back for one more brief, fierce hug, this time half love and half anger. Then, just like her five-year-old self, she breaks away before I am ready, and turns to her new world. Just like that, my Hannah is gone again.

Chapter 10

Hannah

Order. That's the word I would use as a caption for Vista. It doesn't seem too institutional, nobody's drooling in the hallway or wearing diapers, so I'm relieved. We pass through a living room that must have taken a whole herd of dead cows to furnish, the brown leather couches topped by big woven pillows in shades of beige. There is a mattress on the floor, covered with white sheets turned over a beige blanket, a single pillow on top. We walk past the living room and stop at one of the open doors in a long hallway, and I see that one of the two cork boards fastened to the inside of the door is full of pictures of an Asian family, the other empty except for pin holes. My new room has two single beds, and I recognize the thick, blue comforter and blue striped sheets folded at the foot of one of them. I guess the mother sent bedding ahead, and I wonder how something from home can make this room seem even more alien. The other bed in the room is neatly made up with a striped brown and black quilt. Two tall dressers stand at the far end of the room separated by a long, narrow linen closet. And that door, over there? A bathroom with a sink, shower stall, and flushing toilet!

At least I don't have to shit in the woods anymore. I smile for the first time that day.

Mom

The suite at the hotel is beautiful. Much nicer than we expect. It has a living room and two bedrooms, with pillow top beds and thick comforters in crisp white duvet covers. We try to downsize our room at the front desk, but there are no other rooms available at the hotel. Paul and I take turns in one of the two marble bathrooms, trying to wash away the dirt and grime, and the sense of loss that echoes from the empty bedroom where Hannah should be sleeping. We sit in the little living room and order room service, not wanting to be among normal families while we talk about our good intentions and our disastrous day.

"Susan, how could we know?" Paul holds my hand and leans towards me, into my sadness. "She seemed so strong these past weeks."

We both know now with certainty that we have done the right thing in arranging continuing care for Hannah, but that is surprisingly little consolation for our feelings of defeat. After a while, Paul is deeply asleep in the luxurious bed, and I slip out of the bedroom, pacing the living room as my failings chase after me. Finally, I drift into the room where Hannah should be sleeping, and lie down to cry.

Hannah

If you make a mash up out of a military school, a convent, a juvie hall, and a loony bin, you get Vista Residential Treatment Program and High School. Shit, it's hard. The first night here is terrible. I have to sleep on the fucking mattress in the middle of the living room, with a camera pointed at me. So creepy. Who is watching me and why? Do they think I'll off myself or something? I don't expect a big welcome sign and confetti, but this intro to residential treatment seems a little harsh. None of the chicks here are even supposed to look at me as they go marching back and forth to do whatever it is they do, although I get some stares and a couple of secret smiles. Where are they going? Maybe there are twice a day cult meetings in the cafeteria, where they offer sacrifices to a big statue of the Alcoholics Anonymous dude or something.

Mom

I should feel better, knowing that Hannah is not sleeping out in the cold and digging her own latrines, so why am I so jittery? Maybe it's the "not knowing." I am used to getting letters and journal entries from her every day, seeing her picture on the Second Nature web site, and talking to her every week. Now they tell us we won't be able to see Hannah or talk to her for a whole month. I knew that in the wilderness, Jason and the staff were taking good care of her, and she was making progress. Now she's working with some therapists that I haven't even met yet.

Hannah

My mom told me a story once about my Auntie Robin. That she was in labor with my cousin Jason for thirty-six hours. Every little while a doctor or nurse would come in to check on her and see if her hoo-hoo was doing its thing, getting ready for the baby to come. After about thirty hours, a dude in scrubs comes in and she assumes it's a doctor, so she throws off her blanket and spreads her legs wide, but it turns out that the guy was a janitor. That's sort of how it is here. There are so many different kinds of therapists that I just assume that anyone who talks to me wants a look at my private parts, I mean thoughts. Here some therapists want to talk to me about addiction, some about my relationships, and some lead group. Everybody has a role here, though I'm not sure what mine is yet.

Mom

Hannah's life at Vista is about chores, exercise, school, and therapy. Life at home is much the same. While we wait to reestablish contact with our eldest daughter, Paul, Camilla and I continue our own family therapy here in California, delving into our mistakes, alone and with each other. Our growth is intertwined like the vines of jasmine lining our front walk, though sometimes it seems more like the poison oak that grows rampant on our mountain property. To be healthy, we all have to stretch together, in the same direction.

Finding a family therapist is more difficult than we expect. We follow the breadcrumbs of recommendations to a therapist in Santa Cruz, and after a lengthy intake process, find ourselves in her small office. Paul and I will see her once a week as a couple while Hannah is away. Camilla will see her separately, to battle the miasma of sadness that seems to be overtaking her.

I get to know the waiting room intimately, waiting for Camilla. Each week I slip a check into the utilitarian gray metal desk that is there for that purpose. We've already reached the insurance limit for our sessions, and Hannah's. After feeding the drawer, I lower myself into one of the waiting room's wicker chairs, wondering if the bright cushions and pretty photographs ever really cheer anyone.

Sometimes, when Camilla is in her session, I walk the unkempt little courtyard outside, the dying winter plants matching my mood more closely than the cheery office. I pace back and forth in the garden, ugly with its sole survivor of tough ivy. I peek furtively at the other tenants of the small office complex as they come and go, avoiding eye contact so they won't see my shame.

When Paul and I go to a session, we sit in that same waiting room, silent except for the creak of wicker and the snap of pages as Paul leafs through the old magazines. Finally the therapist peeks out of her office, beckoning us in with a smile and some perfunctory courtesies. I always choose the chair, sitting rigid and upright with my notebook and pen, but Paul sprawls on the loveseat, his tall frame and big feet hanging over the edge of one arm, looking as though he should have a beer and a baseball game going.

Our postures aren't the only differences in those sessions. It doesn't take long for the accusations to fly.

"You are too lenient," Paul states, catching me off guard.

"Well, I'm not like your mother, if that's what you're saying," I respond defensively, aiming right for the most vulnerable spot I can find.

"No, you're not," he acquiesces triumphantly, shutting down the dialogue and leaving me red-faced and angry, the doctor jumping in to calm us, to try to make us more communicative, or at least more effective.

After several nonproductive sessions, she seems ready to judge us. "It seems that you both go for the clever answer rather than working through the issues at hand." It is time for new rules. No more repartee. Paul is asked to say three positive things before he criticizes me. I have to wait until the count of five before responding. Tedious and frustrating, it feels fake and wrong, and I am surprised when sometimes it works.

"Is this the way you interact with Hannah?" There it is, the question that was bound to come up. Paul and I look at each other guiltily, knowing how sharp, sarcastic retorts had become the end game in many of our arguments with Hannah—a sick competition with our quick-witted daughter. "You need to shut it down," counsels the therapist. "Keep your objective in mind. You want her to open up, to grow, to feel safe with you."

It is devastating to realize that our jousting has pushed Hannah away, that our communication has created an arena where words trump substance. We do a lot of work, Paul and I, to modify our communication style. I vow to be calm, to listen, to respond directly, and to never, never, let my emotions rule my communication with my daughter again. Maybe I take the therapist's advice too far, absorbing rather than reflecting, suppressing rather than speaking. I find it a relief in the end, the permission to subdue my emotions, to tuck them away for later, maybe for the shower, where I can cry under the stream of water, letting my snarky retorts and emotions swirl away, leaving me clean and ready to face the impossible world in which I now live.

Hannah

I never wanted to be one of those kids—"therapy kids," I called them. There were bunches of them at my elementary school. "A statistical anomaly," Mother-person called it. About half the brats in my class needed some kind of therapy. We had biters, pissers, kids who couldn't sit still, and kids who swore at the teacher and ran out of the room. Well here I am, and they followed me, they found me—the biters and the pissers and all the rest.

Mom

"A letter!" I yell for Paul, who comes running up the stairs from his office and perches on the edge of a living room armchair while I fumble with the #10 envelope, slipping my thumb under the flap and peeking inside for a bit of Hannah. It has been a couple of weeks since we left her at Vista, and I am surprised and a little nervous to see her handwriting on the front of the envelope.

Hannah

After that sucky transition from Second Nature to Vista, I just want a couple of minutes to talk to Mom and Dad, and tell them that I'm sorry, and that I figured out that I probably need to be here in this army barrack of addicts for a while. *Army* is a pretty good description. You get promoted and demoted depending on how well you follow the rules, and get more or fewer privileges. I can tell you that when you don't have any privileges, even the smallest ones seem big. Anyway, they say, "No phone calls for thirty days," but before I can screw myself by whining, they tell me I can write a letter instead.

Mom

It is lined binder paper, and the writing is a scrawl, as though she is trying to get out all her thoughts at once:

> Dear Mom,
> Well, I miss talking to you guys already. Mostly everything is good here, though there are a LOT of rules. Some of the rules that get me in trouble all the time are my clothes. I know that you sent a big box full of stuff, but I guess I gained a lot of weight in the woods and mostly nothing fits me. Do you think you could pick out some really conservative things in bigger sizes? I'm thinking maybe some plain, long sleeve Ts, and maybe some slippers to wear around the house since we all take off our shoes inside? I don't have a lot of time to write, they keep us busy. But I will try. Would you send me stationary?
> Hannah

My first thought is that the letter isn't what I had hoped for, but I catch myself. What had I hoped for? I study the single sheet, trying to read between the lines.

Hannah

That's not really what I want to say to them at all, but it feels good to just be normal and casual. I really don't want to ask Mom to shop more either, but I have no choice. My old schools all had dress codes, but I don't remember anyone getting called out. The schools at home wanted us to be "individuals" and didn't want to bother with how long our shorts or how wide our shirt straps were. That wouldn't be the Santa Cruz way. So we all blurred the line with our purple hair and gauges and ripped clothes. Now the lines are sharp and clear. My panties can't peek at my waistline, my shirts have to cover my belt, even when my arms are up in the air. No armpits (not my best feature anyway) and no slogans on shirts. Hair neat and clean and out of my face. Mom being a shopping machine, it doesn't take too long to get a big box of clothes and a letter.

> Dear Hannah,
> I hope this package helps keep you out of trouble. No belly, no armpits, no slogans. How are you settling in? How are the girls there? Who is your roommate? What is the program like?
> Love,
> Mom

The box has a bunch of shirts and pants, some pretty blue stationary with sparkles on it, and at the bottom some bunny slippers that make me laugh. I put them on right away.

Mom

Less than a week after sending off Hannah's package, a sparkly blue envelope appears in our mailbox. Paul isn't home, but I don't wait, dropping the rest of the mail on the hall table. I open it standing up.

> Dear Mom,
> Thank you for the package. Most of the stuff fits. I think I'll keep my other clothes here in the attic because we exercise every day and now that

my new shrink is getting me off the Depakote, I might be able to get back to my normal size. The stationary is pretty, I like it a lot. The bunnies are warm.

Hannah

I smile as I fold the note back into its envelope and put it on Paul's placemat, a special treat. Grabbing some notepaper and sitting down at the dining room table, I reply to my new pen pal, asking her how she is spending her day.

Hannah

Ugh. Sunday. That means deep clean. When we got here, Mom said it was "so clean," and now I know how it gets that way, and it isn't an ultimate cleaning lady, it's me and the other bitches here. Every Saturday we have to clean our rooms and our bathrooms, and every Sunday we have to clean the rest of the house. And I mean clean. We pull the couch cushions off and vacuum underneath them, bleach the toilet bowls, and use toothbrushes on the grout. I never had to clean before.

There's a shit ton of rules here. When I first arrive, it takes me a whole week just to figure out how to get off "orientation," which is the most basic level with no privileges. It's hard cuz every time I blow one of the gazillion rules, I get bumped back down to RO . . . re-orientation. I call it the silent zone, since nobody is supposed to talk to you when you're there. I've already been bumped down three times. One time I don't finish my homework and lose a shit ton of points. I look at a boy and get dinged for that . . . unsanctioned lust is out of the question here in Mormonville. I also forget to keep track of my points sometimes, and lose points for that, which seems redundant to me. Anyway, now that I have been here a couple of weeks, I'm definitely getting the hang of it. Pretty soon I'll have enough points to earn a five-minute call home once a week. I never thought I would be excited about calling home.

Mom

Moving Hannah to Vista is like sending her away all over again. It's the calls I miss the most now that she's out of the Wilderness Program. Even though they were mostly therapeutic and moderated by Jason, I could hear her voice over the SAT phone, and know she was really okay. No phone calls allowed now, until Hannah earns them, and I check our big mailbox daily in case there's a letter. I gather our three big dogs around me and walk the long drive, downhill and then uphill to the street, a long tenth of a mile away through the redwoods that line our driveway. It always makes me smile to see the dogs sitting pretty while I fumble for the key and open the box, shaking each piece of mail in case there are spiders, stopping to look for anything that might be a card or letter from Hannah, my mood shifting, depending on what I find. I push the mail into my bag and start the walk home, the dogs growling and nipping at each other in play, oblivious to how I am feeling.

Hannah

I miss my family, and that surprises me and makes me feel good at the same time, but what surprises me even more is how much I miss the bitches from Wilderness. Maybe it's how we always watched out for each other, or maybe it's because I don't like Shelly, the roommate they gave me here. She is so crabby! She's been here a couple of months, and she's a level two, which means that she has a bunch of privileges, like phone calls and taking visitors around. She struts around, tossing her long black hair and rolling her eyes at me every time I make a mistake.

Mom

I'm working on a long letter to Hannah. It's more of a journal, really, and whenever I can't sit in the loneliness anymore, I go back to it. I close my eyes and try to picture her at Vista, in that sparkling clean house, sitting down on her bed to read the mail, already opened and checked by the office for contraband. I write about the little stuff she's missing, thinking how life is in the small things we do each day. I tell her about my walks along the ocean path, and about how Camilla is starting to run track, and how we had an earthquake—a 4.5 magnitude—and our dogs did not even wake up, which begs the question of animals sensing disaster. I add cartoons and poems. I write until the letter is unwieldy, and I have to use a big brown envelope with a clasp to send it.

Hannah

I guess I better get used to Tater Tots and veggie burgers. It seems that's what passes for vegetarian cuisine here, and I'm not about to throw away the last three years of being vegetarian. What they lack in culinary imagination they make up for with discipline. These cats are strict! Today I lose points for taking a long shower. Then my therapist starts digging in to see if I am being secretly oppositional with my water use. Christ!

Mom

Today is Camilla's first visit to the rabbi to start individual study for her bat mitzvah. She's reading from a Torah portion called Pinchas, and she'll be expected to teach the portion at her coming of age service. We sit together in the rabbi's office, at a round table covered with books. The rabbi tells Camilla that most young women talk about the feminist ideas in the portion, but she has already read the work and decided that for her, it is about sacrificing rewards today for rewards in the future. She tells him this, looking down at her hands, and after a long discussion where she fails to be persuaded, he tells her that what matters most is that it be meaningful for her, and she should take the direction that feels right. She responds in her whispery voice that she will.

Hannah

I make my first unsupervised phone call in over four months, and I can't believe how nervous I am. I feel like a middle-schooler calling a boy for a date or something. I plan out exactly what I am going to say to the parents before dialing the little black portable phone that the students use here, but when Mom picks up the phone, I just forget it all and just sort of grunt stuff at her for a few minutes. Something about what I'm doing in the gym, and what it's like to go to school every single day, and how everyone speaks therapy here. I can complain a little, it's safe, and that's a relief. Dad isn't home, so I get to spend the whole five minutes with her. It goes fast, and when the staffer gives me the "five" sign, I can't believe that I have to cut the connection.

Mom

> *Dear Hannah,*
> *It was such a joy to be able to speak with you about non-therapeutic things again, with nobody listening and evaluating our relationship. I can't wait to talk to you again on Monday. I love you and miss you.*
> *Mom*

Hannah

I think I'm getting the hang of this. I am figuring out how things work around here and remembering to tally my points. I've met most all the girls now. Most of them are okay, just one or two bitches, like my roommate Shelly, but I guess they are trying to deal with their own shit, and I sure know what that feels like. I think that the girls who went to Wilderness are calmer because they have a head start on therapy, but really everyone seems to need a lot of support.

We have a cool bunch of therapists here; they are all no bullshit. My main therapist is Bobbi. She is a hot blond mama, with pretty clothes and shoes that don't seem to belong here. Holy hell, I found out that she's Jason's wife! I believe it though. Just like Jason, she doesn't let me get away with any kind of crap. Sometimes she calls me out on my crap even before I know it's crap! Then I think, "Wow, that really was some kind of crap." Amazing. I dig it. My big problem? Group therapy.

Mom

Monday comes and goes and no call from Hannah. I pace the floor in the kitchen, moving between the counter and the refrigerator, nibbling and worrying about what she might have done to lose her phone privileges.

Hannah

Group therapy here is a bitch. We have it every day. Everyone sits on the big "U" of brown leather couches and stares at you while you talk about what landed you here. Even when I participate, they keep pushing at me, and the girls tell me that I'm not honest, and that I won't ever move forward this way. I dare you to try to please the therapist and the six bitches in my group. If they're not giving me shit about my own stuff, then they're giving me shit about not giving honest feedback to others. Today they accuse me of bragging, of being proud of my wild life. I guess sometimes girls try to one-up each other, and that's looked down upon here as much as it was in the wilderness. I don't think I was trying to glorify what I did, but maybe I'm trying to show that I belong . . . even here. I guess I still have that over-identification thing going. I should work on that. Anyway my supposed bragging lost me my phone call, and so I spend personal time writing a note to Mom and Dad so they won't worry too much.

> Dear Mom,
> I got busted back to reorientation because I was not mindful of my attitude and my participation in group today. I'm working to improve, and I hope I'll be able to call you soon. I'm also working on being able to sit with myself and my uncomfortableness.

Mom

She sounds so matter of fact about being punished that I feel my eyebrows raise. I read the letter twice and, shaking my head in amazement, put it on Paul's placemat. Lately he's been out a lot on a project he's doing, and so I'm alone a lot wondering if he's just trying to get away from me and find some normal people to hang with. I stay home, not wanting to interact or to explain, preferring my solitude.

I sit at my glass desk in the little alcove I set up after giving my office to Hannah, and stare out the window. I half-heartedly chase leads for a couple of consulting projects and distract myself with planning Camilla's bat mitzvah. Paul warns me that our budget will be less than half of what we spent for Hannah, and I wander around the Internet, putting together budgets and starting the guest list. Camilla could care less about the ceremony or the party. She does seem a little interested in her Torah portion, and when I pick her up from school, we talk about who else in history made sacrifices for future generations, and I hope she will say "you and Dad," but she doesn't. When we get home, she is swallowed by her room and a pile of homework, and I sit at my desk and write up some bullet points on the things she said in the car, and I email them to her to encourage her to begin to write her speech. I know that I should not do this, but I hit "send" anyway, knowing that as far as my many parenting mistakes go, this one is likely to rank rather low.

Hannah

I like my chemical dependency therapist a lot. Her name is Liz, and she's "been there, done that," and no disrespect, but it really shows. Dang, she looks wrung out and hung out to dry. The fact that she knows the life, though, that makes it really easy to talk to her. She has a bunch of books on religion in her office, and is super interested in our religion and our family history. I think she must be soul-searching or something. Anyway I'm going to work the twelve steps with her. I can already see that the hardest part is going to be this higher power crap. I've been off the formal religion stuff for a long time now, and I don't miss it. Liz says that a higher power doesn't have to be a deity. That higher power can be any symbol, even a rock, but that doesn't feel right at all. So yeah, I guess I have to figure that part out. Can I be saved without being "saved?"

Mom

Paul and I go to the bookstore. I haven't been to downtown Santa Cruz in a long time, and I am surprised at how my anger wells up at the drug-addled teens wandering the street. I want to scream at them—did you give my daughter drugs? Paul doesn't notice my angst. As usual he is on a mission, and he pulls on my arm, moving me towards the double doors that lead into the shop. I have a moment's pleasure as we walk through the stacks, reliving the delicious evenings we have had wandering through this shop after a quiet dinner, our problems as yet unimagined. I love to read the little hand-written staff reviews in the independent store, sometimes disagreeing vehemently, but always appreciating how people can read the same book so differently.

My pleasure melts like chocolate in the sun as Paul starts choosing the books we have come for. Alcoholics Anonymous' *The Big Book*, to help us support Hannah as she works the twelve-step program, and *Addictive Thinking* by Abraham Twerski, to help us understand her. Paul also searches the stacks for information on Dialectic Behavioral Therapy. "We'll have to get it online," he says, mouth turned down in disappointment at their sparse selection on the topic. We make our way to the counter, me hiding the books close against my chest as though they were pornography, looking forward to the brown paper bag that will conceal our problems.

Hannah

I've earned the right to talk to Mom and Dad tonight. Camilla won't get on the phone, and I guess I don't blame her and shouldn't expect her to forgive me instantly for all the bad shit I did to her and the family. I ask Mom to send me some pictures of her, and the family, and maybe some of me before all the bad stuff happened. She comes through in a big way; the brown envelope she sends is stuffed with pictures, and I pull them out one by one, like eating candy real slowly to make it last. Then I decorate my door with them. It feels like they are standing guard there, keeping me safe. My favorite is a picture of Camilla and me having a tea party picnic with our teddy bears. We are sitting on a quilt on the living room floor, smiling real smiles, and holding little tiny cups shaped like strawberries. I put that picture of Cammy and me in the middle and surround us with the family.

Mom

It is an unusually nice February day, and I sit outside on a cushioned lawn chair to take advantage of the bright sun and the mild breeze while the dogs sun themselves on the deck. My enjoyment is marred by my reading, and I snap the pages of the Alcoholics Anonymous *Big Book* so hard that I risk tearing the pages, and then I wonder if that isn't my intention. Why am I so angry? Is it because this book is sexist tripe? Maybe it's just the fact that I have to be reading it. I reset my brain and try to find balance in the book. After all, it has helped so many people. I weigh the offensive statement, "Our womenfolk have suggested certain attitudes a wife may take with the husband who is recovering," against another bit that seems like a very good idea: "Take inventory every day." I pull my straw hat over my eyes and try to do that.

Hannah

I have broken down and cried in group therapy every day this week. Not crying like, "Oh, look, she's having a breakthrough" crying, and then everyone hugs you and tells you that you are going to be okay now. No, it's more like, "Oh, she's blocked, she can't get there, she won't touch that thang." I wipe the snot off my face with my sleeve and look down at the tip of my pencil and wonder if I can break my skin with it if I try real hard. I lay the tip against the skin of my arm, and then I think about how hard I have worked and how hard Mom and Dad have worked to get this far, and I drop the pencil into the crease of my journal and look up to see that everyone is looking at me and into me, and nobody is too impressed.

Mom

Bobbi tells us that she is starting Hannah on Dialectic Behavioral Therapy. She's glad that we're reading about it, and suggests more titles. She also tells me that we will start weekly family therapy calls again, and we spend some time figuring out our calendars. I hang up the phone and lie down on the leather couch in our living room, just for a moment, suddenly tired. I wake up when Paul walks in, feeling better than I have in a long time. I sit down at my computer and write Hannah a long breezy letter telling her about my new kick-boxing class, in which an eighty-year-old man named George regularly kicks my ass. I smile at the image and hope Hannah smiles when she reads it.

Hannah

Now they have just gone too far. I am tied to Shelly. No, I don't mean metaphorically. I am actually tied with a piece of string to the fugly bitch. The string is about ten feet long. Long enough for one of us to go to the bathroom while the other one waits outside the door. Long enough to sleep on my twin bed while she sleeps just across the room, but short enough that we have to coordinate rolling over. Long enough to eat at a different table in the little cafeteria, but short enough that we have to coordinate clearing our tables after lunch. That string is always pulling at me and reminding me that I cannot seem to control my emotions around her. I try, but I fail. Then I try again. Getting along with Shelly is like making fire. I work at it constantly, but I keep failing.

Our group therapist decides that we have opposite problems or something. He says that Shelly can teach me about emotional control, and I can teach her about empathy. I think she got all banged up and raped a bunch of times before coming here, and tamped it all down behind this extremely cold and bitchy exterior. I don't want to be all bottled up like Shelly, but I do understand that my daily crying jags are getting old. Maybe they should put us two in a blender to get one well-balanced teen. I lie in bed, Shelly silent across the tightrope of twine, and I clutch the stuffed puppy and soft blanket that came in a package from home today for Valentine's Day.

Mom

Another Hallmark holiday, and though sad, I try to work up enthusiasm for Camilla's sake, baking a heart-shaped breakfast cake and buying a card and a big chocolate kiss to leave at her place at the table. My mood turns all of a sudden with the twist of the mailbox key and a large white envelope decorated with hand drawn hearts. Inside is a big homemade card, with a red foil heart on the cover. Inside is a wonderful gift, the first loving words we have from Hannah in well over a year:

> Dear Mom & Dad,
> Happy V-Day. I know it's been a tough year, but I want to let you know how grateful I am for you always being there for me even when I didn't show you my love in return. I want to let you know how much I really do love you.
> Hannah

The tears come yet again, and I let them, feeling lighter with each one that runs down my face. Smiling and crying, I walk into the house and call for Paul.

Hannah

So I'm learning about this DBT stuff that Jason started in the wilderness. He told me to watch my physical reaction when bad shit happens. Now Bobbi is telling me that it's okay to feel the way I do, and that I should let myself feel it and then let it go. I think that's a good idea, but how do I do that? How do I let it go? I hug the pillow from the couch in Bobbi's office, and she smiles at me and promises me she'll help me figure that part out, and I believe her.

Mom

I put down the Twerski book on addictive thinking patterns and wonder if everyone is addicted to something. When I eat too much or shop too much, isn't that addiction? Don't I justify getting a new dress or having an extra scoop of ice cream the same way a drug addict justifies a fix? I dog-ear the page and close the book, then throw out the rest of the muffin I'm working on and go outside for a walk.

Hannah

Today I take my very last Depakote pill. It's kind of scary getting off meds cuz I wonder, what if they are wrong and I really do have bipolar disorder? Will I go crazy, crazier than I am? But I have had less and less medication over the last two months, and I don't feel any different. I feel pretty happy and even-keeled most of the time, even though I am going to school seven days a week, scrubbing toilets, and eating Tater Tots twice a day.

Mom

Paul is in Cabo San Lucas. I don't much like Cabo, maybe because I don't like the heat or wearing bathing suits these days, but I wish that I were there with him anyway. I wish I were anywhere else, but I'm not. I'm in the school office, talking to the dean of students about Camilla. She has taken a boy's cell phone and dangled it over the edge of the school roof. I ask the dean what the boy did to her to make her so angry, and he looks surprised. He doesn't know, and that makes me more angry than it should. Neither one of us mentions Hannah in this meeting, but we are both thinking of her, and my stare is making him shift around in his chair and promise to find out more about the situation. I am not hopeful. The boy's parents are large contributors to the school, and we've learned what that means the hard way. I take notes so I can give Paul the details, but both of us are pretty tired of feeling beat up.

Hannah

We go to the gym a lot, and I don't really like it, but I do like the way I feel afterwards. I'm losing weight, and I had to get some of my smaller pants down from the attic. I am catching up in school too, though it looks like I'm going to have to work most of the summer to finish eleventh grade. I like that I'm not being looked at like a fuck up any more. Maybe I'm not a fuck up any more.

Mom

People speak in code. At the temple, I sit in the big velvet lobby chairs and wait for Camilla to finish her study session, and I have a conversation with a member I know only a little bit. I answer him in conversation, "Yes, I have an older daughter too. She is at school in Utah."

He replies softly, "My son went to school in Arizona." He looks at me over the top of his glasses, mouth set in a straight line, sadness in his eyes.

At the school picnic, I meet a family who tells me the devastating outcome of their Utah experience. "He's okay now, but we don't speak much anymore." Will we be this family? Will we lose our daughter by helping her find herself?

I write to Hannah often—about the big things, but also the small things, and even silly things, hoping to keep a layer of normality between us.

Dear Hannah,

Things have been quiet here. I continue reading the Twerski book. I look forward to discussing it with you when we are all finished with it.

I'm happy to hear that most stuff is going well, and I know that you will keep working on your group experience. I have been struggling with more mundane things here, getting ready for Camilla's bat mitzvah. I'm excited that so many people are coming from out of town. I'm counting on you being one of them, so keep up the good work and earn enough points!

As an aside, I am rethinking kickboxing. I am examining why I, a pumpkin with legs that barely lift past my hearty ankles, would want to go get beat up by an old man every week. Of course I am bringing joy and laughter to the rest of the class.

Hannah

Mom's letters make me laugh sometimes, even though this place can be pretty grim. Reading her letters is like reading some kind of fiction. I've been away and in such a different place for so long that it just doesn't seem all that real to me anymore. I put her letter down and finish my school reading and assignments. All I have to do now is spill my guts in group therapy, work the twelve steps, take accountability for my life, and make a plan to move forward. Piece of cake.

Mom

We are into March now, and we don't yet have an answer from Vista about Hannah attending her sister's bat mitzvah this summer. Bobbi is making me a little crazy with her calm. "Let's just do the work the best we can," she tells us as I sit tapping my pen on the guest list, "and the answer will present itself." I hang up the phone and try to do the work.

Dear Hannah,
Dad and I just finished Addictive Thinking. For me, it answered how you could continue to hurt us and other people around you in order to justify your drug use. I guess now we'll all recognize "stinking thinking" and how to hear arguments through the filter of an addict, but I hope we'll never have to hear it from you again.

Hannah

I don't know. How can I know what will happen in the future?
I see it all the time here, kids coming back after using again,
shoulders hunched, heads down. I don't want to scare Mom and
Dad—they have been through a lot—but I have to be honest.

> Dear Mom,
> I can't promise that I won't get self-obsessed
> again, since I am an addictive personality. I
> hope I can be more aware of my actions and how
> they are affecting other people, and let people
> help me. You know, Mom, everyone has some of
> these thinking errors. Mine went batshit out of
> control, but like a lot of things we talk about
> here, our destructive behaviors are mostly just
> normal behaviors that go haywire. Then we deny
> them, we justify them, we twist everything up
> around them. Pretty scary shit.

Mom

I wish for easy answers, for miraculous epiphanies, for the end
of our pain—but I get the truth instead, and I sit outside and
try to be okay with it. My big Labrador jumps in the pool, and I
watch her swim around in circles before she gets out and shakes
herself, catching me in the spray of water in spite of my best
efforts. I hold Hannah's letter in my hand and decide that it is
way past time to get in the deep end.

> *Dear Hannah,*
> *Of course you're right. It is not realistic for me to ask*
> *you for guarantees. I agree that we all have thinking*
> *errors. With me it's food and shopping. But my think-*
> *ing errors don't destroy my brain, just my body and*
> *my wallet.*

I stop writing and read my words, and shaking my head, I write on.

> *I can't believe it. I just justified my thinking errors.*
> *I just employed "stinking thinking." I'm wrong to say*
> *my behaviors are not harmful. They are. Twerski might*
> *say they are the result of self-pity, pleasure-seeking, and*
> *maybe a little boredom.*

Yes indeed. The Twerski book was a real eye opener.

Hannah

I am busy every minute here, with a schedule for every fucking thing. We eat and clean and sleep and do exercise. We have two groups a day and we have private therapy once a week. We write letters and we journal. We go to school and we do homework. We go to the shrink once a month and the doctor when we need to. It's funny that with all of this activity, I feel paralyzed as I start reading the twelve steps and start thinking about what they mean to me. The first one is a doozy.

> *Step 1: We admitted we were powerless over alcohol—that*
> *our lives had become unmanageable.*

I am thinking about the word *unmanageable*. Sometimes I'm so impatient with all the ridiculous rules here that I try to figure out what they want me to say so that I can get back to my life. The problem is that I don't know if I would fit into that life anymore, or if I would even want to fit in if I could. From this distance I can see that it revolved around drugs, drinking, fucking, and other misdemeanors.

Mom seems freaked when I call myself an alcoholic, but my CD counselor Liz helps me understand that it wasn't necessarily how often I drank, but how I drank when I did. I drank until I got sick, and I forgot big patches of time. I liked to drink with friends, but also in my room. I would make up all kinds of reasons to justify my drinking, like, "It helps me stay cool with the family." I sit quietly in Liz's office and think that being me has become easier now that I am off alcohol and drugs, even with constant therapy and school. Life *is* more manageable. Am I more powerful, or am I deluded? Am I letting them brainwash me?

Dear Mom & Dad,
I'm working the first step of the twelve-step program now, with my chemical dependency counselor Liz. It is hard to imagine that there are parts of your life that you do not control, even if you think you do. It's also hard to admit that you might not be as smart as you think you are. I am going to work on number four next, the moral inventory stuff, cuz Liz thinks it will help me examine my behaviors and that could help me break through in group.

I know it's got to be hard for Mom and Dad to hear about this shit, and I wonder if they think of me as damaged goods. I don't know if I'll ever be whole again. But brainwash or not, this might be my best chance. I don't know who I'll end up being, but I guess most teens can say that.

Chapter 11

Mom

Let me tell you what people don't understand about having a child in treatment. Everything I see, hear, and do is filtered through a lens of frustration, failure, and shame. I see a mother and daughter bantering, casually arm in arm, and I wish, I yearn, I beg God to let me have that, or at least let me remember a moment in my past when I had it. But the memories don't want to come, because my mind is filled with despair over our family's situation and the need to be practical, to deal with our daily issues of finance, therapy, and a second child's needs. Wearing my despair on the outside is a luxury, an indulgence that does not serve me or my children. I move forward every day because the place I am in is a very bad place, and the place I was before the bad things happened? It was good, but it doesn't exist anymore, that mother doesn't exist. She was a bad mother, look what happened, and that sweet child of the past? She is gone, dead, evolving into something else, someone I don't know yet, except I know I love her.

Hannah is taking a moral inventory of herself right now, and since we told her we would do everything with her, we take one of ourselves too. I am surprised at the ugliness I uncover; it doesn't match the person I think I am. It's little things that hurt no one, like taking the largest slice of cheesecake, or allowing a cashier to under-ring a purchase; but big things too, like judging people by their appearance or their success, and being petty with people. I hang my head at the biggest failing of all, my failure to keep my daughter safe, the times I gave in to her because I was too worn out to fight with her. I try to soothe myself in the face of my discoveries by eating, but my waistband reminds me that the strategy doesn't work. I try drinking, but it works even less, the alcohol watering my budding self-loathing instead of killing it, and I push the bottles back into the deep recesses of the cabinet they came from. Is it very important to always think moral thoughts? I like to think it's more important to do moral things. I am suspicious of my justification, and measure it against my new "stinking thinking" ruler. I can't take it anymore, and so for now I tuck my self-discovery away too, in a place nobody can see, along with my pain and outrage at our family's situation.

We are all hurting, in our corners, licking our wounds. Paul is in his office downstairs until it's time for bed. Camilla is silent, still assaulted by Hannah, all those miles away.

I sit in the therapist's office, disagreeing with her observations, providing dishonest responses to her questions, my distrust heavy in the air. "Yes, I'm fine," I tell her with a smile, glancing at the clock. She sweeps her styled hair out of her face with a manicured hand and suggests a behavior chart for my emotionally injured daughter.

"You need to hold Camilla to standards of your choosing," she proclaims. "You need to be tough. There should be consequences for her failings."

I nod at her. "I'll think about it," I lie. She spends some time explaining methods that have worked for other families with much smaller problems than ours, and I grimace and squirm with impatience, watching the clock hands and keeping my thoughts to myself.

I have a kid in treatment. Don't try to make me smile or feel better about myself. "It took courage," you say.

"You gave up," I hear.

Hannah

When I was in the wilderness, I made a list of how my values and actions don't match each other, but somehow my list has gotten a lot longer between then and now. I did some pretty foul things, and I guess I'm supposed to make amends, but I'm not sure how to do that from here in Mormonville. Liz tells me that the first thing I have to do is think about each thing on my bad girl inventory, and then turn it over in group and let everyone examine it with me. I don't really like to think that much about how I hurt people.

I listen in group to how the bitches talk, how once you are self-obsessed you don't care about shit anymore. I look anywhere but at the other girls, because I don't want them to know how hard I'm listening. I don't know exactly how or when I became that person who didn't care, but when I think about all the shit I did to people, I know it's true. I bury my head in one of the big couch pillows and try to lose myself in the soft leather. I feel like an awful person. I chose drugs and alcohol over everything, and I hurt so many people. I don't want to talk about it in this fucking group, because it feels new and raw every time. Why do I have to say it out loud, why can't I just know and make it better? Saying the words cuts me deeper than any razor ever did, and hurts me more.

I lose it in group, I call Shelly a vindictive bitch, and she calls me a spoiled, snot-nosed ho and shakes the string that connects the two of us like she wants to strangle me with it—a growl, a real growl coming out of her throat. No surprise, we are both busted right back down to reorientation, and I lose my phone call. Later I have to tug at the string that ties us together in order to reach my stationary, my lifeline to home.

> Dear Mom,
> I'm on RO again, but don't worry. I'm not really sad about it and I guess I deserved it. It gives me time to think, and get my shit together and I'm happy about that. Not happy like, "Yay, treatment" or anything, but just appreciating life. I'll talk to you tomorrow in family session and I think that I can earn my phone call back by next Monday if everything goes okay.
> I went to the vag doctor today, and it was weird to go to the doctor with strangers instead of you, Mom. Anyway it was really funny. Not that salad tong part, that wasn't funny, but the doctor's name was—are you ready for this mom??—Dr. Khunt. Really. Did I make you laugh?
> I'm a duck in the New York winter, Mom. I don't belong in Utah, I need to go somewhere else . . . it's too intense here. I miss you guys, and I'll work hard so I can come in July.

Mom

Hannah's letters are a balm, a time when I can be with her for a moment. She writes to Paul and me separately, and I don't ask Paul what she shares with him. I write back.

> Dear Hannah,
> I know you are feeling out of place, but I don't know how you could possibly feel at home in your situation. I'm happy to hear that you feel normal sometimes. Things are pretty stressed around here too. Camilla is meeting with the rabbi weekly to get ready for her bat mitzvah, but she doesn't love

to go and argue Torah the way you did. She's smart and works hard, but it is not her passion. I admit, it gave me such a thrill to pick you up from study, all those books open and scattered around the rabbi's office, you two arguing all the way to the door, and then you telling me about it all the way home in the car.

I am making Camilla's prayer shawl. I plan on burying blessings in all of the fringes when we knot them—a total of 613 knots—because I think she needs them. She just finished her community service at an old age home, and she taught all the old people how to play the card game "Bullshit." I walked into the day room to pick her up, and all these octogenarians are waving cards around and screaming "Bullshit!" at each other, with your sister standing in the middle of the bedlam with that evil smile on her face.

Hannah

Camilla. I hope Mom doesn't run out of blessings at 500 knots or something.

———

Mom

The RSVPs for Camilla's bat mitzvah are growing, and it dawns on me that someone from out of town will probably have to stay in Hannah's room. I sit on her bed holding her Mr. Bear for comfort as I look around. It will be a very, very big job. The first part was the hardest.

Dear Hannah,
This is a hard subject to broach, but I am sitting in your room right now, and I think it's time to do a cleanup. You are clearing the junk out of your life and creating order.

I would like to do the same here, and I would like to do it before our bat mitzvah guests arrive. I admit that I am embarrassed for people to see your room like this, but I am also kind of grossed out and done. You know what's in there. Are you open to this? I do promise to save all your things.

Hannah

I sit on my bed in my sterile bedroom at Vista Residential Treatment Program hugging the stuffed puppy Mom sent me and thinking about how I feel about her going through all my stuff. Since I am now the therapy queen, I understand that this possibly has therapeutic value for me and for her. Now that I have admitted that, I can put it aside and do a mental list of things that mean something to me that are in my room. My art. That's first. I know Mom will save the paintings and sketches; she loves art, and I think she knows what it means to me. Of course she did send me to this school, the equivalent of an art desert. They have a "studio" here and a teacher who has a master's degree in art education, but the materials they give us are crap. The only painting I have done since being here is with tempera paints on cardboard. Kiddy stuff, very structured and supervised. It truly sucks. But still, I trust her to be respectful of my work, even the stuff she doesn't like, cuz she gets what art is all about.

The second thing I guess I'm worried about are my photos and books. I guess there are some I wouldn't like her to see, but after the conversations we've had, I don't really feel like they would be too shocking. Third, well, there doesn't seem to be a third. The rest is just a mishmash of schoolwork, dirty clothes, paint tubes, art supplies, and other assorted junk. So it's not the stuff that bothers me, it is something else. Maybe it's the idea of people imposing order on my life. After sitting with this a while I decide that's selfish and I write to her.

Dear Mom,
It's cool with me if you clean out my room. I'm
really sorry that you got stuck with it. I know
it's gross.

Mom

After I gingerly pick through Hannah's art and photos, her
books and music, and pile her dirty clothes and used cups and
dishes into a laundry basket, I literally sweep the rest of the
garbage left on the floor into a big pile and use a dust pan to
scoop it right into the big gray trash can I have rolled onto the
deck where her doors open to the outside. The *thunk* of debris
hitting the bottom of the can is satisfying for a moment, but
then, recognizing the mess for what it is—my absent daughter's
life—I gently close the lid and walk away. I tell myself that I
should be happy, throwing this past away, but for some reason
it makes me sad, like I'm throwing out part of Hannah. This
will have to be done in small doses, over time.

Hannah

Mom is going through the crap in my room, and I'm going
through the crap in my head. They tell me I was a house terrorist, and I guess that's right. There was a time when I would
get satisfaction from being called that, but now I wonder if that,
right there, is the definition of crazy, terrorizing the people who
love you and want to help you. Funny, of all the people I hurt,
and there were plenty, I keep thinking about my art teacher,
Shirley. She liked to paint side by side with me, and it was cool
to see our canvases come into focus, different but the same,
both of us expressing our different realities. The big clay pot
of brushes would be between us, our palettes covered with the
professional grade paint she let me use because I was special. I
stopped going to Shirley after ten years of painting canvasses
next to her. I didn't even say goodbye. I am an asshole. Huh.

Mom

Saying that you are going to clean something out and doing it is very different. I worry about each artifact. I turn it around in my hands and wonder. Save it? Throw it away? Does it have a hidden meaning of which I am unaware? Will Hannah want this particular doodad? Will she ask for it on her first day home, only to find out that I have thrown it away in the big gray bin? After I clear the floor, I start on the walls, the paint covered with hundreds of images, some beautiful and some horrible, like our life with Hannah. I take them down one at a time. The photograph of the old woman in the park keeps company with the sketch of a limbless monster. Receipts hang next to poems, carved gourd masks vandalized with spray paint perch on the same nails as the dream catchers that guard her nightmarish paintings, and winged angels hover over pornography. I remove the warring images of her drug-addled mind from the walls, and I'm left with holes. Hundreds of small holes of all sizes, from staples, pins, and nails. Hundreds of holes that now need to be filled with something else, something better. I get the spackle and begin.

Hannah

Bobbi tells me that Mom and Dad and Camilla are going to come and see me. I am scared of all of us being together for the first time since they sent me away to Wilderness. I haven't spoken to Camilla at all, not once. She just can't get over the terrible shit I did to her. But then I get my report card and realize that maybe I can change the way things are.

Dear Mom,
Hey, guess who got straight As? This guy. Right
here. And the lessons are not set up for jelly
brains either. So I hope you can be a little proud

for a change. I hear you are coming. I can't wait
to see you guys.
Love,
Hannah

Mom

We have permission to visit Hannah, and have decided to
take Camilla with us. If we want to heal, we have to heal the
whole family.

Dear Hannah,

*We are getting ready for our trip. I am trying to crochet
you a scarf, but at this rate it might be a potholder. We
took the dogs to a cage-less "doggie camp" to see if they fit
in, but of course there was no need to worry—they fit in
wherever there is a ball.*

*Camilla is a little nervous about coming. Please be
gentle with her; remember that she didn't ask for any
of this, it sort of happened to her, this family falling
apart stuff. I am asking you to be patient and sensitive
to her needs.*

Love,

Mom

Hannah

Patient and sensitive is not something I've practiced a lot. But I
really do want this visit to go well. I'm excited to see the family,
but I'm scared too. I feel like they have a lot of good reasons
to throw things at me, and I don't have anything solid to hide
behind. I mean, I know they would never hurt me, but somehow that makes me feel worse. Part of me wishes they would
come and call me every name I have ever called them, and
maybe slap me around too. But I guess I'm going to have to
beat myself up. The bitches in group are happy to help. I pull

out my latest stationary from Mom, black and white graphics with, of course, sparkles.

> Dear Mom,
> I'm excited to see you all. Scared too. It will be all right though.
> Love, Hannah

Mom

I put down the phone softly, not wanting to break the fragile connection I have made on a phone call with another mother. Her sadness hangs in the air, and I close my eyes, breathing it in, sharing her pain. I am speaking to other parents now, who are thinking about sending their children away. I have just spent an hour listening to another tearful, desperate parent. I reread Hannah's letter and sit at the dining room table to write.

> Dear Hannah,
> Yes. It will be all right. We will make it be all right together. I want to share that Second Nature called me and asked me if I would be willing to speak to other parents. Of course I agreed. It's hard, Hannah. Hearing their stories takes me back to our very worst times, and I can hear the terrible pain that they are in. I'm telling you this because even though some weeks have been a struggle for you at Vista, and some sessions have been so difficult for us, I can see after this morning's conversation how far we have come, and it gives me hope that we can find each other again and that you can find the future that you want to have. It gives me new energy to do my part here at home. Just remember that when you come home, we will still all be imperfect, just in new ways. But maybe we will know how to talk about it, and how to help each other.
> I love you.
> Mom

Hannah

It's the big day!

The family doesn't get here until this afternoon, but I stand in front of the mirror and try to make the most out of my personal hygiene time. I touch my hair and sweep it out of my eyes, but it's not cooperating, so I pull out the plastic clips I am allowed to have here . . . little yellow duckies . . . and get my bangs out of my eyes. With my hair pulled back, you can really see the extra weight that's still rounding out my face and blooping over my pants a little bit. I try a smile into the mirror, but what I get back is just some fat chick taunting me. All part of facing myself, I guess. I don't want to scare them or make them feel bad about putting me in this place, so I keep working on my smile until it's time to line up for breakfast.

Mom

Paul is busy at the car rental counter, and I shift back and forth on my feet, wanting him to hurry. Camilla looks like she wishes she could bolt. She says nothing, just looks around the busy Salt Lake City airport, swiveling like a warning lighthouse. Paul turns away from the counter, triumphantly waving the little folder in his hand, and motions for us to follow him to the shuttle that will take us to our car. I reach for Camilla's hand but she shifts her backpack into it so that I reach for air. Our attempts to talk to her about this visit have been distinctly one way, with us doing all the talking. I study the back of her head as she moves ahead of me, her hair swinging in rhythm with her shoulders. I think about Hannah's welcome in the wilderness, and hope that Camilla isn't expecting too much.

Hannah

The day is dragging. All of my counseling sessions have been moved to the afternoon so my family can participate, and so I am left with schoolwork, chores, and personal time. The clock drags like I am in a time warp, every minute seems to take five. I glare at the clock, but it doesn't care, and I feel like I am swimming through molasses. It isn't until lunch cleanup in the downstairs cafeteria that I hear the commotion. A door, people walking and yes, right there, my mom's voice. I start moving towards the stairs, then remember to ask for permission, which is granted by staff even though I haven't finished my work. I run up the stairs and round the corner just as my mom is hanging up her gray coat on the hall rack. Dad has already hung up his ski jacket, and is standing there awkward and dear, his long arms dangling, urging Camilla to take off her jacket. Camilla looks like a scared deer, tensed up, her eyes moving back and forth like the plastic visitor badges that are swinging from their necks.

I don't know who to hug first, and somehow we end up all of us in a big ball of hug like when I was a little kid, and I pretend that we never lost this, I never fucked up, and this was just another day at home with my family. But the staff member's voice slices through my fantasy, urging us into the living room, and revealing the truth. We are here, in Utah, in a residential treatment center.

Mom

Hannah flies at us, her arms flung out in welcome. She pulls us to her, and my heart skips as she whispers, "Momma" into my hair, and then shouts, "Cammy" to her sister, gripping her with one arm and reaching for her father with the other before a staff member shows us into the living room. We all sit on one dark brown leather couch together, Paul and I flanking Camilla like Pharaoh Hounds, the leather of the couch squeaking a little as we settled in closer to each other. After a welcome like this, what could go wrong?

Hannah

Have you ever seen familiar things like you were looking at them for the first time? That's how it is for me that day. I've been at Vista for months, and I've stopped noticing how surreal it is anymore. Suddenly, I'm looking at Vista with an outsider's eyes. The sturdy furniture and the muted tones of the living room. The girls in their gray sweats and slippers, lining up for Dialectic Behavioral Therapy. They strike me as sick looking, though I know that they aren't sick in any physical way. They move into the room with grim faces and messy hair, their lack of makeup highlighting their shortcomings, and the absence of bright baubles spelling out the dullness of our daily routine. I look down at myself, just as plain, with my silly yellow ducky barrettes bravely holding my lanky hair out of my face. Well, I can't do anything about the place, the girls, or the duckies now.

Mom

The wild hugging over, I have a chance to finally study my daughter close up. She is dressed a little nicer than the other girls who walk back and forth through the living room, and I wonder if that's because of our visit. She is wearing a long-sleeve baby blue T-shirt against the still chilly Utah weather. I remember shopping for it, holding it up, and trying to picture if it will fit her new, larger body. It hangs loosely on her, and I notice that she has lost quite a bit of the weight that she put on in the wilderness. Her hair is no longer in dirty dreads, and instead hangs down in lanky waves, two yellow plastic duck barrettes floating above her ears to hold back the curls. "We're free until one," she informs us. "Would you like to see my room?"

Hannah

Of course they want to see my room. I lead them towards the hallway with my new eyes, noticing two girls from another treatment team in punishment scrubs, sitting on the floor waiting to speak with their therapist. I turn down the long hall and suddenly think of the hall in the movie *Beetlejuice*, each doorway leading to bizarre and unexpected horrors. These open doors reveal unnaturally neat beds flashing by, with cheerful pictures of past lives posted on Vista-approved bulletin boards. The bright colors and smiles in the pictures are like exotic collections of pinned butterflies, real at one time, now dried up and delicate to the touch.

We finally come to a room that I share with another drug addict, our mental disarray hidden beneath the neatly tucked covers of our beds, and in our orderly drawers and shelves. I spend a lot of time standing in front of my door, showing them which pictures I hung up, and we talk about where and when they were taken, and Dad is all hearty and tells me stories about them that I already know but had forgotten. Mom is quiet and stands with us but turns in towards the room and finally is the first one to go through the door, and I wonder about that—fuck is everything going to be symbolic for the rest of my life?

Mom

Really Paul? We are going to pretend to be normal? I lose patience with his stories and step into Hannah's neat box of a room. I'm not sure what to do next.

Hannah

Mom looks around and steps over to my bed. It's made up with the blue comforter she sent me, the soft one that was always a favorite of mine. She reaches for the single stuffed animal on the bed, the little dog that she sent me for Valentine's Day. She picks up the dog and combs her short fingers through the black fur of its ears, studying the toy before hugging it and putting it back on my pillow. Suddenly I know for sure that she hugged the dog that way before putting it in the box and sending it to me, and I feel good knowing it had some of those hugs in it when it got to me.

I listen to my father talk and see Camilla peeking into my bathroom and closet and watch my mother sit on my bed, and I avoid looking at the clock on my dresser because I really don't want to move or talk or do anything to make time start again. I never get to be alone or private, and having this short, frozen time with my family is a gift. I breathe in deeply—have I forgotten to breathe? I force myself to look at the clock and I see that it's almost time for group therapy with Marshall. "Time to go, you guys."

Mom

A therapist who introduces himself as Marshall meets us in the living room. He is a big man, youngish, in faded jeans bunched up around the top of dark brown Ugg boots. Marshall waves us over to a couch as though he is showing us to our table at a restaurant, and all four of us sit in a row. I don't realize we will be the main course that evening.

Hannah

Marshall is one of the no-shit therapists they have at Vista. It's like Wilderness in some ways—these therapists have seen it all, heard it all and didn't believe it all or sometimes even a little. These guys at Vista, though, they have you every day, and they dig deep, and of course there are always the ever-present bitches in the treatment group who are digging too, trying to earn points and deflect attention from themselves by putting others in the spotlight. Marshall asks Camilla if she wants to leave, and I wish so hard that she would go, but she shakes her head "no," and instead of leaving, she snuggles so close to Mom that she is almost behind her on the couch.

It is bad. It is so bad. Marshall wants to talk about how I treated my family, and he makes Mom and Dad say how they feel about my idiocy and he makes me go over the worst things I did at home. The bitches, they hold back, and I am grateful, but it is still bad.

Who didn't we have in that group? They are people like me, who are trying to survive all the ways life can hurt you. We are drug addicts and alcoholics, but we are also the molested, the prostitutes, the runaways, the arsonists, the shoplifters, and the house terrorists. Some of us are the disdainful and the distant, and some remorseful and reaching out.

I'm sorry Mom. I'm sorry I didn't do better, that I let the bitches in the group work me over, I'm sorry that I cried and that you had to see Marshall ignore my crying and the snot running down my face. I'm sorry that you know now that I am having trouble clearly seeing, really seeing my past, and figuring out what my future will be.

I was so afraid that this would happen, and it did, and my Mom—well, she looks pissed, and Dad is stoic and thoughtful, and Camilla is quiet and mostly invisible as she tucks deeper into the folds of the couch.

Mom

Can this really be useful? Am I the only one who is shaken by the confrontation that passes as therapy? I look at Hannah, at her red-rimmed eyes, at her lovely hands tearing at the tissues she uses to stem her tears, and she looks away. No, I'm not the only one shaken. The girls are lining up, seeming oblivious of the pain that they have just heaped on me and Hannah, as they march off in a line to write in their journals.

Hannah

I almost cry again with the relief at the session being over. The bitches line up for their next assault, this one on their journals. I am excused because of the family visit, and I ask Camilla if she wants to go outside. She nods at me, and I grab my jacket and hers and ask permission to go. Marshall looks at his watch and tells us to go ahead, and we pass by him on our way out, Mom looking at him like her anger could make him melt away like the snow outside, to be gone for good, and I want to tell her he's all right, but I think deep down she knows.

Mom

It snowed the week before we came to visit, and Camilla was excited to see snow again, but a heat wave washed through Utah and melted most of what was there. I watch Hannah hold Camilla gently by the elbow, walking around the high fence, searching the shady areas for enough snow to form a tiny snowman, and maybe start building a relationship again. A woman with leathery skin and spiky, short blond hair pokes her head out of the door and calls to us. She is Liz, Hannah's chemical dependency counselor. I take another breath of the cool air, grasp Paul's hand and walk towards the facility, desperately hoping that this will not be another session like the one we just finished.

Hannah

The coolness and the peace of being outside comes back inside with us, and I feel a lot better by the time we all sit down in Liz's small office. Mom and Dad sit on blue stacking chairs, and I'm happy when Camilla sits on the small striped couch next to me, scanning the bookshelves full of thoughtful treatise on spirituality. Liz spends most of our hour talking about religion, probing my parents for clues about why I was having so much trouble figuring out a higher power. I yuck it up secretly, watching my rationalist mom and my new age dad smile and nod politely at Liz's enthusiasm for Mormonism. Mom's eyes glaze over. I wonder what she's thinking.

Mom

I am thinking about dinner. Hannah's counselor is passionately discussing angels and golden plates and heaven, but I am wondering if the cafeteria will be serving the Tater Tots that Hannah dislikes so much.

Hannah

I stop to pee on our way to the cafeteria. Mom tells me that they'll meet me downstairs, and I have to remind her that she has to stay with me cuz I'm not in my room, and I have to be supervised. Her mouth opens in an "O" shape, but she doesn't say anything, and I'm hungry so I don't talk any more. I just go pee and wash my hands. I expect dinner to be awkward, since having families visit is kind of a novelty, and that makes it a spectator sport. The girls watch us, and Mom watches them, and smiles at a new girl sitting alone at a table. The new girl looks away quickly and Mom looks confused, so I lean across the wood table to explain to her that the girl is on orientation and isn't supposed to communicate and could be docked points for smiling back. I get the "O" mouth from her again, and go back to my Tater Tots. The food is pretty gross, as usual, and the only really good thing about the meal is that I don't have to clean up because family is visiting.

Mom

Our next meeting is with Hannah's primary therapist here at Vista. It's Bobbi, Jason's wife and leader of the "blue team." I wonder if calling the groups "teams" creates a feeling of competition, and whether that is their intent. I am calm and almost bored as we wait for Bobbi, and I run an emotional inventory. Not much to account for. Mostly I feel dullness. I notice that Camilla has, probably also out of boredom, relaxed as well. She halfway lies down on the brown leather couch, memorizing sections of *Beowulf*. Paul is reading too, gently turning the pages of the *Salt Lake Tribune*. Hannah is actually nodding off, her head on Paul's shoulder. Bobbi walks in, and she smiles like sunrise. We all get up and follow her energetic steps to her office.

Hannah

The meeting with Bobbi is the best one, and who could be surprised about that? She looks so out of place in her soft blue dress and patent leather heels, but so comfortable too. I guess if you like yourself and you know you do a good job, you can wear anything you want and feel just right. The session is sort of different with my family there, but Bobbi is the same as she always is. She catches me in every inconsistency, and using my new eyes, I can actually see how inconsistent I am.

After the session, Mom gives me a box of goodies. Stationary, clothes, some candy—standard prison package minus the cake with a hacksaw. I give her a bracelet that I made for her in art class . . . another effort that looks like a third-grade project. I can tell that she really loves it and is trying not to cry, and I try to remember the last time I gave her something, not counting the leather pouch at transition, but I can't think of anything.

Goodbye, family. I can't believe I did this to us. I have to say goodbye, and they have to go, and we all have to act like this is somehow normal, like I'm in some fucking boarding school or some such shit, and that they came for a nice visit. I wish I had somewhere private to cry.

Mom

It's been four months since I watched Hannah, curled up in a ball in the dirt of the Utah wilderness, crying to come home. I can see that physically she is more comfortable at Vista, but something is wrong. All the confidence she developed taking care of herself in the wilderness has disintegrated, turned to dust under the constant pummeling she takes in group therapy. I wonder what it must be like to live with rules for every action, every moment. To be pelted by the deepest, most personal questions imaginable every single day. "Who did you sleep with?" they ask her. "Did you do it for drugs? How did you feel after? What else did you do for drugs?"

It is miraculous that there is any Hannah left at all, after the grinding session that I have just witnessed. I wonder, as I always do, if we are doing the right thing. I close my eyes and settle into the middle seat between Paul and Camilla for our flight home, pretending to sleep but trying to pray. I picture Hannah's round face framed by her limp hair, I see her sad eyes in my mind and I wonder what to pray for. I turn inward to search for comfort, but find none. God eludes me.

Hannah

This higher power shit that Liz keeps making me talk about is making my brain bleed. I'm still not really sure why AA says you have to admit the exact nature of your wrong doings to God. Shouldn't God already know how you fucked up? It seems redundant. Liz says that it doesn't matter what I choose to represent my higher power. I can call a rock my higher power. I don't really get that. I sit cross-legged and pick up a hand full of pebbles on the driveway. They lie there in my palm, and I know that I'm supposed to have some sort of quantum theory revelation or something, but in the end they are just rocks. I think to myself that if there is a higher power and it is in a rock, then it is probably everywhere. I wonder if I'm allowed to think about higher power as something that's around me and maybe even in me, but not an object or a thing or a person. Holy shit, I think maybe I get it. God is not a single thing, can't be a single thing, has to be all things, so it doesn't matter what object I assign as God. I picture a glowing light bulb over my head and angels singing, maybe a cymbal crash. Ta-da!

Mom

I am in the kitchen, listlessly making a salad, trying without success to think of nothing, when I hear the screams. I run to Camilla, who is standing in the garage over what looks like a prop from a horror movie. "Mom, get it out of here!" she screams, pointing her finger at the mess. The smell assaults me, the stench of rotting meat, and I draw back until Camilla grabs my arm and pulls me towards her and the carnage. "Get it out!" A closer inspection reveals the entire back leg of a deer, all the way up to the haunch, with our senior Labrador proudly grinning and wagging above it. Not only did our poor old dog manage to drag this huge windfall out of the forest, she somehow squeezed it through the dog door into the garage. Camilla stumbled over it when she went to feed the dogs. I stare at my younger daughter, and reply slowly so she doesn't misunderstand, "You're insane. I'm not touching it!"

Paul's car crunches to a halt outside the garage door at that very moment, and Camilla and I fall over each other trying to get out the door at the same time. "There's a dead deer in the garage," we shout over each other, evoking a confused look on his face. Suddenly it becomes funny, Paul in charge now, a deer hoof sticking out of the big grey garbage can, too big by a foot. Paul sets off to scour the trails with a shovel to lay what's left of the poor animal to rest. Only then do I realize that I haven't thought about Hannah or my spiritual emptiness for five whole minutes. All it took was a dead deer carcass to do it.

Hannah

I sit down to write to Mom about my light bulb moment about my higher power and the rocks, but somehow it doesn't want to come out of me yet. I curl up on the couch and decide to enjoy my idea in private for just a little bit. Instead I write:

Dear Mom,

I'm really happy that you visited me, and I really think we had a good time except for the crying and stuff. Next time you are here maybe we will have time to kickbox, and I'll show you some moves you can use against that old fart that keeps beating you up. Anyway, would you believe it, just after you left a snow storm hit, and it was beautiful, everything white. Sorry you missed it, Cammy! It was so pretty you forget where you are and how fucking cold it is. For a while anyway. The girls here were all running around sticking their tongues out to catch these big fat snowflakes. Remember the Barney show, Mom? "If all the snowflakes were lemon drops and milkshakes" or some such shit like that? That's what it reminded me of, and I got a kick out of watching all these hard asses acting like the little kids on that show. It made me see the soft side, or maybe I should call it the "before" side of these girls. I could see that they were once happy but that they loaded crap on top of their happiness until they couldn't find it anymore cuz it was under a steaming pile. Dig, dig, dig!
Love,
Hannah

Mom

Dear Hannah,

I remember that Barney song. You used to sit in your Barney chair in your Barney nightie and hug your Barney toy while you made me sing it with you over and over again. Personally, I consider this proof of my love for you.

May will mark seven months since you've been gone, and it feels like forever.

I miss you,

Mom

Hannah

Dear Mom,

This might sound weird but I have decided that God is inside me, and I hope you don't think I have delusions of grandeur or anything, but when I feel calm or suddenly understand things, I feel like that is why. I believe that when I did awful things, the little part of me that felt bad about it—that was God. What do you think?

Love,

Hannah

Mom

Dear Hannah,

I doesn't really matter what I think, because God is a very personal belief, but since you asked I will tell you. There's this rabbi named David Aaron who doesn't believe in "God" because it's just a word. He writes that God is what we live in and what lives in us. It is the power that connects us to *each other and to the world around us. Do you remember a time when you gave of yourself, or were kind, or practiced justice? Aaron says that feeling is God. If God is a feeling, then it is, as you say, inside of us.*

When you were little, it was hard to give you an allowance, because the next day you would take it all to school and put it in the charity box. You told me you were giving the money to God so he could help people. I believe that child was well connected to her higher power. I don't think you need to find your higher power, Hannah, I think you just need to reconnect with it.

I love you.

Mom

Hannah

Mom doesn't think my revelation is weird, and neither does Liz or even the bitches. They are real quiet, and I just talk and talk and then they all hug me, even Shelly, and Marshall tells me I'm being emotionally authentic and gives me his wise man look. Cool.

> Dear Mom,
> This Aaron dude sounds interesting. Do you think you could send me the book? I don't think they have it in the library here (snark).
> Love,
> Hannah

Mom

Before mailing the book to Hannah, I mark a section about Adam, when he asks God for a helpmate. God answers, "I will find a helpmate against him." In the Hebrew language the root word for "against" also means "opposite," and "parallel." I tuck a Superman bookmark into the pages, trusting Hannah to figure it out. I smile and seal the envelope.

Hannah

It takes me a while to figure out why Mom highlighted this tedious discussion about the Hebrew word *kenegdo*. I sit with the question for a while, and eureka! I figure out that it must be about group therapy. It blows what's left of my mind to think of these girls as parallel to me, against me, and also my helpmates all at the same time. We are going through the same crap, we are hard on each other and demand honesty, and we also comfort each other. I feel my chest flutter a little bit as I ponder the possibility of trusting them.

Mom

May crawls by, and as Hannah finds her stride in group therapy, I find myself incredibly bored and frustrated with our local therapist and our lack of progress. Paul disagrees.

"I don't know what you expect, Susan," he says, after a session that seems exactly like the last. We say how Hannah is doing. We say how Camilla is doing. We pretend that everything is getting better between us.

"Yes, Paul is being much more positive," I lie.

"Yes, Susan is communicating more directly," he lies.

Our expectations are very different. I am looking for some fundamental change in the way our family communicates, and Paul seems sure that I just need to deal with the fact that I have failed at parenting. Camilla is just plain disgusted.

"She wants to play games with me," she complains. "Did you forget to mention that I'm thirteen?"

The failure of our efforts is in stark contrast to the work that Hannah is doing with her therapists, and I marvel at the difference.

Hannah

Therapy is hard, and even harder after I decide to let the bitches and the therapists know what I'm really thinking. I talk a lot about how I never felt like I fit in with other people, and how hard I tried. I tell them about my bad girl antics, the people I hurt, the pain of doing things I knew were wrong, and how I gloried in the power I had terrorizing my family. Honesty hurts, and some of the family sessions we have over the phone every week are pretty rough, because I tell them how they let me get away with things and how that gave me power over them. I feel so bad after sessions, I wish that we were doing the sessions in person so that I could look at my parents and tell them that I love them and hug them until I squeeze out the pain of the truth.

Instead I write them long letters, trying to make them understand that most of the bad shit is about me and my short-comings. That I know they tried. That it wouldn't have been different with other parents, or other friends.

Dear Mom,

I'm sorry therapy didn't go too well last week. I can tell that it upset you, but it was still great to hear your voice and make contact with the outside world. I'm reading Vonnegut's Slaughterhouse 5 again. I love that book. Did you know it has the serenity prayer in it? I think it's interesting to look at time the way Vonnegut does, all existing at once, cuz it means that I'm with you guys! I'm reading The Red Tent next. Did you read that, Mom?

Oh, could you please send me a non-spiral sketchbook? I'm not allowed to have anything with wire, even though I don't feel like hurting myself any more.

Mom

Hannah is making progress, but I am feeling so low that it is hard to get out of bed in the morning. I try not to let my depression sneak into my letters.

> *Dear Hannah,*
> *I read The Red Tent, and I did like it; Ann Diamante is a fine writer. Right now I'm reading The Curious Incident of the Dog in the Night-Time by Haddon. It's an odd book, with lots of little gems. Like the part where he writes about moving forward in the face of too many choices: "... I made my hand into a little tube with my fingers and I opened my eyes and I looked through the tube so that I was only looking at one sign at a time ..." Lovely. New sketchbook enclosed.*

Hannah

Mom sounds a little overwhelmed with the whole tube-hand thing, but we all have to deal with our own shit I guess.

> *Dear Mom,*
> *Thanks for the sketchbook. I'm not sure what I want to sketch, so I'm letting my hands do it without the involvement of my brain right now.*
> *Love, Hannah*

I mean, I like thinking and talking about heavy stuff, but sometimes I just need a break.

Chapter 12

Mom

June sneaks up on us, and as Hannah methodically deals with her issues, I find myself in an escalating storm of Camilla's bat mitzvah planning, end-of-year activities, school issues, and the never-ending therapy sessions. As Hannah softens, Camilla becomes more intractable, settling into an angry silence, broken only by her irritation at the world around her.

Dear Hannah,

As difficult as May seemed to be, I miss it. Today I took Camilla to shop for some sweats. She was in a terrible mood and yelled at me for going into Gap, since they supposedly use sweatshop labor. Then she complained about the birthday party she was going to at the zoo, since it is cruel and unnecessary to capture and hold captive wild animals in inadequate facilities for our own enjoyment. I'm pretty sure that at the birthday lunch, she'll happily lecture the other little girls about the environmental and ethical issues connected to eating animal flesh. Then on the drive home, she can regale them with information about green fuels and sustainability of our energy sources. I'm just not sure why she isn't invited to more parties (snark).

I have enclosed some pretty, yet safe hair ornaments for you.

Love,

Mom

Hannah

Dear Mom,

I'm sorry Camilla is being an asshole. At least she's not committing lewd acts on the streets of Santa Cruz, or robbing banks. She's probably pretty stressed about her bat mitzvah.

I heard you guys had another earthquake. Did the dogs warn you with their super-animal senses? Did anything break?

I changed rooms today. No more creaky bed and cranky roommate! Yay!

I led deep cleaning at the house today and it went well. I learned to clean, Ma! I also led the campus AA meeting and it went really well. That's all that's going on here. I'll call you later.

Love,

Hannah

Mom

Dear Hannah,

Sorry for all the complaining. I guess we are all stressed about the bat mitzvah. The dogs slept through the earthquake. One month until you get to visit, I hope.

Hannah

Some days I get two or three letters from different people in the family, and it's funny how I feel more connected to them here in Utah than I ever did at home. They are my solid matter in this liquid place. Two of my bitches graduated from the Vista high school and went home, and it's weird to see new girls come in and take their places on the big leather couches, and see how raw and hurt they are. It's like looking through time and seeing what I must have looked like when I got here.

There's no end of the school year for me. I'm still trying to fix my fucked up eleventh grade, and it means that I have to go to school every single day through the summer. Except for the days that I visit home. It isn't really time for me to go home for a visit, but it's Camilla's bat mitzvah, which is a big deal, and so they are giving me special permission. Mom seems a little freaked out, but I know it's cool. Bobbi is spending a lot of time preparing all of us for my visit home. She's super clear about the rules:

1. Hannah will be supervised at all times.
2. Hannah will be supervised at all times.
3. Hannah will be supervised at all times.

I guess you might expect me to feel smothered, rankled, perturbed (how am I doing with my SAT vocabulary words?), but I don't. I feel like the rules are my guard rails, and that I won't have to go into the soupy fog that is my Santa Cruz without some safety. I am definitely freaking out about maybe running into my old friends and worried that all the horrible shit I did with them will seem normal again. I know a lot of them probably think I'm being brainwashed here in Utah. I even know some of them who went through programs like this who think it's all bullshit, but they didn't have Bobbi or Marshall or Liz or my family. If some of these people want to step out of that scene and hang with me some day, that would be cool. But not right now. Right now it's still too scary. Bobbi practices with me, pretending to be one of my old friends. "Keep it simple" is her advice. She pretends to be an old buddy who recognizes me and tries to get me into conversation, and then I say, "Hello, I'm out with my family right now." If I feel like it, I introduce everyone, but I don't have to.

Mom

Too much to do and too much to worry about. I wonder if we are doing the right thing, bringing Hannah into such a chaotic situation, with a weekend full of events and family. I am mired in centerpieces, DJs, and caterers. I try to read the book, *Putting God on the Guest List*, to find balance, but lose patience. I sit down at my familiar place at Hannah's scarred desk and write.

> *Dear Hannah,*
> *You are coming home home home home home! Are you scared? I am. But I'm more excited and happy.*

Hannah

Mom sounds as frantic as a swarm of bees, but I find myself getting calmer. I am getting pretty good at using my Dialectic Behavioral Therapy tools, and I'm sort of looking forward to trying them out in the real world. They started teaching us the magical mystery of DBT in the woods, even though we didn't really know that's what we were doing. We just were supposed to notice the way our bodies reacted to our emotional states. Of course back then I was in withdrawal, and my emotional state was pretty much "crisis," so I probably didn't get that much out of it. But here at Vista, there's a regular DBT class and a whole menu full of tools that we can use to deal with our emotions. I really like that they don't tell us not to feel things. They tell us to be mindful and acknowledge what we are feeling, feel it, and then deal with it.

It makes me realize that life isn't comfortable for anyone all the time, and that it's okay to be uncomfortable without being a full on drama queen about it or judging myself for being a pussy. It's hard to do. We are supposed to practice radical acceptance of our situation, and that's supposed to be our first step. I can do radical. Anyway, we accept, then we cope, and then we move forward and let go. It's complicated and simple at the same time, and it's supposed to help us be honest and direct and assertive, but in a more appropriate way. It makes me feel powerful, like I have the instruction book now. I just hope I can find all the tools I need when Bobbi isn't around to hand them to me. I hope I can find the strength and peace to face all these people who know what I did.

Dear Mom,
Don't worry, everything will be fine. I know you're super busy but do you think you might be able to get a dress for me?

Mom

I take Camilla shopping again, this time to pick out her dress, and a dress for her sister. She is more patient than in the past, holding dresses up thoughtfully, making "Hannah" piles and "Camilla" piles. In the dressing room, she works with utter confidence selecting clothes for Hannah. She chooses a simple soft black dress with a subdued ruffled bodice and thin straps for her sister. I know it is perfect right away, and I can't wait to see Hannah in it. Camilla picks black and white cotton for her own temple dress, sleeveless with a wide skirt and a modest little black shrug out of respect to my Orthodox upbringing. Finally, black chiffon for her evening party, the handkerchief hem swinging gracefully as she walks, the halter top showing off her beautiful shoulders, the result of baling hay and shoveling manure at her volunteer job at a horse rescue.

I hand over my charge card and turn to compliment Camilla on her final choices, but she is already gone, walking towards the exit even as the salesperson rings up the purchases. I turn the smile meant for Camilla towards the sales person and pay.

Hannah

It is the day of my first trip home in nine months, and I lie in bed with my eyes wide open waiting for it to be late enough to get up. My roommate sleeps, her breathing deep and regular as though it is a normal day. I gaze at my duffel bag, mentally running through the contents, but I know I have everything I need.

Finally it is time to wake up, go through morning rituals, line up and eat breakfast in the small cafeteria. Afterwards I wait for the van to pull up while Liz stands behind me with her hand on my shoulder. My sendoff is so solemn you might think I am being sent off to war. Or a convent. Or something serious and once in a lifetime-y. The staffer takes me to the airport in the same white van we use to get around town, so it is familiar except for the fact that there is only one staffer and I am sitting in front and nobody is staring at us. In town everyone knows that Vista is where the "crazy" or "bad" kids live, and they all know the van that transports us, always with two staffers, to the doctor, the gym, or, as the townies might tell you, "the loony bin." Sometimes kids walk past our gated and fenced property at night, and you can hear them whispering dares to each other. "Wake them up. See if you can get one of them to look out." But at the Salt Lake City airport, we are just another white van, and at the airport, I am just another traveler.

It seems to take forever for the Great Salt Lake to disappear, but suddenly we are over the mountains of San Jose. And then there's Dad, waiting with a big smile and open arms and a squishy hug. "Mom and Camilla wanted to come, but we didn't want you to be overwhelmed." It's okay with me cuz I haven't had a chance to talk to him alone in a long time, and once we get home the craziness is bound to hit. He tells me that the house is a real circus, and that I'll stay in Camilla's room since company will be staying in my room. It's weird, but I'm actually happy that I don't have to stay in my room. There are just too many memories in there.

When we finally pull in at home, I get about a hundred hugs from the family that is there already, cousins and uncles and aunts who are all crowding into our big house. I also find out that there are no memories lurking in my old room. Mom shoveled most of my shit out of there and painted it a deep slate grey. I hate it.

"I thought it was going to be yellow," I complain. Mom just shrugs. How can my house change so much in just nine months? There seems to be no trace of me, like I don't belong here or like I'm forgotten.

I guess everyone is too busy to notice that I am a little freaked out. I'm feeling tired and maybe a little defeated, so I tell Mom I'm going upstairs to take a nap. She hugs me and says "Okay, honey" or something like that and lets me go, and I step back and we both stare at each other, and I realize that she doesn't know what I am waiting for.

"You have to escort me," I remind her. It's weird, but after a moment she takes my hand and we go upstairs and she settles down to work in the alcove outside of Camilla's room while I rest with the door open.

I lie down on Camilla's "guest bed" that used to be my bed a long time ago, but I can't rest. I keep feeling like there's something I should be doing or not doing, or thinking about or talking about. I guess Vista has me all trained up. Camilla comes in after a while, and she lies down on her bed and sticks her earphones in, listening to her bat mitzvah stuff, I guess. I watch her and push back the tears, remembering all the bad shit I did to her, the stuffed animals and the money and the mean words. Now her earphones are like a wall keeping me and my feelings away. I'm ready to hug and make up, but she's stepped back out of my reach and left me alone. I guess I deserve it. I did try to write to her lots of times though, but I guess it was too late cuz she never wrote back:

> Dear Camilla,
> My six months sober is in two days. By the time you get this, it probably already happened. Tomorrow I get to go downtown with my therapist Liz to look for triggers that will make me go bad again, like vodka or cigarettes. I'm not worried, just excited to be doing something different.

> Dear Camilla,
> How are you? I hear you're doing really well on the swim team. Mom sent me the drawing you did of the dogs and it's really good. I put it up on my wall. I think we should do some art together when I get home. Will you let me do your hair and makeup for your party?

> Dear Camilla,
> I'm so glad that you came to Utah with Mom and Dad. I know how hard group can be. But I had fun with you. Are you reading any good books? I'm reading a lot of therapy books. They are actually pretty interesting. Please write.

It's not that Camilla ignores me completely. Every now and then she gives Mom a drawing to send. But she never writes. I guess she has nothing to say to me. She doesn't say anything to me now either. But after a while, she comes and sits on my bed, at the other end of it, and listens to her music or whatever with her eyes closed. I reach out with my toe and make contact, and she doesn't move away, and that makes me feel happy and hopeful, and I finally close my eyes and rest.

Mom

It's like having a toddler again. I have to know where Hannah is all the time. I think it will be impossible to get anything done, but after a while I realize that the closeness is a comfort to both of us. Hannah stays mostly at my side, or at the side of another family member, working in the kitchen or writing place cards in her beautiful calligraphy hand while she sits on the deck. I look at her across the patio, and see lost treasure, found again after nine months, chipped and battered from trials, its patina making it more beautiful than ever.

Hannah

It's kind of funny. I'm pretty sure everyone thinks it's bizarre that Mom drops everything and goes with me every time I have to pee. I guess they didn't get the "supervised at all times" memo, or they think it's stupid, but to tell you the truth, I don't want to be alone, and I think I might have stayed glued to Mom and Dad even if there were no rules. Everyone tries to act all normal around me, but it's a weird and sort of strained normal, I guess what you might call an elephant in the room normal.

Mom

I don't really know how to act. So I try not to act. I just try to be present in each moment of the weekend so I can tuck it away and take it out to enjoy later.

Hannah

Camilla's bat mitzvah is the reason I get to come home so soon, and it's a wall-to-wall Jew-Rama the whole time. Rehearsals and dinners and lunches and brunches and parties. We finish centerpieces and make out place cards, bake and cook and do dishes and play backgammon. I meet new family and get to see everyone else I love. Friday night at temple, I say the blessings over the candles with all the women in my family, and you can feel the hum of love vibrating right through all of our linked arms, and I think of my higher power again. Saturday morning Rabbi Paula leads us through the service, warm and sweet and deep in her music. You just can't help but know she's the real thing—she practically glows pink.

Mom drapes the prayer shawl she made around Camilla's shoulders, and I cry a little, remembering how that feels like a hug. I get to pray with Camilla during the service, and our voices sound so good and strong together, and when we are done she looks up at me like she used to, her almond eyes seeing the good in me. Camilla does great with her bat mitzvah speech; that must be so hard for her. She speaks about sacrifice, and I remember that I spoke about sacrifice at my bat mitzvah too, and I wonder what it is about our family that makes us both look at our readings that way.

At the party that night, people I haven't seen in a long time come up to me and ask, "What have you been doing with yourself? Have you started looking at colleges yet?" and it makes me realize that Mom must not talk a whole lot about me to other people. That makes me feel good and bad at the same time.

Mom
Most everything goes smoothly. There is some family drama and some catering failures, but I find myself not caring. Nothing can poison my weekend. Except maybe thinking about Hannah leaving for Utah Sunday afternoon. I push the thought away.

Hannah
Sunday comes so fast. The morning is a blur. Camilla and I lie there in our twin beds and laugh about how I started the dancing

at her Saturday night party (I thought the boy I asked was going to pee himself), and we talk about what to wear to brunch, and then all the out of town people meet us at a restaurant and take pictures of each other. Then suddenly my happiness at leaving Utah flips upside down, and I am at the airport with Mom and Dad and Camilla, and I swear I hear the ripping sound when it's time for them to let me go through the security line. I press my six-month chip into Camilla's hand and tell her I'll be getting another one soon. Then I get on the plane.

This time the mountains come first, then the lake, the white van, and finally Vista. Back to lines and learning and truth telling and growth and bitches and bad food and no boys. Back to DBT and daily exercise and making beds and making it to twelfth grade. Back to work. I sit on the edge of my bed after the lights are out, and in the dark I pretend that my roommate's breaths are my sister's and that the stirring in the hallway isn't a staffer, it's my dad checking the doors and shutting off lights. Then I lie down on my bed and try to dream.

Mom

The house is quiet, and I miss Hannah terribly. Her visit was short, and we were all on our best behavior so I can't really tell how she's doing, but I can tell for sure that she was happy to be home and determined to move forward with her life. I wander the house aimlessly for a while, lost in the too-quiet aftermath, missing the loving confusion of family. I look at the sink full of dishes and the mountain of laundry and decide that it will all get done in due time, and I go to bed, forgiving myself for the moment.

Hannah

It's hard to be back at Vista, but I know what I want now, and I know it's not going to be easy. It's taken a while, but I finally realize that I'm in a garden full of lies, and that the person I am lying to, the person I've always been lying to, is me. By the time I decide to make my way out of my garden, my lies have grown into a fucking forest. Mostly it's my bitches and my therapists who are helping me find my way out. They make me look at everything real close, and then help me find the path forward. Turns out it is not okay to act crazy so people will like you or think you're funny. Using drugs as a harmless social aid is not harmless. Cutting doesn't give you control, it just gives you scars, both inside and out.

Mom

I want to move forward, but I don't feel like Paul and Camilla and I are getting anywhere with the therapist we see in Santa Cruz. I tell Hannah about my doubts. "I just don't get anything from her, except maybe bad advice." Hannah asks what our therapy is like, and so I tell her about how the therapist thinks we should make a reward and consequence chart for Camilla, and how Dad is supposed to tell me three nice things before he is permitted to say anything critical. I don't tell Hannah about how Paul counts them off on his fingers: "You're pretty, I liked dinner, and it's great that you go to all the school functions." That buys him permission to say, "I don't like how you talk across the house," or "I can't stand it when you interrupt me," or "You are stressing me with your obsessing about the kids." I tell Hannah that it all feels punitive and awkward and a big fat waste of money, which is becoming scarcer. When I compare our local therapist to the professionals Hannah is working with, it seems like we're being operated on by a clumsy surgeon using a wooden spoon.

"Kick her to the curb, Momma," Hannah instructs me.

Hannah

When I was at home and Camilla finally started talking to me, she told me that creative people make the best evil geniuses and criminals, cuz they can justify all their actions in a twisted way that makes them acceptable in a moral world. It made me think of addiction right away. Now I sit in therapy and listen to the new girls who are just coming in try to justify all the shit they do for drugs—the running away, the stealing, and the sex—and I smile inside and think *Dang!* They are pretty creative! Since I'm trying not to lie to myself or justify my actions any more, I think I'm going to start using all the creative energy I'm saving in some different ways. I pull out my sketchbook and work on cartoons of the new bitches hiding behind their justifications. In my drawings, their justifications are walls, cages, and big boulders that can roll right on top of them and kill them.

Mom

Our therapist doesn't seem surprised when I tell her that we are terminating our sessions. "I'm sorry," I state flatly, "but after a year, we just aren't getting any traction at all." She spends our last session talking about some goals to pursue as a couple and then apologizes, looking at me and touching my arm gently, saying, "I'm sorry I wasn't able to help." Then she glances sideways at Paul. Paul doesn't notice, or pretends not to, just as he has not noticed any need to change his behavior. He has always looked at therapy as something I needed, to deal with my failure as a parent. I wonder to myself about his opinion of me, and with a flash of anger wonder if I will be able to forgive him. We walk out of the office for the last time, and I immediately feel better.

Hannah

Everything reminds me of addiction, it's so sick! We watch *The Wizard of Oz* and notice how once you know there's an old dude behind the curtain, the illusion of the great and powerful wizard is shot. That's how I feel these days, like a curtain has been pulled back and I am peeking around the edges and saying, "Why hello, Mr. Wizard." I tell the girls in group, cuz I tell them everything, the big stuff and the little stuff too, cuz sometimes the little stuff turns into big stuff once the group helps you look at it.

Mom

Hannah is putting in school time seven days a week, trying to finish eleventh grade this summer. Paul and I agree to put off discussing school with her until we're sure that she will be ready for her senior year. Now it looks like she will finish the school year in time to start twelfth grade in September.

Hannah

Going to school seven days a week is like speed dating. You go really fast and learn as much as you can by trying to ask the right questions and using your time well. I surprise myself by doing well, and I'm feeling pretty good about it.

Mom

Hannah is doing great, and Bobbi is talking regularly about next steps in our weekly parent calls. I know that I'm supposed to be happy—"Yay, we did the right thing, it's working!"—but all I really feel is dread. Paul and I find ourselves at yet another decision point about how to help Hannah. I'm sick of talking about it, but we have to come to a decision and so we talk about it some more.

"It feels like Hannah should come home," I say. "She's earned it." We are sitting on the deck on a hot August afternoon with bowls of watermelon, and I find myself feeling impatient and disagreeable overall. I tap my fork on the edge of the bowl, knowing this irritates him. He is level and quiet, as usual, so I try to bait him. "Don't you want her to come home?"

He replies with exaggerated calm, as though to a small child. "Susan, where will she go? She has one year of high school left. Are we going to throw her back into Santa Cruz, with the same friends at the same school?"

I shake my head. "Paul, she's not the same person that we sent away."

He is unmovable, putting his bowl down on the glass table carefully before turning to me to answer.

"You know a transition program will help her readjust to normal life."

I shake my head against the shame of putting my child in a group home.

"How can putting her in a group home help her? We aren't those people."

His answer is soft, but firm.

"I want her home too, Susan. But I want Hannah to stay healthy. This is the last chance we'll have to help her."

How can bringing our child home hurt her? I know the answer before I form the question. I retreat from the deck to Hannah's room, sitting down at her desk, and opening my laptop. I read about sobriety and peer pressure and patterns. I call Bobbi alone, without Paul. Bobbi is a statistics course in troubled teen science. Fifty to ninety percent of teens will relapse at least once, she tells me. Almost anything can trigger relapse, she adds. Being around old friends? Check. But being socially isolated can be just as bad. Hearing a certain tune? Check. Over-confidence? Check. Reintroducing teens to "normal" life slowly increases the odds of success, Bobbi explains. Is this real, or are we the victims of institutionalized money sucking?

I try without success to find a local support group, my hope fading like a sunset turning into night. In the end, we look at our options and decide that we have no choice. Hannah will go to Vista's group home, the Teen Living program. Now we have to tell her.

Hannah

Woo-hoo, I'll be finished with eleventh grade in about three weeks! I ask about what comes next, but as usual nobody tells you anything around here for sure. The standard line is, "That depends entirely on you." I kick back on my bed and glance over at my latest roommate, who is still in the sullen stage. It will be so good to leave here. To wear cute clothes again, to eat fast food at my favorite noodle place, and work on an easel with good paints. I have a little stomach jolt thinking about Dylan, and wonder if he has a new girlfriend, but I push him out of my head and think about my friends and how cool it will be to see them at the farmers' market. I get ready for bed and look around the room. It is neat, and the few things I have will fit easily into one bag. It feels light, living this way. I hug my stuffed dog and wonder if Camilla will let me move into her room for a while if I promise not to borrow money or dismember any of her stuffed animals. I don't think I'm ready to move into my old room, especially since Mom painted it gray. What was she thinking?

Mom

Paul and I sit down at the dining room table like we are lowering ourselves into the front pew at a funeral. Maybe it's our dread that makes the call go so badly. Paul is the one to tell her. I make him do it. He is direct.

"Hannah, we've been talking a lot about how to support you through the end of high school and we've decided that it's best if you finish school in Utah. We're sending you to Vista Teen Living."

He hasn't quite gotten the words all the way out when Hannah starts wailing like a widow. Her shrieks come from some deep primal place, frightening me, bringing back memories from the bad times when she was half wild. I clasp my hands over my mouth as though that can stop her screaming, tears wetting my fingers as they press into my cheeks, the phone large and then small again as I rock back and forth in my chair. I try to talk to her.

"Hannah? Hannah!?" My voice gets louder and louder with panic, but she is gone, she had tried to move closer to us, but we pushed her away, and now the only sounds of grief I can hear are my own. Paul scrapes his chair back and draws a deep breath, as though he wishes he could suck the words back in.

Hannah

No. No. No! No more Utah. No more bitches. No more therapists. I. Am. Done. What more can they want from me? I slept in the snow for three months and ate rice and beans out of an old coffee can most every meal. I hiked for miles and got so filthy that you couldn't see the color of my skin. I came to treatment and did my therapy, I journaled endlessly, I cleaned toilets and scrubbed grout with a toothbrush, I lined up for lunch and ate their crap food, exercised every day, and finished eleventh grade in record time. I gave up my art.

Why are they punishing me? Don't they want me anymore? I throw the phone as hard as I can, but Bobbi's office has carpet on the floor so there is no bang, and no flying parts. She stands as the phone hits the floor, and I hit the door and look for a way out, any way out. Staffers run down the hall from both directions, and I know there's no escape. They take my arms—*Don't touch me!*"—and I scream every bad word that I can think of. "*Niggers! Homos! Fucking whores!*" Then I sink to the floor and let myself cry. I want to go home.

Mom

The letters from Hannah stop, the last few letters she wrote before our disastrous decision dropping out of our big mailbox like confetti after a party is over. I mourn the loss of my daughter all over again, and then I get angry. In the end it takes me almost a week before I can write to her.

Dear Hannah,
I'm sorry that you got busted back to Reorientation after
eight months. That's a long fall. As you might imagine,
I've thought about our last session quite a bit. I love you,
Hannah, but I must say that your tantrum, and that's
what it was, seems pretty self-indulgent.

I take my hands off the keyboard and think about my daughter. I imagine her lying on her bed in her pink punishment scrubs, refusing food, silent. I wipe my tears and think about my mother and how she loved me through my tumultuous childhood. But even she had her limits. This is my limit. I am here. I write without thinking, the words rushing through my shaking hands.

When I am upset, depressed, or even angry at my life,
I end up thinking about your bubbe and her life.

I write to Hannah about her grandmother then, and the sweet family life that she had as a child in Hungary. I drift and float with my long dead mother above the orchards of Sighet, Hungary, trying to recapture the sound of her voice as she told me her story. But my drifting is not getting the point across, and so I move on. There are some things I need to say to Hannah.

Your bubbe was transported to Auschwitz when she
was sixteen. Your age. Bubbe tells me that she was jammed
into a cattle car so tightly that she couldn't even sit. There
was no food, and no water, and mothers gave urine to their
children to keep their tongues from swelling.

I sit back and think about how bitterly Hannah complains about the structure at Vista—the strict dress code, how she has to share her room with a crabby roommate, and how she despises the cafeteria food. I have a surge of anger at her, and at myself for raising such an entitled child.

Your bubbe spent eighteen months in the concentration camp. Her head was shaved, and she was given a tattered gray dress removed from a corpse. She ate bread mottled with mealworms, she drank soups made with gristle and fat, and she worked every day until she was allowed to drop onto a wooden "shelf" with seven other starving and diseased girls to try to sleep.

I tap the keyboard so hard that the clicks of the keys sound like an abacus racking up all Hannah's complaints about moving into a teen living program instead of coming home. We never had a chance to explain our decision before she exploded in anger and grief. How can I explain to her that her struggle is being played out against a larger backdrop of events? That she is part of a whole? That she brought herself to this juncture?

Your bubbe never wanted to talk about what happened to her in the war years. But I begged to know. And when she told me, it changed my life.

I wrote it all down. I told Hannah the stories about mothers forced to choose which of their children would live and which would die. Stories about families who risked their lives for each other. Stories about how people lived with dignity and joy in spite of their terrible circumstances. I wrote about how her bubbe made her way to Canada and started a new life alone. I wrote and I cried, the crumpled tissues piling up on the floor of Hannah's room like my discarded dreams of a perfect family. It was not fair, what happened to my mother. And it was not fair, what was happening to me. And my spoiled, self-centered child is pissed because she has to eat Tater Tots three times a week?

Your bubbe taught me that life is full of impossible choices, Hannah, and that we have to capture joyful moments even in the worst times. She taught me about family and survival, about focusing your energy on helping others and accepting help when offered. Most importantly, Hannah, your bubbe taught me about finding the courage to reinvent yourself and face a new world.

I sit back and reread the pages I've written through tears that won't stop. I need Hannah to know. About choices, family, survival, and courage. I blow my nose, then get up from Hannah's desk and wander up the stairs to the bookshelf in my bedroom. There I gently lift the photo of my mother, my father at her side, her two children in front of her like a shield against all she had endured. I take the picture back to Hannah's room and sit down at the scarred desk.

I'm sure you can understand why my mother has always been my hero.

Would she understand? I stare at the picture on my desk, and let a mental collage of my childhood form in my mind; my mother smiling and laughing.

Bubbe taught me what the human spirit can overcome, that harshness in life makes happiness more full, that living among hateful people does not diminish one's capacity for love.

Bubbe taught me to live life in a practical manner, to accept what cannot be changed, to move forward in the best way possible, with all the speed I could muster. She showed me it was of no use to dwell in the past, or to yearn for what might have been. Instead, she always encouraged me to look forward, to fight for what I wanted and believed in.

I remember my mother, holding her first grandchild. Hannah was only hours old, and all the smiles I have ever seen fade next to the smile that lit up my mother's face that day. She loved Hannah completely at that moment, and every moment after that until she died, when her first granddaughter was eight.

You, Hannah, were the culmination of Bubbe's dreams to rebuild the family she lost. I think that gives you a responsibility for how you choose to live your life.

Crying again, this time with the fear that I will drive Hannah away, I wipe my eyes one more time and finally find the courage to write the hard truth of what I'm feeling.

So, for all of these reasons, I am incredibly ashamed, Hannah, when you call someone hateful names as you did during your tantrum. I am upset and angry when you indulge yourself in melodrama, and I am frustrated when you allow yourself to stagnate. I acknowledge that you are challenged to find your best self right now. I understand that Teen Living is not what you want. But I do not accept your anger, your reticence, your drifting, and your laziness. I am shocked and furious that after all we have gone through as a family you could threaten going back "to the way things were," as you screamed over the phone.

Life, a happy life, takes work and forward motion. It takes both joy and sadness, and the ability to live in both of those states without being incapacitated. We are responsible to those who came before us, and to those who love us now.

The things that happened to you were tough, Hannah. The drugs, the social scene, the abusive boyfriend, the betrayal. You need to talk about these things, put them in perspective, and put them behind you. I have spent my life

*holding up my own fears and my tears against the back-
drop of what my mother went through. Perhaps you should
try that, and see if it doesn't give scale to your problems.*

I stop typing, anger drying my tears, and wonder how honest I dare to be with her. I decide then to give her the whole truth, hoping it would be a gift, and not a burden.

*Dad and I are going through tough times right now,
Hannah. You are in a treatment center in Utah, and
Camilla is going through her own personal version of hell.
The economy went bust, and Dad's business hit a big stall
just as our expenses skyrocketed. Dad and I are both dealing with health issues. I live with shame and frustration.
But we still try to measure our good fortune instead of our
bad and make every day as good as it can be. The point is,
we each have a choice to make, every day. Even if it is in
our nature to be pessimistic, we can still choose to live as
optimists. We can take charge of the things that we can
control, and move forward.*

Why waste time with misery?

Hannah

Bobbi brings the letter to me herself, and drops it on the bed next to me. I uncurl out of my fetal position as she walks out of the room, and pull the letter out of the envelope. No stationary this time, no funny pictures, just a lot of type on white paper, and a plain white envelope. I sit up and get ready to read the letter, expecting to get mad, formulating a nasty response before I even unfold the thick sheaf of paper. Then I read.

I read the letter again, and then I fold it up, but the truth doesn't get any smaller. I go to the bathroom to wash my face and I look in the mirror for a long time. I step into the hall and see Bobbi leaning against the wall, waiting.

Mom

I try on words for the way I'm feeling, but none of them fit, and I discard them lazily, one at a time. I sit on a lawn chair, the mesh scratchy and uncomfortable in the late August heat, and wonder what Hannah is feeling instead. She would be uncomfortable too, sitting on the floor in pink punishment scrubs, making up for the crazed tantrum she threw earlier in the month. She isn't allowed to use the phone for personal calls anymore, but Bobbi tells us that she is making amends to the people she hurt with her ugly words and behaviors. We wait to hear of the things that will create her future. Is she participating in her therapy? Will she still finish eleventh grade? Is there an opening at Teen Living, the euphemistic name for the group home affiliated with her program? Will the local charter school accept her? We try to feel good about Hannah "graduating" from residential treatment, but we are tired. Paul and I lie in bed at night, talked out and tuckered out from the long year we've spent in twice-weekly therapy, silently holding hands. We have nothing left to say. We wait for news.

Hannah

Dear Mom and Dad,
I will graduate in time. No words. I love you.
Hannah

Mom

If August was like walking through sucking mud, September is like running fast on dry track. In the first week of September, Hannah finally finishes eleventh grade, and an opening comes up at Teen Living. Paul, alone this time, is going to check Hannah out of Vista Residential Treatment Center and into Teen Living. I will stay home and get Camilla settled into eighth grade in Santa Cruz. Paul packs with grim determination, zipping up his little bag as though securing our decision to move Hannah to a group home. I try to reassure him.

"She sounded fine in last week's session."

He doesn't say anything, but nods and kisses my lips lightly. His "Bye, Camilla" is absorbed into her silence, and he hits the stairs and starts the long trip to Utah.

Hannah

Wow, Dad is really on edge. I guess the Teen-zilla act I pulled last month did that. I feel like a jerk, but I don't know how to tell him that, so I take his hand and pull him into the living room, where the rest of the bitches are waiting on the big leather couches for our very last session.

Mom

I don't want to pick up the phone when it rings. But I think of Paul, doing the dirty work in Utah and so I do, sitting on the sagging edge of our bed. "Paul?"

There is a pause, and then a broken voice, rippling through what sounds like tears. What has Hannah done? Has she hurt herself? Has she hurt someone else? Is she crazy again?

"I'm here. It's been a long day, but I got Hannah settled in to her new place. It's nice. Comfortable." Nice? Comfortable? He could be talking about a Hilton. I ask why he's upset.

"I'm not upset."

"You're crying."

"Not really. I mean not because I'm upset. It's Hannah." I want to shake the answers out of the phone. I take a deep breath instead.

"Tell me what happened."

"When I got there, they had session like usual, but because it was Hannah's last one, every girl was supposed to end by letting Hannah know how she affected her. I was floored. They all look up to her, even with all the crap she's pulled. I guess Hannah spent the last month telling them she's sorry, she's scared, she's lost, and working really hard. They said they watched Hannah pull it together. One girl said Hannah saved her. That she saved her life. That she wants to be like Hannah."

Hannah

It's pretty profound to hear that you made a positive difference in someone's life. I felt stupid crying, but when the girls hugged me, their cheeks were wet too, and I could see that Dad was crying too in that man way, when they're trying to look like they're not crying but just have something in their eyes. I'm pretty proud and ready and okay, but a little scared to leave this place that kept me safe while I figured out my past and maybe a little bit of my future too.

Mom

The girls in her group hugged her and whispered promises that they would be strong and they would work hard. Like her. I feel the tingling of a sensation I thought was long gone and when I look for words to fit what I am feeling, this time I find them. Hope. Pride. Relief.

Chapter 13

Hannah

I thought I would be upset, watching Dad's rental car pull out of the driveway of my new suburban digs. But now that I'm here, I'm a little excited. And maybe nervous. Teen Living is different from Vista in a lot of ways. First of all, it's an actual house, a big one, with a door that opens onto a street in a neighborhood. It's stucco and wood, with neat flower beds and a green lawn. There are no locked gates, no cafeteria, and no gym. Instead there's a kitchen, and a family room with a big TV, and a living room with beige carpeting on the floor, and big tweed couches that are a little scratchy. There are seven bedrooms, not unusual in Salt Lake City I'm told, and two twin beds per bedroom. Only three of the bedrooms are for residents, and the dude that meets us, Joshua, tells us they are all occupied.

"Everyone's at school right now, Hannah," he says, "including my daughter. She's three now, and she lives here too, with me and my wife, Karyn."

Dad takes my bag and a box of bedding stuff downstairs to my new room, and I follow after him. The walls are plain white, and there's a window that looks out to the backyard. I open the window and look out at the patch of backyard, complete with a barbeque on the patio, and notice that there are no locks or bars. I guess they actually trust us by the time we get here. I'll have to share a bathroom with my roommate and two other girls down the hall, but the bathroom is bigger than the one at Vista, and nicer, with a double sink and white tile floor.

The house starts to fill up around 3:30, right after Dad leaves, hugging me quickly in his way, making me a little relieved that Mom didn't come. The first person home is Karyn, a plumpish, thirty-something with a wiggly little kid.

"I'm Vicky," the imp screams at me, blond curls bouncing as she jumps on and off the couch. "Are you going to live here now?"

I nod, not knowing the rules about interacting with her, but the next people who come through the door yell right back at her.

"Hi, Vicky, who did you bring home today? Where did you find her?"

Vicky points at me. "She was here already. I don't know who brunged her!" I laugh for the first time in a long time, and then see a familiar face come through the door. It's Katie, from Wilderness, and right behind her is Maggie.

"Maggie! Katie!" I rush them like a rabid pit bull, and they catch me in a group hug, talking all at once and introducing me to the other girls. Katie will be my roommate, and Maggie is just down the hall, and suddenly, just like that, I know it's all going to be okay.

Mom

Paul is bone tired by the time he gets home, but I grill him anyway.

"What was her room like? Are the house parents nice? Did you meet any of the girls?"

He can't tell me much, he had to leave before anyone was there, but he tosses me a handbook that details the expectations of the Teen Living program. There will be six girls living there, and they'll take turns cooking. They will be expected to clean their rooms every Saturday, and the house's common areas on Sunday. Two hours of study time a day is enforced during the school year, but she has no other scheduled activities or obligations, except for a weekly therapy session with her Teen Living therapist, Aaron, and a weekly session with her new chemical dependency counselor, Tammy. The residents have a 10:00 p.m. curfew on weekdays, and 12:00 midnight on weekends. Something catches in my throat. Is she ready for this?

Hannah

Dear Mom,

It's actually pretty cool here at Teen Living. The neighborhood is normal, and there are no gates or alarms on the doors. There are six girls including me. We all get along pretty good, and it's nice to be a roommate instead of a patient, though we still have to pee in a cup for drug testing whenever they ask us. The food is decent. More family style than cafeteria. No Tater Tots—yay! We take turns cooking, and we all clean up. Joshua and Karyn are the house parents, and they're okay. They have this little kid named Vicky. I have been calling her Icky tho, cuz she's always sticky and snotty. She's about three and a future inmate of the Vista program for sure. Honestly I don't know why people would want to raise their kid around a bunch of recovering addicts, but hey, it's a living. I'm excited about starting school.

Love,

Hannah

P.S. They let me have a razor! No more Jungle Jane.

Mom

Arrangements are finally complete for Hannah to start at a local charter school that promises a college prep education. Our choices are fairly limited, but that's okay, since it limits the amount of agonizing we have to do. As out-of-state parents, we are expected to pay, but the fees seem reasonable. The group home will "only" cost six thousand a month, and the school's tuition is less than three thousand for the year. A bargain.

Hannah

It's exciting to be normal-ish and devoid of life-shattering drama. I get up and get dressed and get in a van and go to school a lot like normal people do. It's a pretty small school and pretty new. I guess they've only been open for a few years, and the building is really nice and really clean, with wide halls and gray metal lockers inside. I'll take all the normal classes, plus a leadership class that they require, which is pretty cool. There're only about five hundred of us here, and looking at the family resemblances makes me wonder if they got the word that polygamy is illegal.

Mom

I'm glad that Hannah likes her new school. Study time is a part of her daily life at the group home, so she's doing very well. I suppose that the handsome Italian exchange student probably has something to do with it too. She reveals to me that she plans to kiss him before she graduates in June. I laugh, but I'm nervous, hearing about boys, about her walks to the ice cream store and out to the movies with her friends. She's earned a cell phone now, but she still writes, a habit I'm happy for, because it's nice to have days-long conversations on paper, and to be able to revisit them. I write to her too.

Dear Hannah,
I have to get used to hearing about your shenanigans. You were so young when we sent you to Vista. It freaks me out to know you are allowed out until 10:00 p.m. every night and midnight on weekends. I have trouble remembering you are a high school senior now!

Dear Mom,
Things are going great. I walked to the store with Maggie today and then I peed in a half-pipe.

Dear Hannah,
Why on earth would you pee in a half-pipe?

Dear Mom,
I had to go.

I fold her letters, with their doodles and sketches, into their envelopes and smile at the fact that Hannah is still going to be Hannah. And then the letter I am hoping for and dreading arrives.

Dear Mom,
Do you think I can go to college?

Mom

I talk to Hannah's new therapist, Aaron, about Hannah's interest in college. He is open to following Hannah's lead. "Susan, she has to be able to stand success and failure." I finally send her a letter with as much enthusiasm as I can muster.

Dear Hannah,
I definitely think you should apply to go to college. Have you thought about which schools?

That stops me in my tracks. Realizing that she might never come home, that she could pick a school far away from us and all her bad memories. And then I wonder about the money. Where would we get the money? I decide to worry about that later, if she gets in. Her answer comes fast, the writing bold and sure on the note card.

> *I want to go to an art school, Mom. I know that's not smart and it might not be possible, but that's what I want. I don't think I can be anything else. I don't want to be anything else.*

I put the letter down and flip open my laptop. It takes Google a whole .42 seconds to spit out over a million results and I feel my eyebrows rise. Is there that much demand? That many talented young people? I start mining the results, and discover that lots of the programs are quickie degrees, designed to help students get jobs in graphic design, or marketing. I wonder if that's the way to go, and I prepare to swallow my academic snobbery as a final course to all the crow I've eaten over the last few years.

Hannah

I know Mom and Dad have spent about a billion dollars on me over the past couple of years, but I don't see any way I can do this without asking them for more. I sit in front of the computer staring at pictures of college students in front of easels, in glass blowing studios and lounges. I try to see myself.

Mom

Hannah sends me a list. I could have saved some time and just printed out the "top-ranking art schools" from *U.S. News and World Report*. Hannah is aiming high, and I don't know if it's smart to support her, or maybe try to manage her expectations.

Aaron reminds me, "It's her decision, and her consequences, and you can't and shouldn't protect her." Can that be right? Hannah wants to apply to schools in Rhode Island, Illinois, Georgia, Florida, and California. But she has a problem. She hasn't produced work in almost two years. She is acutely aware of her disadvantage.

> Dear Mom,
> Yes, I would like to see some schools over break, but I am worried about portfolio reviews. I mean I would have to use art from when I was fifteen really. How would that work?

I decide to go all in, and I write what I believe to be the truth.

> *Dear Hannah,*
> *You were more talented at fifteen than most people ever are. If you really want this we will help you.*
> *Love,*
> *Mom*

Hannah

I ruined a lot of the work I had at home in drug-driven frenzies, so I ask Mom to contact my high school art teacher to see if she held on to anything. I start sketching a lot, and it's like opening a creaky door, I can practically hear the hinges in my head. I figure I need some new stuff, some good grades, and a killer essay to even have a chance. I talk to Aaron about how I will feel if I crash and burn, and then I realize that even if I fail, I'll feel better than if I never try at all.

Mom

Hannah's art teacher has everything! She lays the fat brown cardboard portfolio down on one of the big studio tables, and unwinds the string closure. Out comes a tumble of pieces. Some are sharp and angry reflections of Hannah's fifteen-year-old state of mind, but there are also some softer works, reflective of the peace she found here in this art studio.

I haven't seen any of this work before, and I am stunned. The teacher goes over each one with me, making suggestions on which to choose and why, and giving me the name of a good photographer to transform them into portfolio pieces. She hugs me hard as I leave. "Please let me know what happens."

Hannah

I know I have to do well in school, and high school here is okay. Pretty basic. I'm an outsider at this school, and I pretty much stick to my roomies and some other outliers like the foreign exchange students. Who leaves Italy and goes to Utah, anyway? Weird. My last semester at Vista I got straight As, but I didn't completely trust the report card since I thought maybe they dumbed down shit for our drug-ravaged brains. But I get straight As again the first semester here at Paradigm, and I'm stoked. Maybe somebody at some college will notice.

> Dear Mom,
> I feel like a genius here at Paradigm, but I guess all it really takes is sitting down every night and doing two hours of homework in a structured environment during quiet time at a group home. Who knew?
> Love,
> Hannah

I know that Mom and Dad are worried. I mean, who goes to art school? Most of the kids I took art with didn't. Their parents convinced them to major in something "real" and take an art minor or something. Even Mom takes a shot at it.

Dear Hannah,

Dad and I have known you were an artist since you held your first chubby crayon. I respect that art is not something you do, but who you are. But I want you to think about how life is. If you go to a mainstream university and study art you can also find a way to support your art. You've always been great at web design and digital art. What do you think?

Love,

Mom

Dear Mom,

Don't worry, a good art school probably won't even accept me, but I want to try. I don't care about having money or a corporate job or some shit like that. I just want to make art because art helps to make me whole.

Love,

Hannah

Mom

Hannah is just about to turn seventeen, but she's more sure of her direction than I am today. I ask Paul, and he seems sure too. "She's young. She has time to try. She should try." I give up.

Dear Hannah,

Okay, art school it is. But you are whole no matter what you do. Just sayin'.

Love,

Mom

Hannah

My SATs come back good but not Einstein, and I think I should probably go face a portfolio review before I get my hopes up too high. And that's how I find myself at LAX, wandering around baggage claim looking for Mom, who is flying down to meet me for my first portfolio review at Otis College of Art and Design.

Mom

It's been over two years since I've been completely alone with my daughter. Even before we sent her to Utah, Paul would avoid going out of town, or out to dinner, or working long hours so that I wouldn't have to be. He never said anything; he just did it, hovering around us ready to rescue us from the breaking waves of anger and mistrust that always seemed to engulf us.

Now I find myself standing alone in the roiling mess of LAX baggage claim, digging for my phone. Hannah should be here already, but I don't see her, and I want to call her. The therapist-approved plan is for us to meet here and go to my brother's house for the night, before attending a portfolio review at Otis College of Art and Design in the morning.

My heart races at the thought of all the things that could go wrong. Will I say or do something to upset her? It's always hard to know exactly what will set her off. I set down my bag and the little gifts that I brought for my brother's children and dig deeper into my purse. Before I can find my phone I glance up and see Hannah across the vast baggage claim area. I freeze in place, hand in my purse, people flowing around both sides of me. Hannah looks stressed, chewing on the ends of her fingers and looking around at the sea of people separating us. As I straighten I flash on an unwelcome memory: our ill-behaved dog at obedience class. The dog behaving perfectly in class (blue ribbon winner!), but then snarling and snapping when we got home. Is Hannah going to be different here in Los Angeles, away from her support structure? Will her violence resurface? Will I know what to do after two years of having only supervised visits? I absently rub at the spot where she once punched me and realize with horror that I am afraid of my own daughter. I take a deep breath and raise the arm I was rubbing, and she spots me.

Hannah

It's way cool to be away from Teen Living and the dead zone that is Utah, and I feel all urban and adult-y, carrying my bag and following signs to the baggage claim area where I'm supposed to meet Mom. LAX is a carpet of people and bags and carts, and I have a moment of panic until I see Mom smiling and waving across the big space. She smooshes me a little too long, and then we grab our carry-on bags and hit the door. She talks nonstop.

"I rented a car. Uncle Butchi wanted to pick us up, but I thought we needed our independence." Once we are on the rental car bus, Mom reaches into her bag and pulls out the portfolio that we worked on together over the phone. It's a nicely bound black book, plus a few loose sheets with some digital stuff she wasn't sure about. I'm not sure about it either. Suddenly I'm not sure about any of it. I feel my throat closing as I leaf through the pages. These are definitely not good enough. These are frozen bits of time preserved in plastic sleeves like processed food, representing me the moment before everything went rotten. A fourteen- and fifteen-year-old's version of art. Jesus, there's a piece in here I did when I was nine. Fuck.

Mom

I'm an idiot. It didn't occur to me that Hannah might be unhappy with the portfolio, since she guided me in putting it together. My fear melts into concern, and I study her, her eyes wild and her arms molded unnaturally against her chest. She clutches her portfolio like it's a life preserver, one inadequate to the task. I do the only thing I can think of. I try to distract her. "We'll look at these later," I tell her, gently prying the book out of her arms, gathering the loose pages and tucking everything back in the bag, "when we can spread everything out."

Hannah

Does Mom not notice how upset I am? Doesn't know me anymore? I've been gone too long. I turn away so she doesn't see my hurt. It's weird, she knows my deep shit—the therapy shit—like what drugs I took, how I cut myself, how I begged in the streets, and who I slept with, but she doesn't know what I eat for breakfast or what kind of deodorant I like. And obviously she can't tell how I feel about this art. She keeps talking as the rental bus drops us at our car. She talks about the weather and the flight and the family. She talks about traffic. She is a small-talk demo reel. I feel lost and sick as she gets us on the road.

Mom

I talk and talk and I can't stop, even though I'm saying nothing over and over again. I will myself to get a grip.

Hannah

At least we don't have too far to drive. We're staying with Uncle Butchi and the family, and they live pretty close to the airport, and near the art school I pick to visit. Otis is a good school, but not one of my top choices. I picked it for my first review just in case I fuck up royally. I don't mention this strategy to Mom, who is busy envisioning my new life. "You can have Shabbat dinner with the family every Friday," she says. A snarky answer automatically starts to rise up, but I push it down. After all, I'm not going to be out drinking on the weekends, so maybe that would work out.

Mom

I wish I had waited to show the portfolio to Hannah. I think it's gorgeous. Digital work that she didn't bother to ruin, some old watercolors that I had framed behind glass before she got destructive, her first big oil, forgotten in the guest room downstairs. All of these had somehow slipped past her raging tantrums, as she slashed paint across years of canvasses that dared give us a peek at her secrets. These few pieces, along with the tenth-grade work she left at school, are all that she has. I know she's frightened. I live in awe of Hannah's talent, but watching her reaction makes me wonder if I am seeing her art with a mother's eyes. How can I know?

Hannah

Uncle Butchi twinkles with happiness. Mom says it's because he's figured out what's important in life. But I think some people are born that way, and some people, well, they're born like me. He's standing on the front steps when we get there, even though he already called Mom twice to make sure we're okay. Mom says it's because he's her big brother and mostly raised her after their father died and Bubbe had to go back to work. I have a flash of knowing how badly I treated Camilla, but put it aside, too busy for guilt.

Mom

A moment after we park the car, we are in a pile of cousins, all talking at once, telling us about important things, like soccer and school and how the dog pooped in the house. It's a relief to be in my brother's home, in a place where everything is going right. I let myself relax and enjoy the normalcy of their family life.

Hannah

It's fun to see everyone. I draw cartoons and play sword with my little cousins, and then join them to pick the last of the green beans from their little urban garden. I help set the Sabbath table, my first one in so many years, and listen to talk about politics and science and travel, and I realize how small my world's become.

There's no wine on the table like there usually would be, just grape juice, and I try hard not to think about all the things we're not talking about, knowing my story isn't exactly suitable for children under the age of thirteen, even with parental supervision. Instead, I let myself get lost in the Sabbath candles my aunt is lighting. Mom stands close enough for me to lean against her, and we circle our hands around the flames and invite peace, eyes closed, hands over our faces as we chant the blessing. My cousins sing the Sabbath service in their pretty pixie voices, and I float along the melody back to my years in Jewish Day School. I think about how it was to be a kid who spoke two languages and cared about charity and got As and won first place in art at the county fair, and I have a pang of regret about my choices, but I let it go. I watch my Uncle Butchi bless each of his kids one at a time, whispering into their ears, a special blessing just for them. Mom had blessed me that way when I was a kid, but even then, I used to squirm and pull away from her. I turn to her and see the candlelight reflecting tears in her eyes. I reach for her hand.

Mom

We're staying in the little guest quarters behind the house, and that's where Hannah and I finish her portfolio, sitting on top of the fluffy down comforter, its cheerful floral pattern arguing unsuccessfully with the edginess of Hannah's work. I wonder if I'm supposed to have some words of wisdom, or at least comfort, but since I come up empty, I decide not to worry about it and feel the relief of letting go.

I am just a passenger now, helpless to change the course of what is about to happen. I watch Hannah handle the pages of her new-old portfolio, chewing on her cherub lips and making low noises of disapproval in her throat as she reviews her art.

Her hands clench and unclench, forming fists, and my throat catches again as I remember those fists coming towards me. I go to brush my teeth, running the water in case I cry, but I don't.

Hannah

Mom and I are sharing a bed, and she's still talking as she gets under the covers. She falls asleep fast, leaving me alone in the dark to think about tomorrow's portfolio review and my childish art. I fight down panic and try to lie still, and Mom begins to snore. Not feminine little snoring, but loud, throaty rumbles that come from being a little too heavy and a lot too tired. I snuggle close behind her, bury my face between her shoulder blades and wait, with my eyes wide open till morning.

Mom

I wake up the next morning to see Hannah sitting in the lone leather armchair, leafing through her portfolio for what I guess is the hundredth time, her long artist's fingers massaging the pale skin at her temple. By breakfast time Hannah is a wreck. I shake my head at my brother, warning him with my sister-telepathy to leave her be. We pass out hugs and thanks and promises to see each other soon, and Hannah and I are off to Otis.

Hannah

Otis is tiny. It's only four acres, but it feels enormous to me, as big as my dreams if I'm going to be corny, and I guess I am. I look for a bathroom, in case I get diarrhea or have to vomit or cut my wrists or something.

Mom

There is a fan of people converging on a large square building, and I tap Hannah's arm. "Oh look, honey, there's the auditorium, right there." It comes out in a kind of fake upbeat voice that you use when you are visiting someone who's really sick in the hospital, and you don't know if they're going to make it. Hannah is pale, her eyes enormous, her full lips pressed into a fine line.

Hannah

Art is a funny thing. It's something you do, but it's also who you are. If you let someone tell you things about your art, you may have to listen to some things about yourself, and that's pretty uncomfortable coming from a stranger. Especially if that stranger has power over your life. Think about it. If this dude tells me that I'm going in the wrong direction, then what direction do I have left? There is no other direction for people like me.

Mom

I know Hannah is nervous, but I don't notice when she crosses over into distress, and so I miss the opportunity to help my daughter before she spirals into full on crisis. I am busy people watching. The trendy, the unusual, and even the occasionally scary wannabe art students are lining up gripping every form of portfolio imaginable. I crane to peek at the art that they flip through in line, trying not to be obvious. Hannah does not flip through her book. She is still and quiet behind me. It isn't until we enter the final waiting room that I turn to Hannah and see her quietly struggling to breathe.

Hannah

The panic attack I have that day at Otis is the panic attack against which all future panic attacks will be measured. Holy crap, I really can't catch my breath, and then I am crying, and then comes snot plugging up my breathing even more. I gasp, "Momma, please, get me to the car, I can't do this." I tug on her arm, but she doesn't move, she just stands there frozen, looking at me with a grim look on her face, the one she used to wear at meetings with the dean of students when I'd fucked up, when I came home drunk or high, every time I was a bitch to Camilla. I know I have to get it together, because she's already done enough, she's gone through so much because of me, and some of fixing this has to be up to me. But how can I fix things? Can things be fixed?

Mom

Not now, not at this moment, I pray, please don't let me say the wrong thing. I wait for some wise words, some idea of how to calm my daughter, and the last two years telescope into all the inadequate things I've said and done to put us in this time and place. To my horror, nothing comes at all, and I pull Hannah close to me, near the cool concrete of the hallway wall. I put my hands on her shoulders and touch my forehead to hers, so she can feel that I love her and maybe somehow hear my thoughts.

Hannah

I lean against the wall and my mom, trying to catch my breath. We're in a big gray concrete hallway that was cool looking before, but suddenly makes me think of what a coffin might look like from the inside. A girl with purple hair comes up to me with a bottle of water, and looks away as I take it, mumbling, "no prob" to the snot-soaked "thank you" I manage to hiccup out. I drink and breathe and look through the mental toolbox that Bobbi has given me over eight months at Vista. Yes, there are some things in here I can use. I will not judge myself. I will allow myself to feel panicked. I will put my panic aside and move forward. Somehow I pull my shit together enough to move out of Mom's grip and into the little space where you go when it's your turn next. It's at the base of some steps, just outside two blue double doors leading into an auditorium where future artists try to sell themselves and their work to a bunch of bored faculty sitting behind tables. I think this is what it must look like at the pearly gates, walking up to some head angel seated at a folding table who looks through your portfolio of good deeds and decides if you can get into heaven.

Mom

Hannah seems calmer, but her hair is wild, sticking out at every angle around her flushed face and red-rimmed eyes. I pull my shoulders up around my ears and hold my breath. There is nothing to do but wait. I put my hand on her shoulder, and she doesn't pull away.

Hannah

Mom touches me and I almost start blubbering again but the man who comes up to us just then is wearing a black beret, and it makes me laugh. I mean I actually laugh, and that must make me seem really crazy, but it's his fault. Seriously, a beret?

He gives a little speech. "You'll be seen by the next available faculty member. You will be given approximately ten minutes to review your best pieces. Feedback will be immediate, and your visit will be noted for your file." He barely gets done saying it when a beefy old dude with a white beard raises his hand in our direction.

Mom takes a step back but I grab her hand. Somehow I find myself teleported over in front of his table, with Mom standing behind me.

Mom

The professor looks kind, and that's good because he has to ask Hannah for her work twice before she hears him. "Is that your portfolio?" Finally she nods and mutely drops the book in front of him. He must be used to nervous students because he doesn't react, just pulls the portfolio close and opens it. I wedge my hands in the pockets of my jeans, and resolve to be silent.

Hannah

Santa Claus—that's what I name him in my head—looks through my portfolio slowly, and I regret every choice I made last night about what to include. He doesn't say anything at all until he finishes, and then stabs me with his question. "Do you have anything else?" Shit. I knew these weren't good enough. What was I thinking?

I nod at him, and pull my backpack off my shoulder, digging for the sketchbook I always carry. I am embarrassed to watch him flip through my latest doodles and sketches, and he looks at every page hard, like he's trying to find just the right words to let me down. I am surprised when he closes my sketchbook and pulls my portfolio back and opens it again. Then more questions come, fast. He looks at all the digital stuff first. "What program did you use for this one?" "How did you get this glow?" Then he turns to my painting. "What were you thinking when you drew this?" I mumble my replies. I'm pretty sure my ten minutes are up, so when he leans over to reach under the table I figure he's going for the paperwork that the beret-dude told us about. But it's his sketchbook.

Santa hands it to me, and I look at it page by page the way he looked at mine. I see unformed pencil doodles, and finely rendered ink drawings, cartoons and even some beautiful little watercolors scattered through the pages like jewels. His mouth is moving, and he's pointing to his pages and my pages and I hope he isn't saying anything important cuz I miss every word. By the time I come back into my right head he's wrapping up with the most beautiful words I ever heard in my whole entire fucking life.

"You should definitely be in art school."

Oh, thank you, Santa.

Mom

A lifetime of Hannah's art dances through my head, from her first nubby crayon crocodile to her beautiful watercolors, her edgy digital art, and her soulful oils. I tip my head back with the memories and close my eyes against the tears. Of course she should be in art school. Hannah opens her arms to receive her portfolio like it's some kind of Eucharist, and the man from the double doors appears to encourage our reviewer to wrap up. He's been with us for forty-five minutes. There are people waiting. The faculty member nods and smiles at Hannah, white beard waggling.

Hannah

I can hardly wait to get outside. I have Mom by the elbow and I'm pulling her out of the room. I might have knocked over a couple of artists on the way out. "SORRY!" I fill the outside air with my shouts, I can't help it. "I SHOULD DEFINITELY BE IN ART SCHOOL MOMMA. DEF-IN-ITE-LY." I grab Mom and squish her for all I'm worth. Maybe I can squeeze out some of her sadness and doubt and replace it with something better. I should definitely be in art school, and everything is going to be okay. I'm crying again, but with happy, and I don't care if everyone is looking at me weird; they just can't know what we've gone through, what I've gone through. They've never had to give up their art to find their sanity, never had to secretly draw with a stick in the snow, or give up oil paints for temperas because you can't huff tempera. Mom puts her arm around me, and we walk away from the review and into the next part of my life.

Afterword

"You should definitely be in art school." Words that changed Hannah's life. She applied and was accepted to the art school of her choice, a magical moment I missed, like so many others in that senior year of high school she spent in Utah. I had to make do with the leftovers of her excitement, when she calmed down enough to make the phone call.

"Mama, they want me and they're giving me money!"

Hannah would come back to Santa Cruz for an awkward, tender summer and invite her "bitches" to an overnight reunion at our home that included pizza, a long night of laughing, and a sunrise AA meeting at the beach. She took a lengthy road trip back to Utah, this time entering the residential treatment facility with a plastic visitor's badge and some inspirational words for the next group of young women taking their turn at recovery. Then in just a blink, she would leave us again, for art school.

Hannah earned her Bachelor of Fine Arts degree, graduating with distinction from the California College of the Arts as an award-winning print maker, and everyone's favorite designated driver. She is currently making art in Oakland, California, trying to find her way as a working artist. She takes odd jobs to make ends meet, she travels extensively, she is in love.

By most standards, you can call what happened to us a happy ending, but we are all left scarred and battle-weary in different ways. For years, Hannah wore the effects of lingering neurotoxicity from her drug use, stuttering badly when nervous or excited. Camilla often didn't get the attention or resources she deserved during those years because of our focus on Hannah, and remains withdrawn and introverted.

Paul and I managed to hold on to each other through the strain of those years, transitioning from a life of parties, shows, dinners, and travel to quiet hikes, backyard barbeques, and discovering a better way to be together.

I still regret so many of the mistakes I made as a parent, and there will always be an ache in my heart for the two years we gave our daughter into the care of others. I continue to learn the difficult details of my daughter's treatment, and I try to balance that pain with the good choices we made to keep her from harming herself, so she could become the unique individual she is today. I am so proud of her, and grateful for the love she brings into my life every day.

People often ask me what we did that made it work. I'm not sure, but I think it has a lot to do with Hannah's resilience and our family's collective stubbornness. We also feel lucky, and grateful, for the talented professionals we met along the way, and their unflagging commitment to the young women and men in their care.

Finally, and most importantly, Hannah insisted we do everything along with her, that we had to grow and change together as a family. Her letters were clear. "One person can't make a family change," she wrote. "We have to find a new way to fit together." Thus, she laid the groundwork for finding a better way for us to love and support each other.

Looking back it feels like we've been submerged under water for two years, our flailing raising mud, everything murky and distorted in the waters of addiction and emotional instability. Air tastes sweeter when you finally break through the water's surface, breathing in the life so recently denied. Tides tug, but we remain afloat, one day at a time.

Hannah

So, I guess I get the last word.

It sucks, what happened to me and my family. Knowing I had a leading role sucks even worse. Some of my drug-induced adventuring has no up side at all. For one, my parents' life has never been the same, and I know it's because they spent a shit ton of money on making me whole again. They can't help me in life as much as they want to now, because they helped me so much during those years. I know that Camilla is getting a lot less, because I got more, and that's not fair either. I'm also sad that I was never really able to go home again, and I know that hurts Mom. I know they all love me, and I love them back, but sometimes I feel like a visitor when I'm there, like when I had to "meet" the new dog. Mom writes in my old room, so when I visit, I get the feeling it's more her room now than mine. I haven't really found or made another home yet. I guess some of that is because of what happened to us, but some of it is just growing up and starting my own life and is probably pretty normal.

In spite of all that, I think some good things happened to us too. I'm really proud of spending almost three months in Wilderness with Second Nature. It was hard, but it makes me know how strong I really am.

After Wilderness my time at Vista gave me tools to stay steady, and I made really great friends. I got to know them and myself pretty well. I'm grateful to be able to see—actually see— the kind of love my family feels for me, even when my brain had the consistency of a Slurpee and I became a violent moron. I try to live up to their trust that I was still "in there somewhere" by loving them back with all my might, and I think—I hope—they feel that.

At Vista, and afterwards too, I've had the opportunity to help other people change their lives for the better, so my experience with recovery could be part of a positive ripple out there in the world and maybe that will bring some balance to what happened to us. I also learned a lot of life skills through the two years I was in Utah. I still dig through my DBT toolbox to help me when I feel down, or doubt my life decisions or my work. Overall, I think I ended up better for the experience, but I'm crushed flat when I hear about my friends who didn't make it, who made it just for a while, or who carry scars from their time in these programs.

Mom wanted to write this book, and I told her she could, because I thought she needed some kind of catharsis, and I owed her that. But I'm glad it's all written down. People need to know how tough these programs are, and that they're only for last-resort situations, when the fucked-upness is extreme and nothing else works. In the end the telling of our story reminds me again of how much I'm loved, and I hope it reminds you of how much love counts.

I hope our story helps you. If you've fallen off the rails, I hope that you can find your way, on your own path, back to your loved ones. Most of all, I hope that you never give up on each other.

Discussion Guide

1. During Hannah's decline, her family worked hard to keep her at home, with behavior contracts, bribes, restrictions, and interventions. What do you think of the various methods that were used, and why were they not successful?

2. Mom's shame at her inability to parent her daughter effectively is palpable. To what extent do you think parenting decisions drove Hannah's decline? What other factors may have contributed to Hannah's downward spiral?

3. Hannah goes through sessions with three psychologists and a psychiatrist before overdosing. Why did this "local" therapy fail her? What made the therapy at wilderness and residential treatment different?

4. Critics of wilderness and residential treatment programs call them "brainwash mills." After reading the book, how would you characterize this type of treatment?

5. Hannah notes that most of the teens she encountered at her rehab programs are privileged, white kids. What does this say about access to care?

6. Hannah lived outdoors in a freezing expanse of snow and ice for over three months. What part, if any, did the harsh conditions in Utah play in her recovery?

7. Much of the treatment Hannah underwent in the wilderness program was experiential. For example, trying versus succeeding, making your own outcomes, resisting temptation, and earning privileges were all demonstrated in different ways. Why do you think Hannah and the other girls benefited from this approach?

8. After mulling it over, Hannah comes to trust Mom enough to allow her to clean out Hannah's bedroom at home. What progress does that show in the relationship between Hannah and Mom?

9. Hannah is both grateful and upset when she visits home and learns how few people know of her treatment. Why is she so conflicted?

10. Hannah believes there are teens in wilderness and residential treatment programs who don't belong there. Why does Hannah feel this way? What legitimate factors do you think should be taken into account when programs accept teens?

11. Some residential treatment facilities have been shown to be abusive to their patients. What kind of oversight is needed to assure the safety of children who are sent away for intensive therapy?

12. Hannah melts down when she learns that she will not be going home after residential treatment. She lashes out at those around her, and succumbs to anger and depression. What happens to change Hannah's outlook?

13. Did the friendships that Hannah formed in the wilderness and residential facilities validate Mom's concerns that Hannah would be poorly influenced? Why or why not?

14. Sadly, at the time of Hannah's treatment, only two out of every five teens managed to achieve sobriety for a substantial amount of time. For Hannah, what do you think made the journey a "success"?

15. One very difficult moment in the book is when Mom realizes that she hasn't been alone with her own daughter for nearly two years, and she is afraid. Do you think her concerns are valid? Explain.

16. At the portfolio review, Mom has no words to comfort Hannah when Hannah experiences a panic attack. How does Hannah manage to pull it together? What does that say about her?

17. Tragically, as this book goes to print, Hannah has learned that several of her group have relapsed, committed suicide, or disappeared. Does this change your opinion of the treatment experience? Why or why not?

18. Hannah insists that if she is expected to change, the whole family needs to change with her. Do you agree with Hannah? How was this change apparent in the book?

19. Hannah finished residential treatment at age seventeen, but except for the brief summer between treatment and college, she never really lived at home again. Discuss the long-term effects of this type of intervention on a family.

20. What are the primary messages of the book for families?

Acknowledgments

To the fine friends, old and new, who read the first drafts of this book, a heartfelt thank-you. This book would not have come to life without you. I would like to thank my earliest readers, Kathy Long, Robin Shine, Megan Ackerman, Tor Valenza, and Tasia Stern. You had the hardest job: part diplomat, part cheerleader. To those who read through later drafts, including Kristen McCandless, Christie Danner, and Catherine Towson, my gratitude. Having the perspective of professionals who work with teens helped bring our family's experiences into focus.

I'm lucky to be part of a weekly writing group, a supportive community of talented writers. Though not nearly a complete list, over time I've worked with Vanya Erickson, Cathy Krizik, Renee Winter, Magali Morales, Sheila Coonerty, Jen Astone, Danilyn Rutherford, Melinda Luster, Gavriella Delgado, Nancy Brown, Mary Ashley, Claire Lovell, Eileen Tejada, Tony del Zompo, Paula Mahoney, Larae Ross, Christine Holstrom, Veronica McGlynn, and Paldrom Collins. I especially want to acknowledge my teacher, Laura Davis, who has worked hard for years to make me a better writer.

I am indebted to the professionals who worked with our family and especially need to thank Bobbi Carter, who read the residential treatment portion of the book and updated me about some of the changes currently taking place in the organization's therapeutic approach. Of course, any inaccuracies in the description of treatment or medication is mine alone.

My extended family and friends were my support structure, always there, before, during and after the events described in the book, like Cory Skook, who has stood by me for more than fifty years. Much love to my brother Harvey Stern, who continues to listen to me endlessly with great patience.

More than anyone else, I acknowledge my daughter, who wants readers to know that treatment of this nature is not a decision to be made lightly, or experienced alone. She brought our family together and made meaning out of the things that happened to her, and to us as a family.

I am so grateful to my younger daughter, who has come into her own so fully since the writing of this book; her quiet strength and determination brings me tears of pride. Thanks as well to my still stoically supportive husband, who listened to every version of every section and gave me good advice along the way.

Eternal gratitude to my beautiful family; may they be blessed for their willingness to sacrifice their privacy for the benefit of others.

Finally, to all of the families who came to us asking questions and spurring the writing of this book, my hopes and wishes for your success, on whatever path is right for you.

About the Author

SUSAN BURROWES is a presenter, teacher, trainer, and project manager. She holds a master's degree in communication, but took enough time out of her studies to produce the two extraordinary, challenging children who continue to define her life. Her career spans fifteen years in advertising, eight years teaching in the college classroom, and another ten years training professionals in organizations how to communicate with each other, an irony that was not lost on her as she struggled to reach her addicted daughter. Burrowes currently works with a team of high-achieving young adults in Admissions at the University of California Santa Cruz, where she ponders the question of teen success on a daily basis. She writes about the strength and determination of troubled teens and special needs children.

Author photo © Jon Covello

Selected Titles from She Writes Press

She Writes Press is an independent publishing company founded to serve women writers everywhere. Visit us at www.shewritespress.com.

Searching for Normal: The Story of a Girl Gone Too Soon by Karen Meadows. $16.95, 978-1-63152-137-9. Karen Meadows intertwines her own story with excerpts from her daughter Sadie's journals to describes their roller coaster ride through Sadie's depression and a maze of inadequate mental health treatment and services—one that ended with Sadie's suicide at age eighteen.

Blinded by Hope: One Mother's Journey Through Her Son's Bipolar Illness and Addiction by Meg McGuire. $16.95, 978-1-63152-125-6. A fiercely candid memoir about one mother's roller coaster ride through doubt and denial as she attempts to save her son from substance abuse and bipolar illness.

A Different Kind of Same: A Memoir by Kelley Clink. $16.95, 978-1-63152-999-3. Several years before Kelley Clink's brother hanged himself, she attempted suicide by overdose. In the aftermath of his death, she traces the evolution of both their illnesses, and wonders: If he couldn't make it, what hope is there for her?

Scattering Ashes: A Memoir of Letting Go by Joan Rough. $16.95, 978-1-63152-095-2. A daughter's chronicle of what happens when she invites her alcoholic and emotionally abusive mother to move in with her in hopes of helping her through the final stages of life—and her dream of mending their tattered relationship fails miserably.

Breathe: A Memoir of Motherhood, Grief, and Family Conflict by Kelly Kittel. $16.95, 978-1-938314-78-0. A mother's heartbreaking account of losing two sons in the span of nine months—and learning, despite all the obstacles in her way, to find joy in life again.

Make a Wish for Me: A Mother's Memoir by LeeAndra Chergey. $16.95, 978-1-63152-828-6. A life-changing diagnosis teaches a family that where's there is love there is hope—and that being "normal" is not nearly as important as providing your child with a life full of joy, love, and acceptance.